The **Sounds** of

German

How are the sounds of German produced? How do German speakers stress their words? How have the sounds of German developed over time? This book provides a clear introduction to the sounds of German, designed particularly for English-speaking students of the language. Topics covered include the role of the organs of speech, the state of the vocal cords and the differences between vowels and consonants. The articulation, distribution and spelling and the major variants of each sound are examined in detail. The book also discusses the regional differences between dialects and between the national standard varieties in Germany, Austria and Switzerland. Students are encouraged to put theory into practice with end-of-chapter questions. Setting a solid foundation in the description and analysis of German sounds, *The Sounds of German* will help students improve their pronunciation of the language by introducing them to the basics of its sound system.

CHARLES V. J. RUSS was formerly Reader in German Linguistics in the Department of Language and Linguistic Science at the University of York.

The **Sounds** of

German

Charles V. J. Russ

CAMBRIDGE
UNIVERSITY PRESS

CAMBRIDGE UNIVERSITY PRESS

Cambridge, New York, Melbourne, Madrid, Cape Town, Singapore,
São Paulo, Delhi, Dubai, Tokyo

Cambridge University Press
The Edinburgh Building, Cambridge CB2 8RU, UK

Published in the United States of America by Cambridge University Press, New York

www.cambridge.org
Information on this title: www.cambridge.org/9780521694629

First published 2010

Printed in the United Kingdom at the University Press, Cambridge

A catalogue record for this publication is available from the British Library

ISBN 978-0-521-69462-9 Paperback

1006548102

Contents

Figures

Preface

This book was written in response to an invitation by Helen Barton of Cambridge University Press, to write something on German to fit in with the series on the *Sounds of* .... In my treatment of this topic I had to deal with a number of problems apart from the main one of describing the sounds of the language. The controversial theme of addressing what is the 'best' type of German forms the subject of Chapter 1. Discussion of this goes back to Goethe and is further complicated by the political development of Germany: unification in 1871 under Prussian, therefore North German, hegemony and the development of two German states between 1949 and 1989.

Chapter 2 swings back to looking at the basic concepts of articulatory phonetics, more detail being given for vowels in Chapter 3 and Consonants in Chapter 4. I have tried to find a wide range of examples, sometimes resulting in rather obscure words that are translated into English. For the most part I have assumed that the reader will either know sufficient German or have access to a good bilingual dictionary. Having described the articulation of the vowels and consonants I then show how they contrast with each other in a phonological system in Chapter 5. Much of this chapter consists of lists of oppositions exemplified for different phonetic contexts and is intended to be used as a reference resource rather than read straight through.

Like the other major European languages German has an orthography that stretches back to the eighth century. Since the beginning of its written tradition there has been a great variety of letters and their usage. Chapter 6 surveys different orthographic principles that have become important in the development of German and how well they reflect the sound system. In recent years there have been new changes and this will continue. Politics and bureaucracy have locked horns with linguistics!

But segmental sounds that were the subject of Chapters 3, 4 and 5 can be combined together to form larger units such as syllables. In Chapter 7 I look at what sounds can combine together to form the beginning and end of syllables and in polysyllabic words form medial clusters.

German has never existed apart from other languages and Chapter 8 deals with the different ways other languages have influenced German: introducing sounds that didn't exist before (nasal vowels) or consonant clusters, for example the *Ps* in *Psalm*. Also some clusters that have disappeared because of sound changes have been re-introduced, for example *Tw* in *Tweed* and *-mb-* in *Bombe*.

Another facet of sounds is that they may alternate with related sounds in different contexts: *Tag*, but *Tage*. These alternations can be described by phonological rules. Different types of phonological alternations, such as umlaut and ablaut, and their origins are the subject of Chapter 9.

In language use sounds are strung together in phrases and sentences. Chapter 10 deals with this aspect of their use, including the array of unstressed 'weak' forms. The use of contrastive stress to mark semantic difference is copiously illustrated. Intonation is dealt with rather briefly and the reader is referred to the secondary literature.

German is, however, not simply spoken in Germany but also in Austria and German-speaking Switzerland. The differences of pronunciation form the subject of Chapter 11, in which there are also some samples of dialects that form the basis for the differences in the standard.

All that we have described up to now is the result of long phonological development over the centuries and these changes form the subject matter for Chapter 12, including such iconic changes as the High German Sound Shift. There are some sample texts for Old High German and Middle High German. The illustrations, tables and maps are to make the text more accessible and the CD provides some exemplification of basic sounds in the standard language.

My introduction to phonetics and the sounds of German was in my first term as an undergraduate studying German and Swedish at King's College, Newcastle, later Newcastle University. Professor Duncan Mennie maintained in his inaugural lecture that I heard in my first term, almost fifty years ago, that 'the student must be taught practical phonetics on the basis of [their] own spoken English and of German as German is recommended to be pronounced today'. I then taught German phonetics and linguistics at Southampton and York. This book is the fruit of those long years of teaching and publishing on this subject. I am grateful to many linguists who have encouraged me over the years, Professors Gerhard Augst, Friedhelm Debus, Walter Haas, Herbert Penzl, Stefan Sonderegger and Peter Wiesinger. I am also endebted to many German-speaking friends who have, very often unwittingly, acted as informants to my phonetic studies.

I am very grateful to my wife Jenny, who has shared the love of the German language for over forty years and also to our son, Jamie, who is now a head of modern languages, and our daughter-in-law, Kate, who also teaches German. Our other son, Thomas, found that knowledge of German can help in a practical way in the medical world. I am grateful for all their patience and understanding during the production of this book. But it is to our grandson, Oliver, born 30 September 2008, that I would like to dedicate this book. He loves making sounds and maybe some day these will be the sounds of German.

Abbreviations

acc.	accusative case
ASG	Austrian Standard German
CG	Central German
dat.	dative case
DAW	*Duden Aussprachwörterbuch*
DG	*Duden Grammatik*
ECG	East Central German
ENHG	Early New High German
gen.	genitive case
GSG	German Standard German
GWDA	*Großes Wörterbuch der deutschen Aussprache*
IPA	International Phonetic Alphabet
LG	Low German
MHG	Middle High German
NHG	New High German
nom.	nominative case
OHG	Old High German
pl.	plural
sg.	singular
SSG	Swiss Standard German
UG	Upper German
WDA	*Wörterbuch der deutschen Aussprache*

1 Standards of pronunciation

1.1 Introduction

1.1.1 Sounds and language

Sounds are part of the communication system between human beings that we call language. One of the main characteristics of language as against other communication systems is that it is transmitted through the medium of sound produced by air from the lungs being expelled through the mouth and nose and modified by the so-called organs of speech. The sounds that are produced in this way are also heard by other speakers. Users of language are therefore normally both speakers and hearers. This medium of transmission we shall call the vocal-auditory channel since language is both produced by the vocal apparatus and heard by means of the ears. In addition language has meaning, i.e. its use can 'cause' other speaker/hearers to perform certain actions. For example, the instruction 'Sit down!' will be produced by one speaker/hearer and another will understand it and carry it out by sitting down. Language differs from other communication systems that are transmitted in different ways, e.g. visually, such as semaphore signals or smoke signals. The combination of sounds produced as language have meaning as we have seen in that they can communicate instructions. This is, of course, only one aspect of meaning. Others include expressing emotions and social interaction. Another function of individual sounds is that they can be built up into larger meaningful units. Words are the basic building blocks of the grammar and lexicon/vocabulary of a language.

In the command *Sit down!* we can distinguish two words. These words furthermore comprise smaller units, letters, that themselves have no meaning but serve to distinguish meaning. These letters in our spoken language represent sounds. In these instances *s* and *d* each represent a single sound but in other instances more than one letter can represent one sound: *sh* in *shine, ng* in *ring.* As we shall see the inconsistency between letters and sounds has led to the development of a phonetic alphabet designating one sound by one letter (see 1.1.6).

This facility of sounds, that have no meaning by themselves, but are used to construct larger units that do have meaning, is called duality of patterning. However, although sounds do not have meaning in themselves they do serve to distinguish meaning (Chapter 5). Thus *down* is different from *town* and *sit* from *fit*. In this book we shall be concentrating on the sounds of German.

The relationship of these meaningful elements/items and what they refer to is arbitrary. There is no compelling reason why a 'window' should be represented by *window* in English and *Fenster* in German. Even seeming exceptions such as onomatopoeia are arbitrarily different (if only slightly!) in different languages: the cock crows *cock-a-doodle-doo* in English, *kikeriki* in German and *cocorico* in French. A further characteristic of language is that language is not genetically transmitted down the generations. It is acquired by a process of learning and teaching in which the ethnic background of the speaker/hearer is irrelevant. Although the ability to acquire language seems a universal characteristic, an infant will normally learn a specific language from the social milieu they are being brought up in. The language of an ethnic Chinese or African child brought up in an English-speaking milieu will be indistinguishable from that of an ethnic British or American child brought up in the same language milieu. Equally an ethnic British or American child brought up in a different language milieu would acquire the language of that milieu. To sum up: language is transmitted through the vocal-auditory channel, has meaning, has duality of patterning, and the relationship between its units and the things they signify is arbitrary. It is transmitted by teaching and learning. Within language sounds are without meaning in isolation but serve to distinguish meaning. Some apparent exceptions are the indefinite article *a* in English or the preposition *a* in Spanish. There seem no examples of this in German. The nearest thing is the word *Ei* 'egg', comprising a diphthong.

1.1.2 Spelling and writing systems

Speaker/hearers learn to speak and listen before they learn to read and write. Unfortunately some speaker/hearers never learn to read and write but they still speak fluently. There are also some several thousand languages in the world that are still unwritten and consequently have no writing systems. Thus we may conclude that writing comes second but speech comes first. In other words we learn to speak before we learn to write.

Linguists and phoneticians are interested in all the possible sounds used in the world's languages. They study their articulation by the organs of speech using scientific methods, such as taking X-ray films of sounds being articulated. They also use palatography, taking a photograph of an artificial palate used by a subject in an experiment. They record utterances and examine spectrograms of them, showing the acoustic features of the sounds. In this book our goal is much more modest and we will only treat a small sub-set of possible sounds, those that are used in German. We will look at basic concepts such as how sounds are produced by the organs of speech interacting with air-flow from the lungs (see Chapter 2).

Sounds are being produced all around us but we early learn to recognize those that are relevant for language and speech. Thus coughing, clearing one's throat, sniffing, clicking our tongue, smacking our lips are normally not part of the speech sounds of German and English. (Clicks are used in some languages of southern Africa.) We usually have no difficulty in understanding the fellow speakers of our native language even though the pronunciation of each sound we use is slightly different every time it is used. We 'tolerate' these slight differences and each sound seems to us to 'sound the same'. It is only when the pronunciation of a sound changes significantly, such that the *s* in *sit* is heard instead of the *f* in *fit*, that we know that we are dealing with a different word with a different meaning. The differently pronounced sounds are now in contrast.

Sound differences in one language may, however, not be the same in another language. In English the two consonants spelt *k* in *kill* and *skill* are different, the first being aspirated and the second one unaspirated. Aspiration can be felt as a puff of breath if a speaker puts their finger in front of their mouth when pronouncing sounds such as *k*, *t* or *p* in English. In the case of *skill*, however, there is no such puff of breath after the *k*. Most English speakers are unaware of this difference but in Hindi these two different articulations of *k* contrast in meaning: *khiil* (with an aspirated *k*) 'parched grain' contrasts with *kiil* (with unaspirated *k*) 'nail'. Conversely, the initial sounds in English *den* and *then* are in contrast, distinguishing the two words. In Spanish, however, they do not have this function: the two sounds represented by *d* in *donde* 'where' are the same as that in English *den* but the *d* in *nada* 'nothing' is the same as the initial sound in English *then*. In English these two sounds contrast, and are phonemes, whereas in Spanish they are positional variants, allophones. In initial position and after *n*, the *d* sound occurs whereas medially between vowels the *th*-sound occurs.

The phoneme system of German will be in described in Chapter 5. The phoneme systems of English and German do not show as wide a difference with regard to phonemes and allophones as our Hindi and Spanish examples but nevertheless there are some parallels. In English the pronunciation of *l* at the beginning and the end of *little* is quite different. The final *l* is pronounced in the back of the mouth and the *l* at the beginning is pronounced in the front of the mouth. These are positional variants in English. In German the *l* phoneme has only one pronunciation in the standard, the front pronunciation. In English there is a contrast between the *w* in *wine* and *v* in *vine*, i.e. they are phonemes (/w/ : /v/). The former is pronounced with both lips, bilabial, and the latter with the upper teeth and bottom lip, labio-dental (for details of these terms see 4.2.1). In German the *w* as in *Wasser* is pronounced in the standard like the *v* in English *vine*, labio-dental. The bilabial pronunciation of *w* exists only as a regional pronunciation in south Germany or in the consonant sequence *qu*, *Quelle* 'source'. Moulton (1962: 26–51 and 91–112) deals in detail with the contrastive analysis of the English and German sound systems.

In this book we will deal not only with the articulation of the sounds of German, but also with their status: whether they are phonemes in contrast or positional variants, allophones (Chapter 5). We will also describe other aspects of sounds such as their alternation (Chapter 9) and their occurrence in loan words (Chapter 8). These are principally segmental sounds. In addition we will treat suprasegmental phenomena such as word stress and intonation (Chapter 10).

1.1.3 The German language

The language of which we shall be describing the sounds is German, more specifically New High German (NHG). The term 'High' refers not to any social or 'higher' prestige model of German but to that variety that was used in the centre and south of Germany and formed the basis of the standard language. It is used in opposition to Low German, the dialects used in the north of Germany. NHG (or Present-day German) is the continuation, albeit with changes, of a language that has been used since the fourth and fifth centuries AD in a wide area, whose central portion lies between the Rhine in the west and the river Oder in the east, the Alps in the south and the area north of the river Schlei in Schleswig-Holstein in the north. This core area has expanded and contracted over the centuries. Figure 1.1 shows the extent of the German-speaking area in the tenth and eleventh centuries and how it expanded to its greatest extent in the nineteenth and twentieth centuries, when German was used in large parts of eastern Europe. Also during that century millions of German speakers had arrived in the USA and Germany possessed colonies in Africa. Since 1945 the German-speaking area has contracted, with

Figure 1.1   The expansion of German from the 10th and 11th centuries to 1900

territory lost to Poland, Russia and the Czech Republic in the east and to France in the west (Fig. 1.2).

It is usual to divide the historical development of German into four periods: Old High German (OHG) (750–1050), Middle High German (MHG) (1050–1350), Early New High German (ENHG) (1350–1650) and New High German (NHG). This division into periods is for the most part arbitrary, being based on linguistic or cultural criteria; it must not be supposed that the periods are separated from each other by rigid boundaries. Present-day German is also a language that is not standing still. It has developed continuously over the centuries and is still evolving. The present-day written language emerged only in the period from the second half of the seventeenth century to the first quarter of the eighteenth century. Authors and grammarians turned their attention to the proper pronunciation of German in the latter part of the eighteenth and the nineteenth century. The best-known comments on pronunciation from this time are 'Rules for Actors' (*Regeln für Schauspieler*) from 1803 by Johann

Figure 1.2   The present-day extent of German

Wolfgang von Goethe (1749–1832) that are recorded in his conversations with Johann Peter Eckermann (1792–1854). In them Goethe maintains the following:

Daher ist das Erste und Notwendigste für den sich bildenden Schauspieler, dass er sich von allen Fehlern des Dialekts befreie und eine vollständige reine Aussprache zu erlangen suche. Kein Provinzialismus taugt auf die Bühne! Dort herrsche nur die reine deutsche Mundart, wie sie durch Geschmack, Kunst und Wissenschaft ausgebildet und verfeinert worden.

(Therefore it is the first and most necessary [requirement] for the actor in training that he tries to free himself of all dialect errors and arrive at a completely pure pronunciation. No provincialism belongs on the stage! Let only the pure way of speaking German rule there, as it [has] been developed and refined through good taste, art and scholarship.)

(Beutler 1964: 72ff.)

1.1.4 Spelling and writing in German

German first became written in the eighth century and we shall be looking at the relationship between the sounds of German and their orthographic representation in Chapter 6. The main motive for writing German at that time seems to have been the educational and ecclesiastical reforms put into place by Charlemagne (747–814). Latin had been the only written language up to then and it was the Latin alphabet that formed the basis for writing Old High German and its successors. This had two principal drawbacks: (1) There were some sounds in OHG that were not present in Latin: the diphthongs *uo* (*guot*, NHG *gut*), *ie* (*ziegel*, NHG *Ziegel*) and the complex sound (affricate) at the beginning of OHG *pfad* (NHG *Pfad*), *pflanza* (NHG *Pflanze*); and (2) some Latin letters were used in ambiguous ways, thus <k> and <c> stood for the same sound: OHG *calb* (NHG *Kalb*), *kind* (NHG *Kind*), *crippa* (NHG *Krippe*), *keisure* (NHG *Kaiser*).

NHG in both its spoken and written form is the result of cumulative changes since OHG times. In the modern period we are able to access the speech of German speaker/hearers directly, make recordings of their speech, transcribe and thus study the sounds in detail. In earlier stages of German we only have indirect evidence of how the language was pronounced. We have to deduce from the orthographic record how sounds were pronounced, helped by rhyming schemes. The strict division between sounds and their spelling that we shall be able to make for NHG is not so easy to make in the past. Indeed, one of the founders of German linguistics, Jacob Grimm (1785–1863), headed a section in his *Deutsche Grammatik* (Germanic Grammar) 'Von den Buchstaben' (Concerning the letters) and treated letters as if they were the same as sounds, although he is aware of this shortcoming: 'Zur darstellung der laute in sämmtlichen deutschen sprachen bediene ich mich meistentheils der heutigen gangbaren buchstaben, deren unzulänglichkeit für alle fälle leicht einzusehen ist' (To represent the sounds in all the Germanic languages I mostly use the usual present-day letters, whose insufficiency is clearly seen) (Grimm 1870: 2). For instance, this insufficiency can be seen in the pronunciation of the consonant at the beginning of *Schritt* and *Stadt* that is pronounced the same but spelt *sch* and *s*.

When students have read through Chapters 2–4 and 7–10 then they will have established a foundation of the phonetics and phonology of German vowels and consonants. Building on this foundation the variation of German sounds in national and regional varieties treated in Chapter 11 can be understood and similarly how this sound system developed in the history of German, which will be the subject of Chapter 12.

1.1.5 The science of studying sounds

The detailed study of the pronunciation of sounds goes back to ancient times with the studies of the Sanskrit grammarians. Greek and Roman scholars were also active in describing the pronunciation of sounds. It is, however, not really until the middle of the nineteenth century that the scientific study of sounds starts to have a firm base. The physics and anatomy of sounds advanced from their treatment as part of natural science to form a new discipline, phonetics, describing not only how speakers pronounce sounds but how these function in specific languages and develop over time.

One of the first influential books on phonetics was *Grundzüge der Laut-physiologie* (Principles of Sound Physiology), published by Eduard Sievers (1850–1933) in 1876, which shows in its title the influence of natural science in emphasizing the physiological description of sound production. In the second edition in 1881 the title was changed to *Grundzüge der Phonetik* (Principles of Phonetics). The word *Phonetik* itself is a learned formation of the nineteenth century from the Greek roots *phone* 'voice', *phonein* 'to speak' and modern Latin *phoneticus* and together with *phonetisch* and *Phonetiker* form a word family. These words are labelled generally as nineteenth-century forms (*DE* 2007: 606; Pfeiffer 1993: 2005) and not dated exactly. Indeed, some dictionaries, including the *Deutsches Wörterbuch*, have no entries for them! In English the words *phonetic* and *phonetician* pre-date *phonetics*. In England Henry Sweet's *Handbook of Phonetics* appeared in 1877.

Historical linguists and dialectologists used these newly gained phonetic insights to describe the development of sounds and also the occurrence of sounds in different dialects. Jost Winteler, who was one of the first dialectologists, produced a monograph of the Swiss German dialect from Kerenzen in the canton of Glarus in 1876, in which he used detailed phonetic description of the sounds (Kerenzen has now been divided into three municipalities: Filzbach, Mühlehorn and Obstalden). In the remaining quarter of the century phonetics became widely researched. Some well-known phoneticians are Daniel Jones (1881–1967) and Henry Sweet (1845–1912) in England, Wilhelm Viëtor (1850–1943) and Otto Bremer (1862–1936) in Germany and the Dane, Otto Jespersen (1860–1943). Chapters 2, 3 and 4 will deal with the basic concepts of phonetics and more specifically with the vowels and consonants of German.

1.1.6 The development of the International Phonetic Association and its alphabet

The interest in phonetics and the teaching of the spoken language led in 1886 to the founding in Paris under the leadership of Paul Passy (1859–1940) of an association that in 1897 became the International Phonetic Association. One of the great needs in the study of phonetics was a system of recording speech which was much more reliable than traditional spelling systems. As we have seen, Jacob Grimm had recognized the insufficiency of spelling systems. There must be no confusion of spelling and sounds! To remedy this shortcoming the first International Phonetic Alphabet (IPA) was proposed in 1887. The following principles that underpinned it were first published in 1888:

'(1) There should be a separate letter for each distinctive sound, that is, for each sound which, being used instead of another, in the same language, can change the meaning of a word.

 (2) When any sound is found in several languages, the same sign should be used in all. This applies also to very similar shades of sound.

 (3) The alphabet should consist as much as possible of the ordinary letters of the alphabet, as few new letters as possible being used.

 (4) In assigning values to the roman letters, international usage should decide.

 (5) The new letters should be suggestive of the sounds they represent by their resemblance to the old ones.

 (6) Diacritic marks should be avoided, being trying for the eyes and troublesome to write.'

(International Phonetic Association 1949)

The 1888 alphabet was extended in 1900 and presented in its familiar chart form. A further revision in 1932 led to the form it took for over half a century. The next major revision was not until 1989. The chart (Fig. 1.3) includes the latest revisions up to 2005. It is, of course, the IPA that will be used for the phonetic transcriptions in this volume. All phonetic transcriptions will be enclosed in square brackets [. . .].

In the field of German linguistics in the nineteenth century there was a rival system that was especially used in dialect studies and in many cases continues to be used. It was codified in the German dialect periodical, *Teuthonista*, after which it is named. It is basically a broad, simple transcription that uses diacritics, such as commas or dots under the basic vowel symbols, to show degrees of openness or closeness. The consonants are mostly represented by different symbols. Eugen Dieth (1893–1956) was a Swiss phonetician who studied both English and Swiss dialects, producing a transcription system for recording Swiss dialects. He contrasts the IPA and *Teuthonista* system and recommends the former most strongly (1968: 43–50). It is the IPA, of course, that is used in the *Survey of English Dialects*, of which he

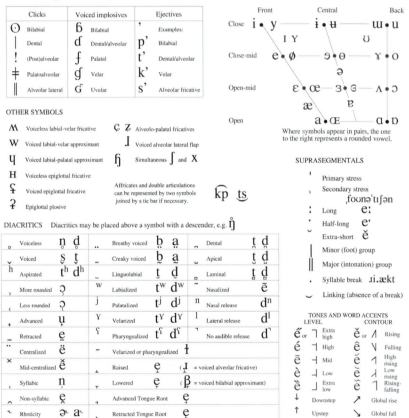

Figure 1.3   Chart of International Phonetic Symbols

was a co-founder with Harold Orton (1898–1975). Anyone reading about German sounds will encounter the *Teuthonista* system sooner or later so it is as well to be aware of it and how it differs from the IPA. The *Sprachatlas der deutschen Schweiz* uses a modified *Teuthonista* system, represented as Fig. 1.4.

Tabelle der phonetischen Zeichen

Konsonanten

Verschlußlaute　　　　　　**Engelaute**

		Verschlußlaute			Engelaute							
Fortes		p	t	k		f	ϑ	s	$\dot{s}$	$\check{s}$	χ'	χ x h
Lenes	{ alem. stl. roman. sth. }	b	d	g	{ alem. stl. roman. sth. }	v	δ	z	$\dot{z}$	$\check{z}$	j	γ

Sonorlaute

m η n $\underset{.}{n}$ η

l $\underset{.}{l}$ $\dot{l}$ r $\underset{.}{r}$ R (uvular) $\underset{.}{R}$ j w { alem.: labiodental, bilabial / roman.: bilabial (labiovelar) } $\ddot{w}$ labiopalatal

---

Länge: $\bar{p}$ $\bar{m}$ ... *Halblänge:* $\hat{p}$ $\hat{m}$ *Geminate:* pp mm *(schwach gem.)* $p\breve{{}}p$ $m\breve{{}}m$ *(stark gem.)*
Aspiriert: ph th... *schwach aspiriert:* p^h t^h... *Affrikaten:* pf ts $t\check{s}$ kx $\underset{.}{t}\chi'$ dj *Implosive:* $\mathring{p}$ $\mathring{b}$...
Sonorisiert: (alem.) $\underset{.}{b}$ $\underset{.}{d}$ $\underset{.}{g}$ $\underset{.}{z}$ $\underset{.}{v}$... *Entsonorisiert:* (rom.) $\underset{.}{d}$ $\underset{.}{g}$ $\underset{.}{v}$... *Sonantisch:* $\underset{.}{l}$ $\underset{.}{m}$ ...
Palatalisiert: $\underset{.}{t}$ $\underset{.}{k}$ $\underset{.}{d}$ $\underset{.}{g}$ $\underset{.}{l}$ *Velarisiert:* $\dot{l}$ *Frikativiert:* $\underset{.}{b}$ $\underset{.}{d}$ $\underset{.}{g}$ *Ohne Vibration:* $\underset{.}{r}$ $\underset{.}{R}$
Mittelwerte zwischen Lenes und Fortes: $\underset{.}{p}$ $\underset{.}{t}$ $\underset{.}{k}$ $\underset{.}{f}$ $\underset{.}{s}$ $\underset{.}{\check{s}}$ ... $\underset{.}{b}$ $\underset{.}{d}$ $\underset{.}{g}$ $\underset{.}{v}$ $\underset{.}{z}$ $\underset{.}{\check{z}}$ $\underset{.}{\dot{v}}$
Mittelwerte zwischen s und $\check{s}$ bzw. z und $\check{z}$: $\acute{s}$ $\acute{z}$

Beispiele für:

	Lenis	Halbfortis		Fortis	Länge	Geminate
	dazi	*dazṣi = daṣzi = dazzi = daṣṣi*		*dasi*	*daṣi*	*dassi* $das\breve{{}}si$
	daß ich	daß sie				

Vokale

Einfache				**Diphthonge**		**Modifizierte**	
geschlossen	neutral	offen		fallend	ie ua ea $\ddot{o}\ddot{u}$ ...	nasaliert	$\tilde{a}$ $\tilde{e}$ $\tilde{o}$ ...
i $\underset{.}{i}$	i	$\underset{.}{i}$ $\dot{i}$		schwebend	ie ua ea $\ddot{o}\ddot{u}$ ...	schwach nasaliert	$\tilde{a}$
e $\underset{.}{e}$	e	$\underset{.}{e}$ $\underset{.}{\varepsilon}$		steigend	$i\underset{.}{e}$ $u\underset{.}{a}$ $\underset{.}{e}a$ $\ddot{o}\ddot{u}$ ...	zentralisiert	$\hat{i}$ $\hat{e}$ $\hat{u}$ ...
pal. $\underset{.}{a}$ a	a	$\underset{.}{a}$ $\underset{.}{a}$ vel.				reduziert	ϑ α $^{a\ o\ e\ \jmath}$
o $\underset{.}{o}$	o	$\underset{.}{o}$ $\underset{.}{o}$			**Mittelwerte**		
$\ddot{o}$ $\underset{.}{\ddot{o}}$	$\ddot{o}$	$\underset{.}{\ddot{o}}$ $\underset{.}{\ddot{o}}$					
u $\underset{.}{u}$	u	$\underset{.}{u}$ $\underset{.}{u}$			$\ddot{\imath}$　$\underset{(.)}{e}$　$\acute{u}$　$\acute{o}$　α　$\mathring{a}$		
$\ddot{u}$ $\underset{.}{\ddot{u}}$	$\ddot{u}$	$\underset{.}{\ddot{u}}$ $\underset{.}{\ddot{u}}$		zwischen	$i...\ddot{u}$　$\underset{.}{e}...e$　$u...\ddot{u}$　$o...\ddot{o}$　$\underset{.}{e}...a$　$\underset{.}{o}...\underset{.}{a}$		

Länge: $\bar{e}$ $\bar{a}$ $\bar{o}$... *Halblänge:* $\hat{a}$... *Kürze:* unbezeichnet oder $\breve{u}$ $\breve{\imath}$ $\breve{o}$...
Pausen: | *(kurz)* || *(lang)* *(sehr kurze Pause oder neuer Stimmeinsatz)*

Betonung: Der Akzent (ˈ für den Haupt-, ˌ für den Nebenton) steht vor der betonten Silbe; besonders starker Druck wird mit ǁ bezeichnet.

Figure 1.4　　The phonetic signs for use in the *Sprachatlas der deutschen Schweiz*

1.1.7 The wish for a standardization of pronunciation

Another factor that went hand in hand with the study of German sounds was their spelling in the written language. Although we can speak of standard German from the middle of the eighteenth century there was still no completely uniform spelling system for German in the middle of the nineteenth century (see 6.5.1).

Thus at the end of the nineteenth century three streams of scholarly activity come together to form the basis and starting point for our study of the sounds of

German. Firstly, there is the establishment of scientific articulatory phonetics. Secondly, we have the development of the International Phonetic Alphabet and thirdly, the desire arises after the unification of Germany for standardization not only in spelling but also in pronunciation on the basis of the German spoken on the stage that we will consider in 1.2.1.

1.2 Standards of pronunciation for German

In this section we shall look at three approaches at establishing a standard pronunciation for German: (1) the stage pronunciation developed in 1898 by Theodor Siebs and others; (2) the Duden model described in the *Duden Aussprachewörterbuch* and also in the *Duden Grammatik* in West Germany from the 1950s and 1960s, building on the stage pronunciation, with its latest edition published in 2005; and (3) the *Wörterbuch der deutschen Aussprache* developed in former East Germany, based on empirical studies, but now chiefly of historical interest.

Summaries of the historical development of the standardization of pronunciation are E.-M. Krech (1961a), Kurka (1980) and Besch (1990, 2003).

1.2.1 Stage pronunciation (*Die Bühnenaussprache*)

This model has developed from that proposed in 1898 by Theodor Siebs called *die deutsche Bühnenaussprache*. When simply the work is being referred to we will use *Siebs* but the person who initiated its introduction will be referred to as Theodor Siebs.

With the unification of Germany in 1870–71 and the establishment of Berlin as the capital, there arose a desire not only to standardize the spelling of German but also its pronunciation. Never before had there been so many German speakers in one political unit. There were also the German speakers in the Austro-Hungarian Empire as well as those in German Switzerland. The standardization of spelling was achieved by 1901 after several conferences and the initial blocking of reform by the Chancellor Count Otto von Bismarck (1815–98) (see 6.5.1). The standardization of pronunciation on the other hand was something rather different. Pronunciation belongs to speech, which is not subject to the controls that a spelling system can be subject to.

Since the beginning of the nineteenth century it had been suggested that the best type of German pronunciation was to be found among actors on the stage (see 1.1.3). In 1898 Theodor Siebs (1862–1941), a professor of German at the University of Greifswald, initiated a conference in Berlin in the Apollosaal of the National Theatre that was attended by two other academics, Eduard

Sievers (1850–1933), of Leipzig, and Karl Luick (1865–1935), from Austria, as well as three representatives from the *Deutscher Bühnenverein*, Graf Bolko von Hochberg (1843–1926), Berlin, Karl Freiherr von Ledebur (1844–1922), Schwerin and Dr Eduard Tempeltey (1832–1919), Coburg. The resulting publication, edited by Theodor Siebs, was entitled *Deutsche Bühnenaussprache*, with the sub-title *Ergebnisse der Beratungen zur ausgleichenden Regelung der deutschen Bühnenaussprache*, published in 1898. The task of the participants was to propose forms that should be levelled out among the variants used in the national theatres: 'die Unterschiede der Aussprache zwischen den einzelnen Bühnen des ober-, mittel- und niederdeutschen Sprachgebietes auszugleichen' (to level out the differences in pronunciation between the individual theatres of the Upper, Central and Low German speech areas) (Siebs 1905: 6). It was taken for granted that the model for a standard pronunciation was to be found on the stage.

There was also a political dimension to the proposals:

Die so von uns erhoffte Einwirkung der Bühnenaussprache auf die weiten Kreise unserer Nation hat auch eine politische Bedeutung. Ein jeder guter Deutsche, dem die völlige gegenseitige Durchdringung unserer Stämme am Herzen liegt, wird sich über diesen weiteren Schritt zur vollkommenen Einigung freuen.

(This influence of the stage pronunciation on large sections of our nation, which we had so hoped for, also has a political importance. Every good German [citizen] who has the complete infusion of our different ethnic groups [*lit*. tribes] will rejoice at this further step to complete unity.)

(Siebs 1905: 9)

Siebs was a description of carefully pronounced language on stage. It also reflected North German features such as the aspiration, i.e. the production of a puff of air, after *p*, *t*, *k* in initial position before vowels, the labio-dental pronunciation of *w* as in the initial sound of English *van*, and the voiced pronunciation of *s* in initial position before vowels as in English *zoo*.

Theodor Siebs asked the *Allgemeiner Deutscher Sprachverein* to discuss the proposals. They were reviewed by five referees – Prof. Oskar Brenner (1854–1920), Würzburg, Karl Erbe (1845–1927), a head teacher from Ludwigsburg, Prof. Friedrich Kluge (1856–1926), Freiburg im Breisgau, Prof. Hermann Paul (1846–1921), Munich, Prof. Joseph Seemüller (1855–1920), Innsbruck and Vienna – and discussed in the session of 2 October 1898 (*Gutachten* 1899). All the referees advanced various criticisms except for Seemüller, who gave a positive report. The criticisms were made under several headings:

(1) North and Central Germany were adequately represented but not South Germany. This was formulated in the assertion that a real fault was 'die

Umgehung süddeutscher Sprechweise' (the avoidance of South German ways of speaking). It was pointed out that five out of six of those present in Berlin were from North Germany. There was only Luick from Austria. Brenner and Erbe pointed out that several recommendations were strange to speakers from South Germany, e.g. pronouncing the *s* at the beginning of a word such as *sein* like *z* in English *zoo* and the pronunciation of the final consonant in the suffix -*ig* in *zwanzig* like the *ch* in *dich*.

(2) Furthermore schools and other institutions were not represented. The whole endeavour was rather impractical. It would be a long time before these suggested pronunciations would become familiar and acquired by the majority of speakers.

(3) Perhaps one of the most damaging of the critical comments was made by Hermann Paul, who considered the recommendations to be the 'private Ansichten eines Einzelnen' (the private views of one individual).

The committee opted for a compromise: they would publish the referees' reports and ask the local branches of the *Sprachverein* for their opinions. However, these were never forthcoming. The work was republished in 1900 and 1905 and in a concise edition. Wilhelm Viëtor (1850–1918), the influential language teacher and phonetician, supported the main points of the *Bühnenaussprache*. However, he had used the IPA transcription in his pronouncing dictionary (Viëtor 1885), which pre-dates Theodor Siebs' dictionary (1905). Viëtor's dictionary had its last edition in 1941 but has tended to remain in the shadow of *Siebs*.

Theodor Siebs and the original members of the committee had offered no empirical evidence of actual pronunciations, so in 1907 questionnaires were sent out to over 200 theatres and the results collected and studied by a commission of the *Kammerspielhaus des Deutschen Theaters* in Berlin. The recommendations were only changed in a few minor details and a fourth edition appeared in 1909 which, for the first time, also contained a pronouncing dictionary of words and names. The transcription, however, was not the IPA but a system peculiar to *Siebs*, which used letters of the alphabet but modified them with diacritics to show openness and closeness in vowels. An elongated *s* was used for [ʃ] and *ch* was used for the velar fricative, the final sound in *Dach*, but *c´h* for the palatal fricative, the final sound in *dich*.

The work was re-examined in 1922 and remained virtually unchanged although the title was extended to include the term *Hochsprache*. It was also recommended for use by the recently created new medium of radio. In the 1930s the commission accepted two innovations: firstly, the omission of a glottal stop in words beginning with a vowel was permitted as was, secondly, the use of a uvular *r*, produced in the back of the mouth, similar to the French *r*, as against the dental *r* produced in the front of the mouth, similar to the Scots *r* in *ran*. Various other suggestions for revision were made in the 1930s and 1940s but were never carried out.

It wasn't until after Theodor Siebs' death in 1941 and the end of World War II in 1945 that the work could be revised (E.-M. Krech 1961a: 18–22). Committees and commissions were set up in the early 1950s. The eighteenth edition of 1955 was entitled *Siebs Deutsche Hochsprache: Bühnenaussprache*. It was edited by Helmut de Boor (1891–1976) and Paul Diels (1882–1963) and a number of other scholars. The IPA was introduced but the general content was much the same. It was maintained that 'die hier niedergelegten Regeln kein starres Gesetz sind, sondern ein Ideal, das als Ziel und Maßstab für alles gebildete Sprechen aufgestellt ist' (the rules laid down here are no fixed law, but an ideal that is set up for all educated speech) (de Boor and Diels 1955: 6). This ideal was intended not only for the stage but also radio, teaching German to foreigners, school and telecommunications and singing.

The nineteenth and last edition appeared in 1969 and brought the linguistic content up to date with the introduction of the phoneme. It combined the word and name list, adding new words and deleting others. A new distinction was introduced between *reine Hochlautung* (pure standard pronunciation) and *gemäßigte Hochlautung* (moderate standard pronunciation) but it was still the largely prescriptive North German work describing the most formal pronunciation that had started life in 1898.

Linguists describing German pronunciation for foreigners generally support the *Siebs* model, or that which has evolved from it in Duden. Egan (1927: vff.), Wardale (1961: 3f.), Moulton (1962: viiif.), MacCarthy (1975: 5ff.), C. Hall (2003: 5–7), Fox (2005: 32ff.) all mention *Siebs*, albeit with caveats.

1.2.2 The Duden and pronunciation standards

The model of pronunciation that is widely accepted as being standard in the German-speaking countries is known today as *die Standardlautung* (Standard Pronunciation). An easily accessible description of this is in the *Duden Aussprachwörterbuch* (*DAW* 2005). There is not only a description of which pronunciations are considered standard but also a dictionary containing words and names in IPA.

The editors of *DAW*, Max Mangold and anonymous members of the Duden editorial board, concede that it is difficult to implement a standard for pronunciation. They also maintain that the *Bühnenaussprache*, discussed in 1.2.1, has been succeeded by a new norm, *Standardaussprache* or *Standardlautung*.

They contrast this norm with the non-normalized pronunciation of colloquial speech (*Umgangslautung*) and the over-exaggerated pronunciation used for dictation, singing etc. (*Überlautung*). It is the *Standardlautung* that we will take as the basis for our description of German sounds in this book.

They describe it in the following terms (being a free translation and paraphrase of *DAW* 2005: 34f.). This norm has five characteristics:

(1) It is a norm based on usage (*Gebrauchsnorm*) that is close to real speech although it cannot hope to reflect all the nuances of spoken language.
(2) It is supraregional and has no features that are regionally restricted.
(3) It is uniform. Any free variation or variation between phonemes in different words is either eliminated or reduced to a minimum.
(4) It is close to the spelling and is largely determined by the orthography.
(5) It is clear, distinguishes sounds more strongly than the colloquial pronunciation on the one hand but on the other hand it is weaker than the *Bühnenaussprache*, which tends to be more exaggerated in pronunciation.

Any stylistic levels within this norm are largely ignored since the attempts to distinguish them have not resulted in uniform and clear results.

In Chapters 3 and 4 the actual details of the articulation for each sound will be described.

1.2.3 Pronunciation standards in former East Germany as reflected in the *Wörterbuch der deutschen Aussprache*

The question of a standard for pronunciation was also being researched in East Germany from the 1950s (E.-M. Krech 1961b: 22–37). The result was the *Wörterbuch der deutschen Aussprache* (*WDA*), whose first edition appeared in 1964. The authors acknowledge their debt to Wilhelm Viëtor and Theodor Siebs but since the nineteenth century the pronunciation model has been extended to the alliterative 'Funk, Film und Fernsehen' ('Radio, film and television'). The editors of the *WDA* wanted to extend the relevance of their description to school and the teaching of German to foreigners. They also wanted to set up a description that reflects linguistic reality (*Sprechwirklichkeit*). The *WDA* was based on empirical investigations, analysing the speech of professional newsreaders among others. The result was a greater tolerance of usage in allegro speech. H. Krech *et al.* (1971) also take up the use of *reine und gemäßigte Hochlautung* as in Duden and *Siebs*.

1.2.4 The terms used in the standardization of German pronunciation

As we have seen in 1.2.1, the first important term to be suggested was *Bühnenaussprache*. To avoid the ambiguity of the word *Hochsprache*, which could refer to the standard language in general and not specifically to standard pronunciation, the term *Hochlautung* was introduced in the 1962 *Duden Aussprachewörterbuch*, for standard pronunciation, as an ideal norm, that was supraregional, uniform, close to the orthography and clear in enunciation. It was also used in *Duden Grammatik* (1966) and then in *Siebs* (1969). Below this norm two levels were recognized, the so-called 'moderate standard' (*gemäßigte Hochlautung*) and the 'non-standard' (*Nichthochlautung*). The term *Hochlautung* is not in fact a creation of the 1960s, although it may have been independently invented. One of its first usages was by Ewald Geißler in 1933:

Soll aus diesen Gründen das Wort 'Hochsprache' aus der Einengung auf die Aussprache frei gemacht werden, so bleibt für diese natürlich noch ein Sondername zu finden. Als solcher bietet sich ungezwungen die 'Hochlautung' an. Ein eindeutiges, schlagendes, auch der Sippenbildung fähiges Wort. 'Der Hochlaut' ist der Gegensatz zum mundartigen [*sic*] und zum Umgangslaut; dazu ergibt sich das Eigenschaftswort 'hochlautig' und sogar ein Zeitwort 'hochlauten', wie es von 'Hochsprache' nicht mehr zu bilden ist.

(If therefore the term 'Hochsprache' is to be freed from its restrictive reference to pronunciation, then a special term has to be found for this. The term 'Hochlautung' is a natural one for this meaning. [It is] a clear, striking word that is capable of forming a word family. 'Der Hochlaut' is the opposite of the dialect and colloquial sound; from this there is the adjective 'hochlautig' and even a verb 'hochlauten', which it is not possible to form from 'Hochsprache'.)

(Geißler 1933: 318)

Needless to say, the other terms have not become part of German vocabulary. The term *Standardlautung* takes over from *Hochlautung* in the 1990s after *Standardsprache* had been introduced in the 1970s on the model of English 'standard language'.

1.3 Conclusion

When Theodor Siebs first proposed the *Bühnenaussprache*, the German Empire was in the ascendant. Nowadays, after two world wars and forty years of division, German and Germany have a very different role and image in Europe and among German-speaking countries. In Austria and Switzerland national norms of pronunciation that deviate from *Siebs* have come into use against the background of German as a pluricentric language (see Chapter 11, Ammon 1995 and Ammon *et al.* 2004) and have become increasingly important.

Against this differentiated background this volume is intended to present the pronunciation of German and the function of its sounds as distinctive units and to illuminate the variation in the language and the historical development of its sounds.

QUESTIONS

1   Describe some of the features of human language. Use Hockett (1958 and 1960). There is a useful summary in Crystal (1987: 395–403). Which to you are the most important and why?

2   What relationship does speech have to writing?

3   Using the following two quotations from Goethe, discuss what some of his goals were in suggesting a model pronunciation:

   (i) Bei den Wörtern, welche sich auf -em und -en endigen, muss man darauf achten, die letzte Silbe deutlich auszusprechen; denn sonst geht die Silbe verloren, indem man das e gar nicht hört. Zum Beispiel: *folgendem*, nicht *folgendm*, *hörendem*, nicht *hörendm*, et cetera.
   (ii) So auch das p und b, das t und d muss merklich unterschieden werden. Daher soll der Anfanger bei beiden einen großen Unterschied machen und p und t starker aussprechen, als es eigentlich sein darf, besonders wenn er vermöge seines Dialekts sich leicht zum Gegenteil neigen sollte.

   (Beutler 1964: 73)

4   Why was it necessary to develop an International Phonetic Alphabet?

5   Construct a chronology for the development of a standard pronunciation for German using Kohler (1995: 25–41) and de Boor *et al.* (1969: 8–15). How successful have the efforts been?

6   Contrast the models of 'best' pronunciation in English and German.

7   How far does the use of standard pronunciation in German depend on the level and social class of the speakers?

8   Ask several native speakers of German what they consider to be the best German pronunciation. Note also how they pronounce: (i) *r* in various positions in the word, (ii) the ending *-ig*, e.g. *König, zwanzig*, (iii) the *s* in *sind*, and (iv) the *ä* in words such as *Käse, spät*. How far do their pronunciations agree?

2 Basic concepts

2.0 Introduction

In this chapter we will describe the mechanisms of vocal communication. This will involve: the organs of speech, air-stream mechanisms, types of sounds, different vowels and consonants and the behaviour of the vocal cords. Many of these basic concepts of speech production are treated in more detail in Abercrombie (1967), O'Connor (1973), Catford (1988), Borden *et al.* (2003) and Ladefoged (2005). Concise and useful accounts are to be found in Crystal (1987: 123–75 and 1995: 236–49).

2.1 Vocal communication

Within an act of vocal communication between two speaker/hearers one speaker/hearer conceptualizes an event and through neural activity in the brain and neuromuscular activity speech is produced and then heard, perceived and understood.

In this book we are concerned with the different phases of speech production: (1) the articulatory or organic phase; (2) the aerodynamic phase; (3) the acoustic phase; and (4) the auditory phase.

The articulatory or organic phase comprises an articulatory component, the positioning and movement of the organs of speech and the spaces within which they operate, e.g. the vocal cavity. The aerodynamic phase is how the air-stream that comes up from the lungs is modified. In the acoustic phase, sound waves are created through the expulsion of air through the mouth and/or nose and these are picked up by the ear of the speaker/hearer. The auditory phase is how the ear registers the sound and interprets it.

Corresponding to these phases sounds can be described in the discipline of phonetics as: articulatory, acoustic and auditory. Articulatory phonetics deals

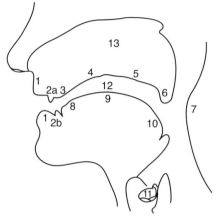

1   Lips
2a Upper teeth
2b Lower teeth
3   Alveolar ridge
4   Hard palate
5   Soft palate or velum
6   Uvula
7   Wall of the pharynx
8   Apex of tongue
9   Dorsum or back of tongue
10 Root of tongue
11 Glottis with vocal cords (within the larynx)
12 Oral cavity
13 Nasal cavity

Figure 2.1   The organs of speech

with how the organs of speech modify the air-stream that comes from the lungs. Acoustic phonetics consists of recording the sound waves so produced and registering their amplitude (strength of articulation) and their duration. Auditory phonetics, how the ear registers sound, is treated in some of the contributions to Hardcastle and Laver (1997), notably Stevens (1997: 462–506), Delgutte (1997: 507–38), Moore (1997: 539–65) and McQueen and Cutler (1997: 566–85). In our treatment of German sounds we will be concentrating on the articulatory side of phonetics.

2.2 The organs of speech

The organs involved in the articulation of speech sounds (Fig. 2.1) are not only used for that sole purpose. Their main functions are breathing and eating. These organs are to be found in the vocal tract that we will take as extending from the lungs to the mouth and nose. The movement of the lungs, their

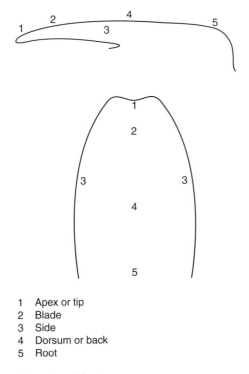

1   Apex or tip
2   Blade
3   Side
4   Dorsum or back
5   Root

Figure 2.2   The parts of the tongue

inflation and deflation, acts as a pair of bellows in forcing air up the trachea, or windpipe, and past the larynx (see 2.3). Above the larynx is the first of three cavities that can change in size or volume according to the movement of the organs of speech. This is the pharynx or pharyngeal cavity. Moving upwards and in the direction of the mouth there is the tongue with its different parts, designated root, dorsum or back, sides, blade and tip, although they don't correspond to obvious anatomical divisions (Fig. 2.2). The tongue is an extremely active organ of speech and moves about in the second cavity, the oral cavity, changing the latter's size and volume, and is involved in the articulation of both vowels and consonants. At the top of the oral cavity is the roof of the mouth, which can be divided into the hard and soft palate. Moving from the back of the oral cavity, the pharyngeal wall, towards the mouth we have the alveolar ridge, the teeth and the upper lip. All of these have counterparts on the base of the mouth, e.g. lower lip etc. The third cavity is the nasal cavity, which can be sealed off from the oral cavity by raising the velum, the moveable part of the soft palate, so that air only flows out through the mouth.

The movement and shape of these articulators modify the shape of the different cavities and help to produce different speech sounds. Articulators

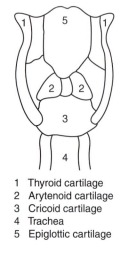

1 Thyroid cartilage
2 Arytenoid cartilage
3 Cricoid cartilage
4 Trachea
5 Epiglottic cartilage

Figure 2.3   The larynx

can be active – the lower lip, the tongue (the most active), the pharynx, the soft palate, particularly the uvula – whereas the other articulators, the upper lip, the upper teeth and the hard palate, are passive.

2.3 The larynx (*der Kehlkopf*)

The larynx is situated at the top of the windpipe or trachea (Fig. 2.3). It acts as a sound box, modifying and magnifying the air-stream from the lungs. It also acts like a valve between the supraglottal cavities and the area below it by moving up and down, controlling the flow of air. It comprises cartilages with connecting ligaments and membranes. At the front is the thyroid cartilage, which sticks out and is called the Adam's apple and is sometimes prominent in men. Above the larynx but below the root of the tongue is the epiglottis, which has no role in speech production but prevents substances from being swallowed the 'wrong' way. Within the larynx, protected by the cricoid and the two arytenoid cartilages are the vocal cords or folds. These are two extremely muscular ledges, rather like lips, that can take up different positions (Fig. 2.4). The space between them when they are not completely closed is called the glottis (*die Glottis*). Normally the glottis is open, the vocal cords are at rest, and the air-stream passes through. This is the position for normal breathing and producing voiceless sounds, e.g. [f s p t k]. If the vocal cords are vibrating, opening and closing at a rapid speed, then the sounds produced are called voiced sounds, e.g. [z v b d g] and most vowels in English and German. If we put a finger and thumb on our Adam's apple we can feel the vibration, or, if

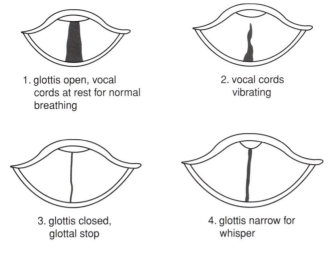

Figure 2.4   Positions or states of the vocal cords

we put our fingers in our ears we can hear a buzzing. If the glottis is closed and then opened, e.g. when we cough or hiccup, we are producing the glottal stop as in the London (Cockney) or Glasgow pronunciation of the medial stop in *better*, or before the initial vowel of the second word in *four apples*, with no linking [r]. The vocal cords can also be narrowed, producing a 'hushing' sound that is known as a whisper. These types of activities of the vocal cords and the glottis are known as phonation.

2.4 Air-stream mechanisms

In producing sounds the air-stream is set in motion by an initiator, in most cases the lungs. As these are deflated they expel air past the larynx, through the oral cavity and out through the mouth. In the case of nasals, e.g. [m n ŋ], the air is also expelled through the nose. This air-stream is called pulmonic since it originates in the lungs (Fig. 2.5). It is also called egressive since it exits through the mouth and nose. Sounds in German and English are normally produced by an egressive pulmonic air-stream. Sounds can also be produced by an ingressive air-stream and by velaric suction, e.g. click consonants in some African languages.

2.5 Some acoustic characteristics of sounds

We have seen that the larynx acts like a sound box modifying the rates of air that are released through the action of the glottis. The rate at which puffs or bursts

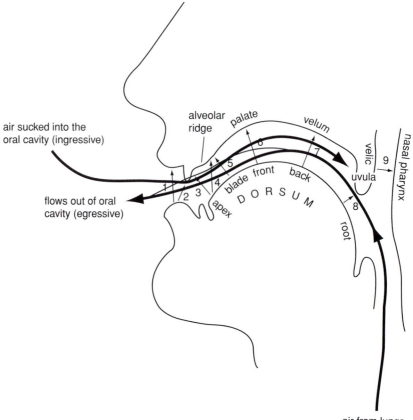

Figure 2.5   Air-stream mechanisms

of air are released through the glottis is measured in openings and closings of the glottis per second. The glottis opens and closes extremely quickly. Every second the glottis will have completed a cycle of 100 openings and closings. The sound wave form will have repeated itself one hundred times a second. This frequency gives the sound its pitch, which is measured in Hertz. The vowel in *father* is normally 100 Hertz. These waveforms will have a constant shape even if they occur with different frequencies. The amplitude, or loudness, of the same sound in *father* will have the same shape as the one used for pitch but will vary in size, being either larger or smaller. This depends on the size of variation in air-pressure. For a vowel like [a] in *father* the oral cavity will be larger than for [i] in *deed* where the oral cavity is smaller (Fig. 2.6). Amplitude is measured in decibels. The quality, or timbre, of a sound shows itself in a different pattern of sound wave. For more information on acoustic phonetics with reference

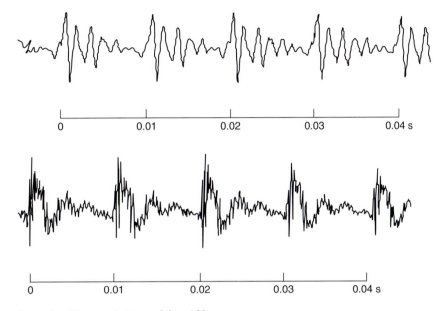

Figure 2.6   Acoustic difference between [a] and [i]

to recent secondary literature, see Borden *et al.* (2003) Ladefoged (2005) and Shadle (2006).

2.6 Types of sounds

Phoneticians distinguish between vowels (*der Vokal, -e*) and consonants (*der Konsonant, -en*). The vowels of German will be described in detail in Chapter 3 and the consonants in Chapter 4.

2.6.1 Vowels

In the articulation of vowels the air-stream from the lungs passes unhindered over the centre of the tongue through the mouth. Vowels are classified firstly according to their tongue height: thus there are high vowels such as [u], mid vowels such as [e] and low vowels such as [a]. Since the oral cavity is modified by tongue height the terms close, half-close, half-open and open are also used (Fig. 2.7). Secondly, vowels are classified according to the position of the tongue in the mouth. Thus there are front vowels such as [i e] and back vowels such as [u o]. Thirdly, vowels are classified according to the shape of the lips, whether these are rounded as is the case in [u o] or spread as is the case in [i e] (Fig. 2.8). Vowels usually form the nucleus, or peak, of a syllable (see 7.1). In German,

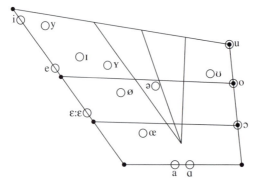

Figure 2.7   Schema for tongue heights

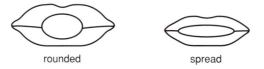

rounded   spread

Figure 2.8   Position and shape of the lips

vowels are always voiced, the vocal cords vibrating. In other languages voiceless vowels occur.

2.6.2 Consonants

Consonants are classified according to whether the air-stream is either completely stopped by a stricture at some point in the oral cavity, or narrowed so that audible friction is produced. In the first case the consonants are called stops or plosives, e.g. [p d] etc., and in the second case, fricatives, e.g. [s v] etc. This is called the manner of articulation. There are other less frequent manners of articulation: lateral, as in [l], where the air-stream is expelled past the sides or one side of the tongue, which makes a closure with its tip against the upper alveolar ridge, or trills or vibrants, e.g. [r] in which the tongue is trilled against the teeth or [R] in which the uvula is trilled against the pharyngeal wall.

It also important to know for consonants where the stricture or friction is taking place. This is known as the point or place of articulation, e.g. with lips (labial), [p b f v]; with the teeth or alveolar ridge (dental or alveolar), [t d s z]; or in the back of the mouth (palatal and velar), [k g ç x].

2.6.3 State of the vocal cords

There is another fundamental distinction in the articulation of obstruents that is created by the behaviour of the vocal cords (see Fig. 2.4). In the pronunciation

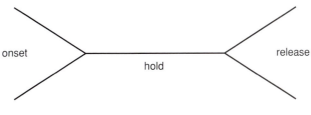

Figure 2.9   Stages in the articulation of plosives

of the plosives [b d g] and the fricatives [v z ʒ] the vocal cords are narrowed so that the air-stream is forced through between them and they vibrate. These sounds are voiced (*stimmhaft*). In the case of the pronunciation of the plosives [p t k] and the fricatives [f s ʃ ç x] the vocal cords are widened and the air-stream flows through without them vibrating. These sounds are voiceless (*stimmlos*). The German affricates [pf ts tʃ] are also voiceless. The nasals and vowels are always voiced. In connected speech, however, voiced and voiceless sounds influence each other.

2.6.4 The release of the occlusion in the pronunciation of plosives

There are three stages in the articulation of plosives: the onset (when the closure or occlusion is made), the hold (the length of the closure) and then the release (when the closure is opened) (Fig. 2.9). When an initial voiceless plosive is released in German a puff of air immediately follows, this being symbolized by writing [h] after the plosive: [ph th kh]. These plosives are known as aspirated plosives. In French, for instance, the initial voiceless plosives are not aspirated, but the vocal cords start to vibrate immediately after the closure is released, whereas in the case of the aspirated voiceless plosives this vibration does not start immediately. Aspiration is acoustically the absence of voicing between the release of the closure and the beginning of voicing in the following vowel. Unaspirated voiceless plosives also occur in some German dialects, particularly in the south, and in these cases the distinction between [p] and [b] is not between a voiceless and a voiced plosive, but rather between different strengths of articulation. The plosive [p] is described as being fortis, that is more force is used in its articulation, and [b] is described as being lenis, less strength being used in its articulation. The terms 'fortis' and 'lenis' are sometimes used without specifying clearly what articulatory or acoustic features they refer to and in general they are best avoided. The terms 'tense' (*gespannt*) and 'lax' (*ungespannt*) have also been suggested to describe the difference in strength

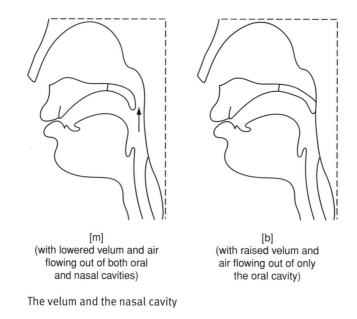

[m]
(with lowered velum and air
flowing out of both oral
and nasal cavities)

[b]
(with raised velum and
air flowing out of only
the oral cavity)

Figure 2.10   The velum and the nasal cavity

of articulation of consonants. We will retain the main features of voiced and voiceless.

2.6.5 The role of the velum and the nasal cavity

The nasal cavity through which air from the lungs is expelled through the nose also plays an important role in the articulation of both consonants and vowels. The entrance to the nasal cavity can be controlled by the soft palate, or velum, which can either seal it off by making a closure with the back wall of the mouth (the pharynx), only allowing the air-stream to pass through the mouth, or it can hang loose and allow the air-stream to be expelled through both the mouth and the nose (Fig. 2.10). Sounds in the production of which the air-stream is expelled only through the mouth are called oral sounds, and those in the production of which the air-stream is expelled through both the mouth and nose are called nasal sounds. In German both oral and nasal consonants exist, for instance the initial consonant in *Bein* is oral and the initial consonant in *mein* is nasal. In the articulation of both sounds there is a closure of both lips but when this is released the air-stream flows only out of the mouth in the case of [b] (see Fig. 2.10). The velum blocks the air-flow escaping through the nasal cavity. In the case of [m], however, after the release of the closure of both lips the air flows out through both the oral and the nasal cavity. The vocal cords are vibrating since both sounds are voiced.

2.6.6 Vowel or consonant?

Sounds such as [j] or [w], depending on how much friction is produced, sometimes act like a vowel and sometimes like a consonant. This ambiguity expresses itself in the use of such terms as semi-vowel (or more unusually semiconsonant) or frictionless continuant. The term approximant, suggested by Ladefoged (2005: 52f.), in whose articulation the organs of speech simply approximate to an articulation and no friction is produced, is to be preferred (Abercrombie 1967: 50). The initial sounds in English *yet* and *wet* are classified as approximants.

The nasal consonants [m n ŋ] can also function as vowels. The vowel in the unstressed ending *-en*, is usually pronounced [-ən], but is replaced in colloquial speech by a syllabic nasal symbolized [n̩] (thus *leben* may be pronounced [leːbn̩]) and in some cases the syllabic nasal is assimilated to the place of articulation of the preceding plosive: [leːbm̩] *leben* in the case of a labial plosive or [dɛŋkŋ̍] *denken* in the case of a velar plosive. The lateral [l] also functions as a vowel. The vowel in the ending *-el* is sometimes replaced by a syllabic [l̩], e.g. *Mantel* [mantl̩]. The vibrant or trill [r] can also function as a vowel in some Slavonic languages, e.g. the Croatian island *Krk*, but not in German.

2.6.7 The case of [h]

The initial sound in German *hat* is classified as a glottal fricative: that is, the glottis, the space between the vocal cords, is almost closed. It is also called a cavity fricative since most of the friction is produced in the throat cavity. The articulation of [h] is determined by the vowel that follows, and there are as many different positions of the vocal tract for [h] as there are vowels.

2.6.8 The glottal stop (*der Glottisschlag, -ë*)

If the glottis is closed completely (see Fig. 2.4) a glottal stop results, symbolized [ʔ]. In English this sometimes occurs instead of the intervocalic plosive [t] in words such as *butter* or instead of the linking *r* at the end of a word when the next word begins with a vowel, e.g. *four apples*. In German it is found initially before a vowel, e.g. *ein* [ʔain] (also called *der harte Vokaleinsatz* or *der Grenzsignal*). It also occurs between vowels as in *Theater* [teʔatər], or after the prefixes *er-* and *ver-*, but before vowels: *erinnern* [ɛrʔinərn], *Verein* [fɛrʔain]. It is typical of North German speech and is often not used in South Germany and Austria.

QUESTIONS

1   Fill in the names of the organs of speech that are numbered in the diagram below:

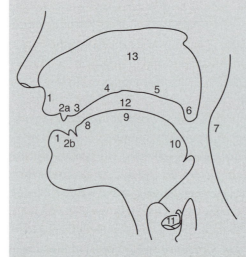

2   In the pronunciation of which of the following sounds do the vocal cords vibrate: [p v z n a l d s]? How can we know that this is happening?

3   Which of the following sounds are voiceless: [n o s t m p]? Sketch the position of the glottis during their articulation.

4   Sketch in the position of the velum in the diagram for the pronunciation of [d] and [n]?

5   How can such sounds as [j] and [w] be classified in relation to the terms 'vowel' and 'consonant'?

6   How far are foreign words used in German phonetic terminology? Is there any trend in an increasing internationalization of this terminology?

7   What are the German terms for: vowel, vocal cords, voiced, voiceless, fricative, front vowel?

8   What are the English terms for: *Verschlusslaut*, *Zäpfchen*, *Glottisschlag*, *Kehlkopf*, *Hinterzungenvokal*?

3 Vowels

3.0 Introduction

Vowels are classified not by different types of strictures as in the case of consonants but by the modification of the oral cavity and the shape of the lips. The oral cavity is modified through the position and height of the tongue. For the vowels there are three tongue heights: high, mid and low, which correspond to close, half-open and open on the vowel diagram (see Fig. 2.7). In the descriptions of the vowels both sets of terms will be used, even though they might appear redundant. According to the position of the dorsum or back of the tongue, vowels are either produced in the front or the back of the oral cavity. The shape of the lips, whether they are rounded or spread, is another important feature in the description of vowels (see Fig. 2.8). Their importance varies from language to language. In English front vowels are always pronounced with spread lips and back vowels with rounded lips, whereas in German there are also front vowels pronounced with rounded lips.

As well as the qualitative differences between vowels, shown by the position of the tongue, its height and the shape of the lips, there is also a quantitative difference between vowels that are short in duration and those that are long. The IPA uses the colon [:] to designate long vowels, e.g. *tief* [tiːf]. In addition, the long vowels are said to be 'tense' (*gespannt*) and the short vowels 'lax' (*ungespannt*). This difference has been ascribed to 'muscular tension' (C. Hall 2003: 76). However, this difference is also 'a matter of dispute' (Benware 1986: 12) and it is not certain what it means (Fox 2005: 41). Kohler (1995: 170f.) uses the feature pair tense/lax as does Becker (1998: 47). He regards them as being realized phonetically by length and lowering, but it is not clear how this relates to muscular tension. The main factor, however, influencing the use of the tense/lax distinction is that it is linked with stress. Stressed long vowels are tense while stressed short vowels are lax.

The high or close vowels are [i y u], which are realized as long tense vowels (*bieten, Tüten, tuten*) in opposition to the short lax vowels (*bitten, Hütte, Mutter*). The mid vowels are [e ø o], which are realized as the long tense vowels (*beten, löten, Boten*) in opposition to the short lax vowels: *Betten, Götter, Motten*. The open vowel [a] shows a minimal difference in tenseness between short *Bann* and long *Bahn*. The front low vowel [ɛ:] is an anomaly, being both long and lax, but it has arisen as a spelling pronunciation for words containing long <ä>. In addition, in north Germany [e:] has largely taken its place.

Another feature of the articulation of both short and long vowels as well as diphthongs in German is that the velum or soft palate is raised and the nasal cavity sealed off. Vowels produced in this way are called oral vowels. Nasal vowels, where the air-stream is expelled through the mouth and also the nose by not raising the velum, only occur in some French loan words in German, e.g. *Teint* 'complexion', *Fonds* 'fund' (see 8.2.1.2).

3.1 Short and long vowels

We will first consider the stressed vowels that form the nucleus, or peak, of the syllable in German. During the production of vowels by the air-stream from the lungs passing unhindered over the centre of the tongue, the height of the tongue may vary, making the vocal tract large or small. The positions and heights of the tongue have been captured by X-ray photography and measured. However, what is important is not any exact measurement of tongue height or frontness or backness but the position of the vowels relative to each other. The description of the relative space between vowels has been made on the basis of the so-called Cardinal Vowels (CVs). These are essentially an ideal qualitative pronunciation of vowel sounds first set out and recorded by the English phonetician Daniel Jones (1881–1967). They can be represented by the well-known vowel trapeze for the primary CVs that gives a number to each vowel from 1 to 8 (Fig. 3.1).

In the pronunciation of the vowel of the German word *Kinn* the tongue is high in the mouth and narrows the vocal tract considerably, whereas in the pronunciation of the German word *kann* the tongue is low in the mouth and the vocal tract is very open. In the pronunciation of the vowel of the German word *Kunde* the vocal tract is very closed and the tongue is high in the mouth.

Thus vowels such as the [i] of *Kinn* and the [u] of *Kunde* are classified as close vowels and [a] of *kann* as an open vowel. The vowels [i] and [u] also differ from one another in that the tongue is positioned in a different part of the mouth during their articulation. The vowel [i] is produced by raising and advancing

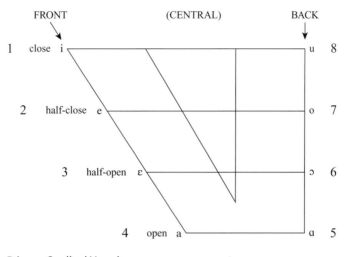

Figure 3.1   Primary Cardinal Vowels

the blade of the tongue towards the front of the mouth whereas [u] is produced by raising the back of the tongue towards the velum. The vowel [a] can also be produced by the tongue being at the front or back of the mouth. Vowels whose articulation is accompanied by a relatively forward position of the tongue in the vocal tract are called front vowels (*Vorderzungenvokale*). Those whose articulation is accompanied by a relatively retracted position of the tongue are called back vowels (*Hinterzungenvokale*). The vowel [i] is therefore a close front vowel and [u] is a close back vowel. In the pronunciation of [i] and [u] yet another dimension can be seen, i.e. the shape of the lips. In the articulation of [u] the lips are rounded and in the articulation of [i] the lips are spread, or neutral, and not rounded.

Between the two extremes of close [i] and [u] and open [a] there are intermediate stages. These intermediate stages are represented by the vowels in the German words *Bett* and *Gott* which are close to the CVs 3 and 6 respectively. The vowel in *Bett* is represented by the IPA symbol [ɛ] and is usually classed as a half-open front vowel. The vowel in *Gott* is represented by the IPA symbol [ɔ] and is usually classed as a half-open back vowel. The stressed vowels in German *leben* and *loben* are long half-close vowels, written [eː] and [oː], close to CVs 2 and 7. (Vowel length is not used in the CV diagram.) The half-open long [ɛː] appears long only in some varieties of German: some speakers distinguish between the stressed vowels in *Beeren* and *Bären* by pronouncing the first as a long half-close vowel [eː] and the second as a long half-open vowel [ɛː], close to a long version of CV 3. The short vowels [i] and [u], corresponding to CVs 1 and 8, have long counterparts in German; compare the pairs *binnen* and

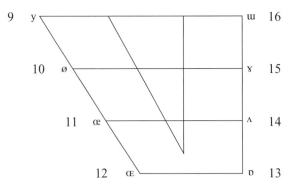

Figure 3.2   Secondary Cardinal Vowels

Bienen, Bucht and *Buch*. It has become usual to consider the short close vowels as being slightly more open with a slightly lower tongue height than the long close vowels and to write the former [ɪ] and [ʊ] and the latter [iː] and [uː]. Although the exact details may not be completely accurate the trapeze diagram for the CVs is a handy way of portraying the relative articulatory and auditory distances between the vowels.

3.2 Front rounded and back unrounded vowels

There are also secondary CVs, again represented by a trapeze diagram where 9–12 are rounded and 13–16 unrounded (Fig. 3.2). These secondary CVs are less frequent, although the front rounded ones occur in German and French. The front vowels so far mentioned, CVs 1–4, are pronounced with no lip-rounding, the back vowels, 6–8, having lip-rounding. The open vowel [a], CV 5, is neutral with respect to lip-rounding. However, the German vowel sounds in *Bühne, schön* and *können* are examples of front vowels with lip-rounding, corresponding to the secondary CVs 9, 10 and 11 respectively. The German front rounded vowels are also distinguished according to whether they are close or open. The vowel in *Bühne* is close, the vowel in *schön* is half-close, and the vowel in *können* is half-open. They are transcribed [yː], [øː] and [œ] respectively. The short counterpart of [yː] appears in *müssen* and is slightly more open, i.e. the tongue height is slightly lower. It is written [ʏ] in phonetic script. The open vowel [a] is a central vowel. During its articulation the main part of the tongue is in the centre of the vowel tract. It is a low vowel. The short vowel in *Ratte* is pronounced with the tongue slightly more advanced than for the long vowel in *raten*. They are symbolized [a] and [ɑː] respectively.

3.3 Diphthongs and sequences of vowels

In the articulation of both the short and long vowels the position of the tongue has remained constant throughout. These vowels are called monophthongs (*der Monophthong, -e*). If the position of the tongue changes during the articulation of a vowel then the vowel is described as a diphthong (*der Diphthong, -e*), e.g. the vowel sounds in *Stein, Zaun, neun*. For purposes of transcription, they are considered as having two components, symbolized [ai], [au] and [oi]. They can be described in the same way as ordinary vowels. German has three so-called falling diphthongs, that is having the stress on the first component. These are the sounds in the words: *mein, Haus, euch*. (For more details on the choice of transcription symbols, see 3.5.3.) Diphthongs must be distinguished from sequences of two vowels, e.g. *a* and *i* in *prosaisch*, *a* and *o* in *Chaos* and *u* and *u* in *Kontinuum*. In these cases the first vowel is usually long, or if short it is close, there is often a glottal stop or a slight pause between the two vowels and they belong to separate syllables.

Another type of vocalic sequence occurs in foreign words where an unstressed non-syllabic vowel precedes another vowel, which is usually, but not always, stressed. To signify that a vowel is non-syllabic the diacritic [ˎ] is used. The most frequent non-syllabic vowels are [i, u], written *i* and *u*: *Studium, Italien; aktuell, rituell*. The vowels *e, y* and *o* do occur, but not so frequently: *Petroleum, Hyäne, loyal, Memoiren*. There is a tendency for the high vowels to become the palatal fricative [j] and the mid back [o] to become the bilabial fricative [w].

3.4 Unstressed vowels

As well as the vowels that bear the main stress in the word there are also unstressed vowels. The main vowel in unstressed syllables is the *-e* of *bitte*, a central unrounded close vowel, written phonetically [ə], called schwa. It occurs mainly after the chief stress in a word, e.g. *bitte, Klasse, Name*, but also before the chief stress in a word in the prefixes *be-* (*bezahlt*), *ge-* (*gegeben*). Schwa also occurs in the careful pronunciation of the unstressed ending *-er*. In colloquial speech, however, the ending *-er* is vocalized to become [ɐ], so-called 'dark schwa', a central half-open vowel (see 3.5.4.2). This pronunciation has now been accepted by *DAW*. In *WDA* it was viewed as an alternative.

Other unstressed vowels do occur, e.g. the final vowels in *Sofa, Kino, Mutti, Uhu*, but mostly in foreign words or, in the case of *-i*, words denoting people (see 8.2.2.2). There are also other unstressed vowels in polysyllabic words through the introduction of Latin and French loan words: *Philologie, thematisieren*.

	Front unrounded	Front rounded	Central	Back rounded
Close (High)	ɪ	ʏ		ʊ
Half-open (mid-low)	ɛ	œ		ɔ
Open (low)			a	

Figure 3.3   Stressed, short, lax vowels in German

3.5 The vowels in detail

Our goal in this chapter is to review the vowels of German one by one and look at them from five different aspects:

(1) their articulation, how they are produced
(2) the main spelling of a particular sound (further details will be given in Chapter 6)
(3) a concise statement of their distribution; a fuller statement will be in Chapters 6 and 7
(4) any similarities with English sounds to help in learning to pronounce them: Received Pronunciation (RP) will be used as a reference point, and readers should refer to the relevant articles in Britain (2007), Cruttenden (1994), Nevalainen and van Ostade (2006: 306–11) and Crystal (1987); for American usage, see Moulton (1962)
(5) what major variants exist in different areas of the German-speaking speech area: these will not be treated in a systematic way and readers should refer to the contributions in Russ (1990).

At this stage we will regard the vowels as sounds and write them in square brackets. In Chapter 5 their phonemic status will be justified with examples of oppositions and distinctive features.

Detailed descriptions of German vowels, often with diagrams and photographs, can be found in C. and P. Martens (1961: 27–107), Wängler (1983: 90–117), MacCarthy (1975: 37–52), Kohler (1995: 169–75), Becker (1998) and C. Hall (2003: 72–108) as well as in this book.

3.5.1 Short lax vowels

There are seven short, lax vowels in German: [ɪ ʏ ʊ ɛ œ ɔ a], as can be seen in Fig. 3.3.

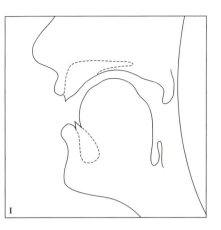

Figure 3.4   Tongue position for short [ɪ]

3.5.1.1 Short high close front unrounded vowel [ɪ]

(i) Articulation

The short vowel [ɪ] is pronounced with the dorsum of the tongue raised in the front of the oral cavity and with spread lips. The tongue height is slightly lower and more central than for long [iː] (Fig. 3.4).

(ii) Spelling

It is normally spelt <i>: *Gift, schwimmen.*

(iii) Distribution

It occurs before stops (*Lippe, kribbeln* 'to tickle', *bitte, Widder* 'ram', *schicken, Riggung* 'rigging'), fricatives (*Schiffe, wissen, wischen, wichen*), nasals (*Zimmer, binnen*), liquids (*Willen, irren*).

(iv) Similarity to English sounds

It is similar to the vowels in English *gift, swim.* It should not be centralized.

(v) Major variants

In southern Germany and Austria short [i] has a closer and tenser articulation whereas in northern Germany it tends to be made more open, sounding like [e]. Also in northern Germany before [r] it tends to be rounded, approaching [ʏ].

3.5.1.2 Short high close front rounded vowel [ʏ]

(i) Articulation

The articulation is similar to [ɪ] as far as the height and position of the tongue, but the lips are rounded (Fig. 3.5).

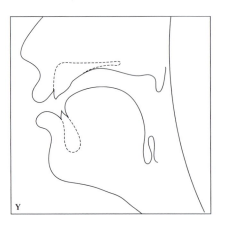

Figure 3.5   Tongue position for short [y]

(ii) Spelling

It is normally spelt <ü> but also <y> in Greek loan words: *Mütze,*
Hymne.

(iii) Distribution

It occurs before stops (*üppig, schütten, pflücken, flügge* 'fully-fledged'),
fricatives (*süffig, Küsse, Büsche, Brüche*), nasals (*dümmer, dünner*),
liquids (*füllen, Dürre*).

(iv) Similarity to English sounds

This vowel does not exist in English but it is similar to the vowel in Scots
look.

(v) Major variants

The short [y] is often lowered to sound like [œ] in north Germany. In
Central and Upper German dialects it is often derounded.

3.5.1.3 Short high close back vowel [ʊ]

(i) Articulation

The sound [ʊ] is pronounced with the tongue position slightly over
half-close in the back of the oral cavity with rounded lips (Fig. 3.6).

(ii) Spelling

It is normally spelt <u>: *Butter.*

(iii) Distribution

It occurs before stops (*struppig, Knubbel* 'lump', *Butter, buddeln, spucken,*
schmuggeln), fricatives (*muffig, Busse, pfuschen, bruchig*), nasals
(*Rummel, Zunge*), liquids (*Stulle* 'slice of bread and butter', *murren*).

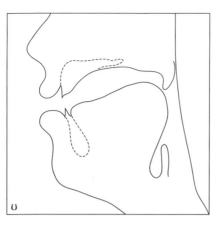

Figure 3.6   Tongue position for short [ʊ]

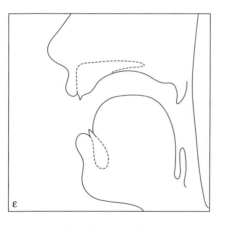

Figure 3.7   Tongue position for short [ɛ]

(iv) Similarity to English sounds

It is similar to the vowels in northern English *butter*, southern English *book*.

(v) Major variants

The short [ʊ] shows no major variants.

3.5.1.4 Short half-open front unrounded vowel [ɛ]

(i) Articulation

The short [ɛ] is articulated in the front of the oral cavity with the tongue in a mid or half-open position. The lips are slightly spread (Fig. 3.7).

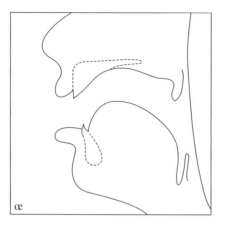

Figure 3.8   Tongue position for short [œ]

(ii) Spelling

It is normally spelt <e> (*Bett*), but also <ä> when there is a morphologically related word with a stem vowel <a>: *Kälte* < *kalt*.

(iii) Distribution

It occurs before stops (*steppen, Ebbe, Wette, verheddern* 'to get muddled up', *lecken, Egge* 'harrow'), fricatives (*treffen, messen, dreschen, Rechen*), nasals (*Lämmer, rennen*), liquids (*Keller, sperren*).

(iv) Similarity to English sounds

It is similar to the vowel in English *bet*. It must not be pronounced closer as in some varieties of English.

(v) Major variants

In southern German, Austria and Switzerland it is pronounced closer and tenser. Sometimes speakers distinguish between two short e-sounds: [e] and [ɛ].

3.5.1.5 Short half-open front rounded vowel [œ]

(i) Articulation

The vowel [œ] is articulated with the tongue in a mid position, half-open or more in the front of the oral cavity, with slightly rounded lips (Fig. 3.8).

(ii) Spelling

It is normally spelt <ö>: *Löffel*.

(iii) Distribution

It occurs before stops (*klöppeln* 'to make fine lace', *Götter, Böcke*), fricatives (*Böschung* 'embankment', *Löcher*), nasals (*schwömme, können*), liquids (*Hölle, dörren* 'to dry').

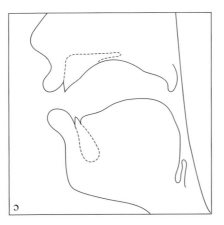

Figure 3.9   Tongue position for short [ɔ]

(iv) Similarity to English sounds
This sound does not occur in southern standard English.

(v) Major variants
The front rounded [œ] is subject to derounding in Central and Upper German dialects.

3.5.1.6 Short half-open back rounded vowel [ɔ]

(i) Articulation
The vowel [ɔ] is pronounced with the tongue in a mid-back position in the oral cavity taking up a half-close position. There is lip rounding, but not as much as in the case of [ʊ] (Fig. 3.9).

(ii) Spelling
It is normally spelt <o>: *Socke*.

(iii) Distribution
It occurs before stops (*stoppen, Robbe* 'seal', *Motte, Modder* 'mud', *locken, Roggen*), fricatives (*hoffen, Rosse, Gosche* 'mouth (vulgar)', *lochen*), nasals (*Sommer, Sonne, bongen* 'to ring up (on a till)'), liquids (*solle, dorren* 'to dry up, wither').

(iv) Similarity to English sounds
It is similar to the vowel in English *sock*. It must not be lowered and unrounded as in American English.

(v) Major variants
The short [ɔ] is pronounced closer and tenser in southern Germany and Austria.

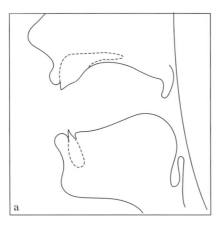

Figure 3.10   Tongue position for short [a]

3.5.1.7 Short open unrounded vowel [a]

(i) Articulation

The vowel [a] is pronounced with the mouth fully open, the tongue low in the oral cavity and towards the front. The lips are neutral and not spread. It differs slightly in quality, being lax, from long open [ɑː] (Fig. 3.10).

(ii) Spelling

It is normally spelt <a>: *hat, Mann.*

(iii) Distribution

It occurs before stops (*Klappe, Krabbe, Ratte, Kladde* 'rough book', *packen, Bagger* 'excavator'), fricatives (*schaffen, hassen, waschen, Rache*), nasals (*Hammer, bannen*), liquids (*fallen, harren* 'to wait').

(iv) Similarity to English sounds

It is the same as the vowel in northern English *hat, man.* It should not be front as in RP [æ] or diphthongized and lengthened as in American English.

(v) Major variants

In north Germany the short [a] is fronted whereas in south Germany and Austria it is retracted and rounded.

3.5.2 Long tense vowels

There are eight long tense vowels in German: [iː yː uː eː ɛː øː oː ɑː] as can be seen in Fig. 3.11.

	Front unrounded	Front rounded	Central	Back rounded
Close (high)	i:	y:		u:
Half-close (mid-high)	e:	ø:		o:
Half-open (mid-low)	ɛ:			
Open (low)			ɑ:	

Figure 3.11   Long tense vowels in German

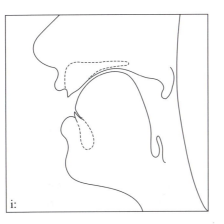

Figure 3.12   Tongue position for long tense [i:]

3.5.2.1 Long high close front unrounded vowel [i:]

(i) Articulation

The front of the tongue arches back towards the front of the hard palate, sometimes towards the alveolar ridge. The edges of the tongue are in contact with the upper molars, whereas the front of the tongue is in contact with the lower incisors. The lips are slightly spread. The velum closes off the nasal cavity (Fig. 3.12).

(ii) Spelling

The long high unrounded [i:] is usually spelt <ie> (*Biene*), but also <i, ih, ieh>: *Tiger, Ihnen, Vieh*.

(iii) Distribution

It occurs before stops (*piepen, lieben, bieten, Lieder, quieken* 'to squeak', *kriegen*), fricatives (*schliefen, Diwan, gießen, bliesen, Nische, riechen*), nasals (*ziemen, dienen*) and liquids (*spielen, frieren*).

(iv) Similarity to English sounds

The vowel is similar to the long vowel in Scots or northern English *mean*. Any over-lengthening or diphthongization as in southern English should be avoided.

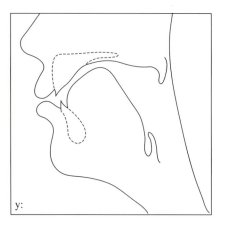

Figure 3.13   Tongue position for long tense [y:]

(v) Major variants

In southern Germany the spelling <ie> is pronounced as a diphthong [iə], e.g. Bavarian *Viech* 'fool, idiot', and in Swiss place names, *Spiez*.

3.5.2.2 Long high close front rounded vowel [y:]

(i) Articulation

The dorsum of the tongue is retracted towards the hard palate while the blade is lowered towards the alveolar ridge and is in contact with the lower incisors. The oral cavity is reduced to a small channel through which the air is expelled (Fig. 3.13).

(ii) Spelling

It is normally spelt <ü> but also <üh> and occasionally <y> and <ui>: *Bücher. rühren.*

(iii) Distribution

It occurs before stops (*trübe, Güte, Süden, Küken, lügen*), fricatives (*prüfen, süßen, Drüse* 'gland', *Rüsche* 'frill', *Bücher*), nasals (*rühmen, grünen*) and liquids (*fühlen, führen*).

(iv) Similarity to English sounds

It does not occur in RP but is similar to the vowel in Scots *moon, soon.*

(v) Major variants

In the spelling < üe> occurs as a diphthong [yə] in Swiss place names, *Flüelen, Rüegsau*. It is derounded and merges with [i:] in Central and Upper German dialects.

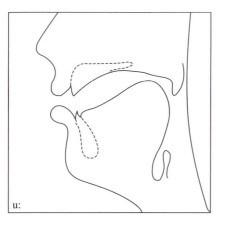

Figure 3.14   Tongue position for long tense [u:]

3.5.2.3 Long high close back vowel [u:]

(i) Articulation

The dorsum of the tongue is raised and retracted towards the soft palate reducing the oral cavity, although not so much as in the case of the front vowels [i:] and [y:]. The blade of the tongue is in contact with the lower incisors. The lips are pushed forward, having a considerable degree of rounding, but form a relatively small oval opening (Fig. 3.14).

(ii) Spelling

It is normally spelt <u> but also <uh>: *suchen, fuhren*.

(iii) Distribution

It occurs before stops (*Lupe, gruben, bluten, luden, spuken, schlugen*), fricatives (*rufen, Muße, schmusen, wuschen, suchen*), nasals (*Puma, Wune* 'hole (in the ice)'), liquids (*Schule, fuhren*).

(iv) Similarity to English sounds

It is similar to the long <oo> of *book* in some northern English varieties. It must always be pronounced as a monophthong and not diphthongized as in RP *soon*.

(v) Major variants

It is often palatalized and centralized in East Central German dialects such as Thuringian and Saxon.

3.5.2.4 Long half-close front unrounded vowel [e:]

(i) Articulation

The dorsum of the tongue is raised and retracted towards the hard palate, reducing the oral cavity but not as much as in the case of [i:]. The

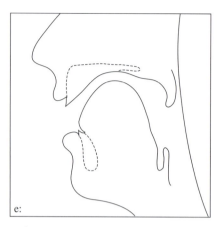

Figure 3.15   Tongue position for long tense [e:]

edges of the tongue are in contact with the inside of the upper molars. The tip of the tongue is on the lower alveolar ridge. The lips are spread (Fig. 3.15).

(ii) Spelling

The long [e:] is usually spelt <e> (*geben*), but also <eh> (*fehlen, mehr*) and <ee> (*Beeten, Meer*).

(iii) Distribution

It occurs before stops (*Reepe* 'ropes', *geben, beten, reden, Ekel, legen*), fricatives (*Hefe, Steven* 'stern', *Wesen, beige*), nasals (*nehmen, lehnen*), liquids (*fehlen, lehren*).

(iv) Similarity to English sounds

It is to be found in Scots and some northern English varieties. It must always be pronounced as a monophthong and not diphthongized as in RP *name*.

(v) Major variants

This long vowel often occurs as the half-open [ɛ:] in Swabian in words such as *treten, Regen*.

3.5.2.5 Long half-open front unrounded vowel [ɛ:]

(i) Articulation

The dorsum of the tongue is raised towards the hard palate but less than in the case of [e:]. The edges of the blade of the tongue are in contact with the lower incisors. The lips are almost as open as for [ɑ:]. This long vowel is an exception, being lax as well as long (Fig. 3.16).

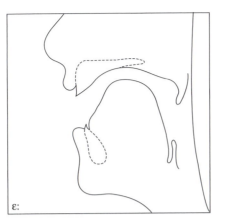

Figure 3.16   Tongue position for long [ɛ:]

(ii) Spelling

The long [ɛ:] is usually spelt <ä> (*Räder*), but also <äh>: *Fähre*.

(iii) Distribution

It occurs before stops (*Säbel, Räte, gnädig, häkeln* 'to crochet', *prägen*), fricatives (*Käfig, mäßig, Käse*), nasals (*schämen, gähnen*), liquids (*wählen, gären*).

(iv) Similarity to English sounds

It does not occur in RP but it does occur in some varieties of northern English in words such as *name, late*. Care should be taken not to diphthongize it.

(v) Major variants

The half-open [ɛ:] is mostly replaced by the long half-close [e:] in the north and east of Germany.

3.5.2.6 Long half-close front rounded vowel [ø:]

(i) Articulation

The dorsum of the back of the tongue is raised towards the soft palate. The sides of the front of the tongue are in contact with the lower incisors. The lips show as great a degree of rounding as in the case of [y:] and are pushed forward (Fig. 3.17).

(ii) Spelling

It is normally spelt <ö> but also <öh>, and <eu> in some French loan words.

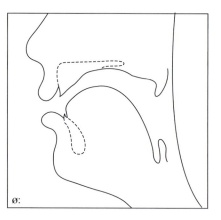

Figure 3.17   Tongue position for long tense [ø:]

(iii) Distribution

It occurs before stops (*Köper* 'twill cloth', *Döbel* 'dowel', *töten, Böden, blöken* 'to bleat', *Bögen*), fricatives (*Öfen, Möwe, Größe, lösen, Ströme, Söhne, Höhle, hören*).

(iv) Similarity to English sounds

It does not occur in RP.

(v) Major variants

The half-close, front rounded [ø:] is often derounded in Central and Upper German dialects.

3.5.2.7 Long half-close back rounded vowel [o:]

(i) Articulation

The dorsum of the tongue is raised towards the soft palate. The sides of the front of the tongue are in contact with the lower incisors. The lips show the same degree of rounding as in the case of the front rounded [ø:] and form an oval shape (Fig. 3.18).

(ii) Spelling

It is normally spelt <o> but also <oh>, <oo> and occasionally <oe, oi>.

(iii) Distribution

It occurs before stops (*Opa, loben, Brote, Mode, Koker* 'worker in coking plant', *Woge*), fricatives (*Ofen, stowen* 'to steam', *Soße, Rose, koscher, Loge, malochen* 'to graft, work hard'), nasals (*Koma, Sohne*), liquids (*Sohle, bohre*).

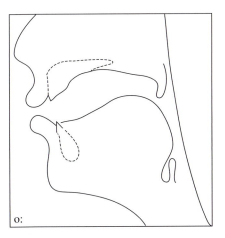

Figure 3.18   Tongue position for long tense [o:]

(iv) Similarity to English sounds

It does not occur in RP. It is used by some Scots speakers. It must always be pronounced as a monophthong and not diphthongized as in RP *stone, moan.* The [ɔ:] of RP *law* and northern English *stone* should also not be used.

(v) Major variants

In East Central German dialects the [o:] is often palatalized and centralized.

3.5.2.8 Long open unrounded vowel [ɑ:]

(i) Articulation

It is the most open vowel, showing the greatest opening of jaw and lips. The tongue lies almost on the floor of the oral cavity and the sides of its front are in contact with the lower incisors. The dorsum is slightly raised. The lips assume a neutral position, being modified by the preceding consonant. It differs slightly in quality from short open [a], being tense (Fig. 3.19).

(ii) Spelling

Long [ɑ:] is usually spelt <a> (*fragen*), but also <ah> (*Rahm*) and <aa>: *Saal.*

(iii) Distribution

It occurs before stops (*Stapel* 'pile', *Gabel, raten, laden, Laken* 'sheet', *lagen*), fricatives (*Hafen, brave, Maßen, Hasen, Rage, Sprache*), nasals (*Samen, Bahnen*), liquids (*fahle* 'pale', *Haare*).

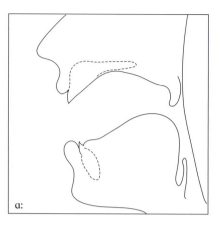

Figure 3.19   Tongue position for long tense [ɑː]

(iv) Similarity to English sounds

It is nearest to the <a> in RP *glass, father* but it should not be retracted. It should also not be fronted as in some varieties of south-west English and American.

(v) Major variants

The long open [ɑː] is often retracted and rounded in southern Germany, Austria and Switzerland. In northern Germany, on the other hand, it is often fronted.

3.5.3 Diphthongs

German has three falling diphthongs, symbolized [ai], [au] and [oi]. These are the sounds in the words: *mein, Haus, euch.* The diphthongs [ai] and [au] start with a low position of the tongue which is then raised to a high front vowel in the case of [ai] and a high back vowel in the case of [au]. The transcription of these diphthongs varies. *DAW*, MacCarthy (1975), C. Hall (2003) and Fox (2005) follow our suggestions but *Siebs* (de Boor *et al.* 1969), *WDA* and Rausch and Rausch (1991) have [ae] and [ao], with a lower tongue height for the second component of [ai] and [au]. There is more substantial disagreement about the nature of the second component of the third diphthong [oi]. According to Moulton (1962), MacCarthy (1975) and Kohler (1995) it is unrounded, whereas for *Siebs* (1969), Benware (1986) and *DAW* (2005) it is rounded, either [ø] or [ʏ]. C. Hall (2003: 105f.) transcribes it as [øy], but concedes that many speakers use [oi]. We will use the transcription [oi]. Diphthongs

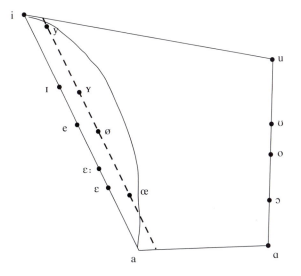

Figure 3.20   Tongue movement for diphthong [ai]

in German dialects show a bewildering variety of forms (see Wiesinger 1970).

3.5.3.1 The diphthong [ai]

(i) Articulation

The diphthong [ai] starts with the tongue at its lowest point and in the central-front of the mouth and then glides upwards towards the highest point. The lips are spread (Fig. 3.20).

(ii) Spelling

It is normally spelt <ei> but also <ai> and occasionally <ey, ay>.

(iii) Distribution

The diphthong [ai] occurs before stops (*Kneipe, bleiben, leiten, leiden, streiken, Geige*), fricatives (*greifen, reisen, reißen, reichen, heischen*), nasals (*reimen, verneinen*), liquids (*feilen, feiern*).

(iv) Similarity to English sounds

It is similar to RP [ai] in *mine* but care should be taken that the [a] is not too fronted.

(v) Major variants

The diphthong [ai] appears often as a monophthong [e:] in some Central German dialects and Berlin: *ik wees*, NHG *ich weiß*. It is also monophthongized to [a:] in other Upper German dialects. In Swabian

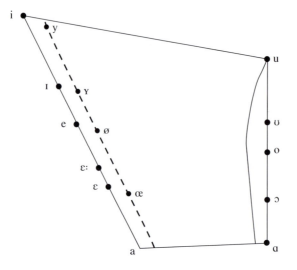

Figure 3.21   Tongue movement for diphthong [au]

the first component is fronted and raised to [ə], giving [əi], especially in those words that come from MHG long *î* (*mîn*).

3.5.3.2 The diphthong [au]

(i) Articulation

The diphthong [au] starts with the tongue at its lowest point and in the central-front of the mouth and then glides upwards towards the highest point in the back of the mouth. The lips become slightly rounded towards the completion of the articulation (Fig. 3.21).

(ii) Spelling

It is normally spelt <au> but also <ow> and <ou> especially in English loans: *down, Couch.*

(iii) Distribution

The diphthong [au] occurs before stops (*Raupe, Tauben, Laute, Stauden, pauken, taugen*), fricatives (*taufen, lausig, draußen, tauchen, tauschen*), nasals (*Gaumen, Gauner*), liquids (*verfaulen, Maurer*).

(iv) Similarity to English sounds

It is similar to the diphthong in RP *mouse* but the first component should be further back.

(v) Major variants

The diphthong [au] appears as a monophthong in some Central and Upper German dialects, particularly before labials. In Swabian the first

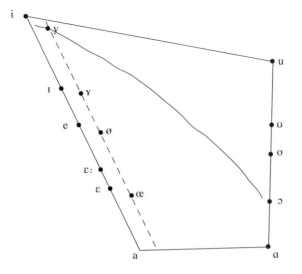

Figure 3.22   Tongue movement for diphthong [oi]

component is fronted and raised to [ə], giving [əu], especially in those words that come from MHG long *û* (*hûs*).

3.5.3.3 The diphthong [oi]

(i) Articulation

The diphthong [oi] starts with the tongue at the position of a half-open back rounded vowel. The lips are rounded during this first part. Then the tongue glides upwards towards the highest point in the front of the mouth and the lips are spread (Fig. 3.22).

(ii) Spelling

It is normally spelt <eu> but also <äu> if there is a morphologically related word with <au> as stem vowel (*Häuser* < *Haus*), and occasionally <oi>.

(iii) Distribution

The diphthong [oi] occurs before stops (*stäupen, Räuber, Leute, Räude, erzeugen*), fricatives (*Teufel, Läuse, äußern, keuchen, täuschen*), nasals (*träumen, Scheune*), liquids (*Beule, Euro*).

(iv) Similarity to English sounds

This is similar to the diphthong in RP *voice* but care should be taken to fully round the first component.

(v) Major variants

In many varieties of Upper and Central German this diphthong is derounded and merges with [ai].

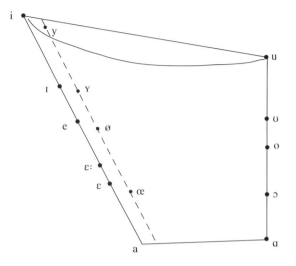

Figure 3.23   Tongue movement for diphthong [ui]

3.5.3.4 The diphthong [ui]

This diphthong only occurs in interjection *pfui!* It starts from a position with the tongue raised in the back of the mouth and the lips rounded. The tongue then glides forward to the front of the mouth and the lips are spread (Fig. 3.23).

3.5.4 Unstressed vowels

3.5.4.1 Schwa

The main vowel in unstressed syllables is schwa [-ə], written <e>. It is a central unrounded mid half-close lax vowel: *bitte, Affe, Name, ohne, Quelle, Beere* (Fig. 3.24). It also occurs before the main stress in the prefixes *be-* and *ge-*: (verbs) *bezahlt, belegen,* (nouns) *Betrieb, Befehl,* (adjectives) *bewusst, bereit;* (verbs) *gezählt, gehören,* (nouns) *Gespräch, Gesetz,* (adjectives) *gemächlich, genau.*

3.5.4.2 So-called 'dark' schwa

The sequence <-er> is often pronounced [ɐ], which is a central unrounded mid-central vowel (Fig. 3.25). It does not occur in Swiss Standard German (see Chapter 11). This vowel, sometimes called 'dark schwa', is also the product of the vocalization of postvocalic <r> after long vowels in the standard and also after short vowels in colloquial speech.

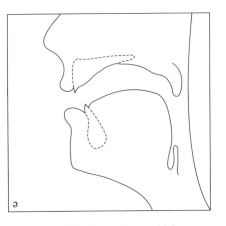

Figure 3.24   Tongue position for unstressed [ə]

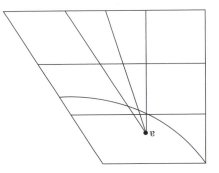

Figure 3.25   Tongue position for unstressed -*er* as a vowel

3.5.4.3 Short tense vowels in unstressed syllables

Many polysyllabic Latin and French words have short tense vowels in their unstressed syllables: *Philosophie, telefonieren*. These vowels represent the full range of monophthongs to be found in stressed syllables. In many cases there are alternations between stressed long vowels and unstressed vowels that retain their quality (close or tense) but simply become short: *Motif > motivieren; leben > lebendig; Drama > dramatisch; Motor > Motoren; Muse > Museum; Asyl > Asylant.*

Other short tense vowels occur in unstressed position but these are mostly in loan words: *Mini, Thema, Kino, Tofu* (see Chapter 8). The unstressed short tense vowels also occur in some derivational suffixes: *langsam, lesbar*. The short tense unstressed vowel *Demut*, as well as in the names *Hartmut, Helmut* should be noted as English speakers tend to make them more open.

3.5.4.4 Short lax vowels in derivational affixes

In derivational suffixes short lax close [ɪ] is the main vowel: *saftig, Kundin, Kenntnis, leserlich*. Unstressed prefixes that end in a consonant, including /r/, have a short, lax vowel. Examples from verbs are: *ent-* (*entfernen*), *er-* (*erweisen*), *miss-* (*missverstehen*), *ver-* (*verkaufen*), *zer-* (*zerbrechen*). Even foreign unstressed prefixes ending in a consonant have a short, lax vowel, e.g. *dis-* (*disqualifizieren*).

3.6 Non-syllabic vowels

These are represented by [i̯ y̯ u̯ o̯] and occur immediately before a stressed vowel in words such as *Nati+on, Reli+ef, Hy+äne, aktu+ell, sumptu+ös*. Normally they form the nucleus of the syllable but in these cases they function as non-syllabic vowels, i.e. like consonants. Fox (2005: 53f.) regards them as being part of the peripheral sound system since they mostly occur in French and Latin words.

QUESTIONS

1   Draw the tongue height in the following diagram for the vowels in: *sieben, Gaben, Bube*.

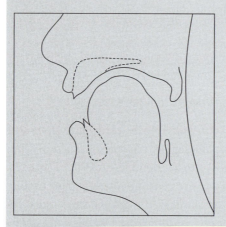

2   What feature do the following vowels have in common: [iː ʊ yː ʏ]?

3   Give the IPA symbol for the vowels represented by the following articulatory description:

  (i)   Short, low, front unrounded
  (ii)   Long, high, back, rounded

(iii) Short, half-open, front, unrounded
(iv) Unstressed, central, low, unrounded
 (v) Short, half-open, front, rounded
(vi) Long, high, front, rounded

4   Discuss the use of 'tense' and 'lax' in describing vowels.

5   Which of the following vowels is the odd one out and why? [i: o: u: ɛ: y:]

6   Give an articulatory description, comprising length, position in the mouth, tongue height and lip rounding for the following vowels: [ɛ o: y: ø: ɔ œ].

7   How do the vowels, in bold, differ from 'normal' German vowels: *Dessin*, *Pendant*, *Filiale*, *virtuos*?

8   Transcribe the following words in the IPA transcription, paying especial attention to the diphthongs: *Ei*, *seit*, *kein*, *neu*, *heute*, *neun*, *Bau*, *Kauf*, *Haus*.

9   Using a pronouncing dictionary transcribe the following words: *flüssig*, *Fußball*, *Igel*, *Optimismus*, *Organisation*, *kolossal*, *Reverenz*.

4 Consonants

4.0 Production of consonants

As we have seen (2.6.2) consonants are produced when the egressive air-stream coming from the lungs is modified in different ways by the articulators in the vocal cavity on its way out through the mouth.

The first feature of consonants is their manner of articulation: how they are articulated, which articulators are involved and how these behave. There can be a complete occlusion of the air-stream, in which case we talk about plosives (or stops). There can also be greater or lesser friction, in which case we talk about fricatives and frictionless continuants or approximants. In both these cases the air-stream passes over the centre of the tongue. If the air-stream passes to one or both sides of the tongue then we term the sound a lateral. In all these cases, if the air is released only through the vocal cavity by shutting off the nasal cavity through lowering the velum then we term the sounds oral. If, however, the air-stream is released through both the nasal and the oral cavity then we term the sounds nasal. The manner of articulation of [r] is rather complicated since it varies from being a fricative to a trill: the striking of the tip of the tongue against the alveolar ridge, or of the uvula against the back of the throat. The [h] is regarded as a glottal or cavity fricative since most of the friction is produced in the throat cavity, in particular the glottis.

The second feature of consonants is that their articulation varies according to where in the vocal cavity they are formed and which articulators are involved. This is the place of articulation (see Fig. 2.1). Proceeding from the front of the vocal cavity to the back we have the following places which are relevant for German: labial, both lips are involved; labio-dental, the lower lip and alveolar ridge; alveolar, the tip or blade of the tongue and the alveolar ridge; palato-alveolar (or post-alveolar or pre-palatal), the tip or blade of the tongue and the front part of the hard palate; palatal, the back of the tongue and the hard palate, and finally, velar, the back of the tongue and the soft palate.

The third major feature is the state of the vocal cords. If the vocal cords are not simply open but are vibrating (opening and closing) very rapidly then the sound produced is termed voiced. Otherwise if there is no vibration then the sound is termed voiceless (see Fig. 2.4).

4.1 Manner of articulation

4.1.1 Obstruents (*der Obstruent, -en*)

In the articulation of consonants either there is a complete constriction at some point in the mouth or the vocal tract is narrowed so much that audible friction is produced at some point along its length. When the air-stream is completely blocked the consonants are called stops (*der Verschlusslaut, -e*), or, in the case of egressive pulmonic stops which are the norm in German, plosives. When the air-stream is forced out through a narrow stricture with friction but there is no complete constriction, the sound is termed a fricative, or spirant (*der Reibelaut, -e*; *der Frikativ, -e*). The initial consonants in *Paar, tun, Koch*; *Bein, dein, Gang* are plosives, as are the medial consonants in *Rippe, Leiter, Brücke*; *Krabbe, Seide, meiden*. The initial consonants in *fein, Wein, Safe, sein, Chemie, Journalist, scheinen, ja* are fricatives, as are the medial consonants in *offen, Möwe, essen, lesen, sprechen, waschen, Boje, Page*. If there is a complete sealing off of the nasal cavity by the soft palate then the resultant consonants are oral: [p t k b d g] or [f v s z ç ʃ ʒ x]. The plosives and fricatives are sometimes classed together as obstruents (*der Obstruent, -en*).

4.1.2 Sonorants

The [r] and [l] sounds are often referred to together as liquids (*der Liquid, -en* or *-a*).

The nasals, together with the liquids, are referred to as sonorants as opposed to the obstruents. They can function in some instances as vowels, e.g. in the reduced form of the ending *-el, -em, -en* (see 2.6.6).

4.1.2.1 Nasals (*der Nasal, -e*)

If there is an occlusion in the vocal tract but the velum hangs loose and does not block off the nasal cavity so that the air also escapes through the nose as well as the mouth when the occlusion is released, then the resultant sound is

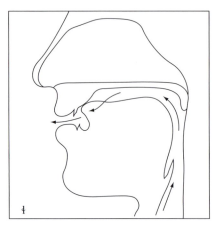

Figure 4.1   The articulation of the velarized [ɫ] in English

called a nasal plosive, or more usually just a nasal (*der Nasal, -e*) (see Fig. 2.10). The initial sounds in *Mut, nein,* and the final sound in *sang* are examples of nasals, symbolized as [m n ŋ]. Nasal (*nasal*) can also be used as an adjective for sounds produced in this way.

4.1.2.2 Lateral

In the articulation of the initial sound in *lassen* the tip of the tongue touches the alveolar ridge and the air-stream flows out past the sides of the tongue. This type of articulation is called lateral (*lateral*) and a sound produced in this way a lateral (*der Lateral, -e*). The lateral [l] in German is pronounced only in the centre and front of the mouth, whereas in English after vowels the [l] is velarized and pronounced in the back of the mouth, symbolized [ɫ], e.g. *ball, soul* (see Fig. 4.1).

4.1.2.3 The *r*-sounds

The articulation of the *r*-sounds in German presents a very complex range of articulations. These depend on stylistic and regional factors. The pronunciations vary from an alveolar trill [r] (*der Vibrant, -en*) in initial position before a vowel as in *Reiter* (Fig. 4.2) to a uvular trill, symbolized [R] (Fig. 4.3). In colloquial informal pronunciation these rolls or trills simply become alveolar or uvular fricatives, in some cases being produced with little or no friction and called frictionless continuants, or approximants (*der Approximant, -en*), symbolized by writing the *r* symbols upside down, e.g. [ɹ], [ʁ].

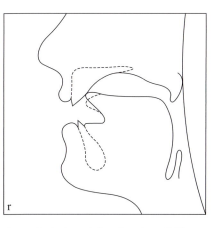

Figure 4.2   The articulation of the alveolar trill [r]

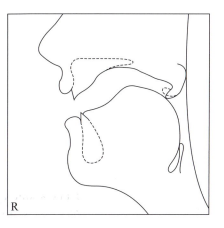

Figure 4.3   The articulation of the uvular trill [R]

4.1.3 Affricates (*die Affrikate, -n*)

Another type of articulation, or rather a combination of already described types, is represented by the initial sounds in *Pferd, Zeit, tschüss* or the final sounds in *Kopf, Satz, deutsch*. Phonetically these sounds, known as affricates (*die Affrikate, -n*), are transcribed [pf ts tʃ] and represent a plosive and a fricative at the same or similar place of articulation. The slow release of the occlusion in the articulation of the plosive produces a fricative before the articulation of the following vowel begins (see Fig. 4.4). There is no voice onset time. The affricate [pf] comprises a labial plosive and a labio-dental fricative, [ts] is an alveolar plosive plus an alveolar fricative and [tʃ] an alveolar plosive plus an alveo-palatal fricative. The status in the phonological analysis of German of

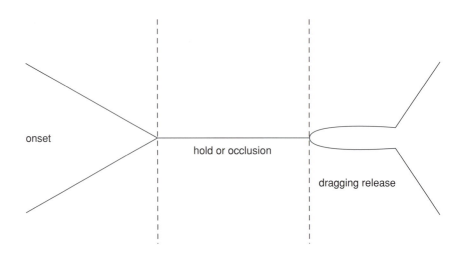

onset

hold or occlusion

dragging release

Figure 4.4   Release of the occlusion in the articulation of affricates

[pf] and [ts] is controversial. Some linguists regard them as single, unitary phonemes, whereas others regard them as being a cluster of two consonants: /p/ + /f/; /t/ + /s/ (see 5.4.1.2). The affricate [tʃ] is less frequent in initial position and is usually regarded as a cluster of two phonemes /t/ + /ʃ/.

4.2 Place of articulation

The plosives, fricatives, nasals, laterals and trills are also divided into several different places of articulation. These are the same for each manner of articulation, although all possible combinations do not exist. There are three places of articulation for voiced and voiceless plosives and nasals, but four for voiced and voiceless fricatives. Usually it is enough to mention one place of articulation in describing the plosive, fricative or nasal. The sounds can be referred to as nouns and adjectives in English and German. In the sub-titles we will give the German terms. The nouns are written with initial capital letters.

4.2.1 Labial (*der Labial, -e*; *labial, bilabial, labiodental*)

The sounds [p b f v m] are labial sounds. In the case of the plosives and nasals in German they are bilabial: both lips are involved in the articulation of the sounds. The constriction is made by the lips. In the case of the fricatives the articulation is produced not by the two articulators in the vocal tract that are exactly opposite to each other vertically but by two that are not exactly opposite to each other. For example, the fricatives [f] and [v] are labio-dental and are produced by the lower lip approaching the upper teeth, creating a narrow stricture through which the air is expelled through the mouth. The *n* in *fünf, Senf* or *m* before *ph, Triumph*, are also labio-dental, symbolized [ɱ].

4.2.2 Alveolar (*der Alveolar, -e; alveolar*)

The sounds [t d], [s z], [n] are alveolar in German, that is the stoppage or friction is made at the teeth ridge or alveoli by the tongue. Therefore [t d] are alveolar plosives, [s z] alveolar fricatives, and [n] is an alveolar nasal. The lateral [l] is also pronounced with the blade (or tip) of the tongue touching the alveolar ridge while the air-stream is released past the sides of the tongue. It is therefore an alveolar sound. As already mentioned, the *r*-sounds are either alveolar or uvular.

4.2.3 Post-alveolar (*der Postalveolar, -e; postalveolar*)

At the next place of articulation there are only fricatives in German. This is the region between the alveolar ridge and the beginning of the hard palate; this is where the initial sounds in *scheinen, Genie*, the medial sounds in *waschen, Gage* and the final sound in *Busch, Beige* are formed. They are termed palato-alveolar fricatives, or sometimes pre-palatal (*präpalatal*) fricatives and are symbolized [ʃ], [ʒ].

4.2.4 Palato-velar

The hard and soft palates, as far as German is concerned, can be taken as one place of articulation. However, the exact place of articulation of the plosive [k] is determined by the following vowel (compare the initial sounds in *Kind, kann, Kunde*): these plosives in German may be called velar or palato-velar plosives. (The parallel term *der Palatovelar, -e; palatovelar* seems to be lacking in German.) The same variation occurs with [g]: *Gift, gab, Gunst*. English has no velar fricative but German has, e.g. the final sound in *Buch, Loch*. This also varies in articulation according to the preceding vowel: *Dach* has a velar fricative after a back vowel, written phonetically [x], and *dich* has a palatal fricative after a front vowel, [ç]. The phonological status of [ç] and [x] is controversial. Some linguists regard them simply as allophones of one phoneme while others regard them as separate phonemes (see 5.4.1.1). German also has a velar nasal, written phonetically [ŋ], which normally only occurs medially and finally: *singen, sang*.

4.3 State of the vocal cords

There is another fundamental distinction in the articulation of obstruents that is created by the behaviour of the vocal cords. In the pronunciation of the plosives [b d g] and the fricatives [v z ʒ] the vocal cords are narrowed so that the air-stream is forced through between them and they vibrate. These sounds are voiced (*stimmhaft*). In the case of the pronunciation of the plosives [p t k] and the fricatives [f s ʃ ç x] the vocal cords are widened and the air-stream flows through without them vibrating (Fig. 2.4). These sounds are voiceless (*stimmlos*). The German affricates [pf ts tʃ] are also voiceless. The nasals and vowels are always voiced. In connected speech, however, voiced and voiceless sounds influence each other.

4.4 The consonants in detail

As in the case of the description of the vowels (see 3.4) we will treat the consonants from five aspects: (1) their articulation, (2) their spelling in brief, (3) their distribution in the word (their occurrence in consonant clusters will be treated in Chapter 7), (4) their similarity to English sounds and (5) their major variants. Spelling is dealt with in a more detailed and systematic way in Chapter 6 and regional variants in Chapter 11. Their phonemic status, including that of the affricates, will be treated in detail in Chapter 5 but references will be given to the relevant sections.

Detailed phonetic descriptions of German consonants, often with diagrams and photographs, can be found in: C. and P. Martens (1961: 108–229), Wängler (1983: 117–65), MacCarthy (1975: 71–97), Kohler (1995: 152–68), and C. Hall (2003: 23–71) and in this book.

4.4.1 Plosives

Other modes of articulation of certain types of consonants that are needed to describe plosives in certain positions of the word are aspiration and strength of articulation (fortis and lenis). Consonant length is also a feature of, particularly, intervocalic consonants.

With voiceless plosives in initial position before a stressed vowel there is a short interval, known as the voice onset time, after the release of the occlusion until the vocal cords start to vibrate in the articulation of the following vowel (Fig. 4.5). The turbulence created then creates a puff of air that is called aspiration. It can be transcribed with [h] or [']. The length of this voice onset time, the amount of aspiration, is greatest before a stressed vowel, as in *Paar*, *Pute*, *Post*. It is also quite strong in word-final position before a pause (*knapp*).

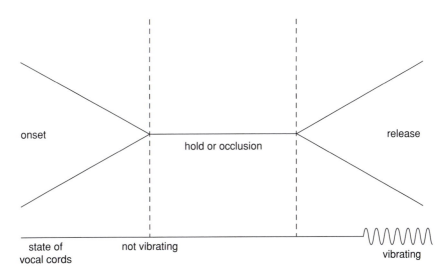

onset

hold or occlusion

release

state of
vocal cords

not vibrating

vibrating

Figure 4.5   Voice onset time in the articulation of plosives

In other positions – after [ʃ], *spät*; before [r] and [l], *Pracht, Pleite*; before unstressed *-e, Lippe* – it is weaker. The more prescriptive works, e.g. *Siebs* (1969), recommend strong aspiration in all positions in the *reine Hochlautung*, although allowing weaker aspiration in non-initial positions in the *gemäßigte Hochlautung* and even no aspiration in *spät*. These differences seem to reflect the fact that aspiration, apart from before a stressed vowel, varies according to the style of speech and whether words are pronounced in isolation or not. *DAW* concedes this (2005: 89) by having strong aspiration in word-initial and word-final position, e.g. [phakh] *pack!*, and medium to weak aspiration elsewhere, [ʃp'eːt] *spät*, using the diacritic ['].

The term fortis is also used to describe voiceless plosives such as [p]. It is a label reflecting a greater energy used in the articulation of the sound. This is due to the greater volume of air expelled after the release of the occlusion and the greater muscular tension of the lips used in the formation and release of the occlusion than in the case of [b] which is labelled lenis. Jessen (1998) is a very full investigation that supports the use of the feature [tense] and wants to link phonetics and phonology more.

4.4.1.1 Voiceless fortis bilabial plosive [p]

(i) Articulation

The voiceless bilabial plosive [p] is articulated by both lips forming a closure that is released after a short hold. The velum is raised so that, when the closure is released, the air expelled flows only through the oral cavity and out through the mouth. The tongue is not actively involved in

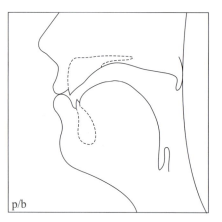

p/b

Figure 4.6   Articulation of [p] and [b]

the articulation of this plosive and rests against the lower back teeth ridge. The lips take up their position to articulate the following vowel, rounded for *u, o, ü, ö* and spread for the other vowels. The vocal cords are not vibrating (Fig. 4.6).

(ii) Spelling

The voiceless, bilabial plosive [p] is spelt <p> (*piepen, Post, Putz*), <pp> (*Lippe, knapp*), or <b> (*ab, Lob*).

(iii) Distribution

The plosive [p] occurs initially before vowels and [r] and [l] and in the affricate [pf]: *Park, Preis, Plan, Pferd*. In medial and final position it appears after short vowels (*kippen*), long vowels (*Rüpel*) and diphthongs (*Kneipe; Tipp, grob, Leib*).

(iv) Similarity to English sounds

It is very similar to the initial <p> with aspiration in English *pack*, German *packen*.

(v) Major variants

In South Germany, Austria and Switzerland <p> is pronounced with little or no aspiration. In Central and Upper German dialects, including Swabian and Central Bavarian, it is weakened to a lenis [b̥] often merging with it. This process of lenition is known as the *binnendeutsche Konsonantenschwächung* (internal German consonant weakening); see also for the historical development 12.7.2.

4.4.1.2 Voiced lenis bilabial plosive [b]

(i) Articulation

Like [p], the voiced bilabial plosive [b] is articulated by both lips forming a closure which is released after a short hold. The velum is raised so that, when the closure is released, the air expelled flows only through the oral cavity and out through the mouth. The tongue is not actively involved in the articulation of this plosive and rests against the lower back teeth ridge. The lips take up their position to articulate the following vowel, rounded for *u, o, ü, ö* and spread for the other vowels (Fig. 4.6). However, in contrast with [p] the vocal cords vibrate immediately before the release of the occlusion. There is thus no voice onset time (Fig. 4.5). The volume of air passing out from the vocal cords and the lungs is relatively small and the muscles are less active than in the case of [p]. The sound is also referred to as lenis in contrast with the fortis [p]. In voiceless contexts this lenis sound is also devoiced, transcribed [b̥].

(ii) Spelling

The plosive [b] is usually spelt <b> (*Bus, binden*) and < bb> medially after short vowels (*Krabbe, rubbeln*).

(iii) Distribution

The plosive [b] has a more restricted distribution than [p]. It occurs initially before vowels: *Ball, Biss, Bett, Bohne, Bude*; and before [r] and [l]: *Brei, braun, Brot; Blei, Blick, bloß*. Medially it occurs mainly after long vowels and diphthongs: *Probe, trübe, Bube*; and less frequently after short vowels: *Ebbe*.

(iv) Similarities with English sounds

It is very similar to the <b> in English *bet*, German *Bett*; English *rubber*, German *rubbeln* 'to rub'.

(v) Major variants

In South Germany, Austria and Switzerland [b] is a voiceless lenis [b̥] but sometimes it is weakened to a fricative [β] medially between vowels.

4.4.1.3 Voiceless fortis alveolar plosive [t]

(i) Articulation

The voiceless alveolar plosive [t] is formed by making a closure in the oral cavity with the tip, or the blade, of the tongue against the alveolar ridge. The sides of the tongue lie against the upper teeth. The velum is raised so that, when the closure is released, the air expelled flows only through the oral cavity and out through the mouth. The vocal cords are not vibrating (Fig. 4.7). The lips take on the features of the following vowel: rounded before front and back rounded vowels, spread before unrounded vowels. In initial position before vowels it is aspirated. The same remarks on voice onset time and aspiration as described for [p] are also valid for [t].

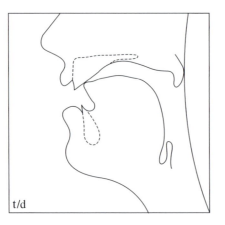

Figure 4.7   Articulation of [t] and [d]

(ii) Spelling
   The voiceless alveolar plosive [t] is usually spelt <t> (*Tal, tun, tragen*),
   <tt> medially and finally after short vowels (*Motte, Blatt*), <th> and
   <t> after long vowels and diphthongs (*Ethos; Vater, Seite, Blut*). The
   digraph <th> is used in Greek loans: *Thema*. Finally <d> is used in
   words that have inflected forms with medial <d>: *Kleider, Kleid*.
   Exceptionally <dt> is used in *Stadt, Städte*.

(iii) Distribution
   The voiceless alveolar [t] occurs initially before vowels: *Tee, tun;* and [r]:
   träge, trübe. It occurs medially and finally after short and long vowels:
   Mitte, Schritt, Miete; and diphthongs: *Streit, leid*.

(iv) Similarities with English sounds
   As with [p] the alveolar plosive [t] is pronounced with aspiration as in
   English *tint*, German *Tinte*.

(v) Major variants
   In South Germany, Austria and Switzerland [t], like [p], is pronounced
   with little or no aspiration. In Central and Upper German dialects,
   including Swabian and Central Bavarian, it is weakened to a lenis [d̥]
   often merging with it in the *binnendeutsche Konsonantenschwächung*
   (internal German consonant weakening).

4.4.1.4 Voiced lenis alveolar plosive [d]

(i) Articulation
   In contrast with [t] the vocal cords vibrate immediately before the
   release of the occlusion. There is thus no voice onset time. The volume
   of air passing out from the vocal cords and the lungs is relatively small

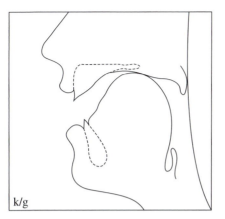

k/g

Figure 4.8   Articulation of [k] and [g]

and the muscles are less active than in the case of [t] (Fig. 4.7). The
sound is also referred to as lenis in contrast with the fortis [t]. In
voiceless contexts this lenis sound is also devoiced, transcribed [d̥].

(ii) Spelling

The voiced alveolar plosive [d] is usually spelt <d> initially (*du,
draußen*), medially after long vowels and diphthongs (*Laden, plaudern*),
while <dd> is used medially after short vowels (*Kladde, buddeln*). The
word- and morpheme-final <d> is always pronounced [t]: *Bad, redlich*.

(iii) Distribution

The voiced alveolar [d] occurs initially before vowels: *Dach, denken*; and
[r]: *Drache, drüben*. It occurs medially and finally after long vowels and
diphthongs: *Lieder, Staude* 'bush'; and less frequently after short vowels:
buddeln.

(iv) Similarity to English sounds

It is very similar to the <d> in English *dumb, rudder*.

(v) Major variants

In South Germany, Austria and Switzerland [d] is a voiceless lenis [d̥]
but sometimes it is even weakened to a fricative or flap [ɾ] medially
between vowels.

4.4.1.5 The voiceless palato-velar plosive [k]

(i) Articulation

The voiceless palato-velar plosive [k] is produced by the back of the
tongue making a closure with a point on the hard and soft palate
(Fig. 4.8). The term palato-velar represents this variation. The exact

place of articulation varies from a palatal stop [k+] in *Kind, kennen, Künstler, können* through a more central stop in *kann* to a clear velar stop in *Kunde, konnte*. Most phonetic descriptions of German describe this variation but 'work with a single point of articulation, the dorsovelar position' (Benware 1986: 22). C. and P. Martens use 'post-palatal' and 'velar-post-dorsal' (1961: 130). The lips take on the features of the following vowel: rounded before front and back rounded vowels, spread before unrounded vowels. In initial position before vowels it is aspirated. The same remarks on voice onset time and aspiration as described for [p] are also valid for [k].

(ii) Spelling

The voiceless palato-velar stop [k] is spelt <k> initially (*können, klein, Kreis, Knie*) in native German words but <c> or <ch> in loan words (*Computer, Chor*). Medially between vowels it is usually spelt <ck> after short vowels (*Brücke, lecker*) and <k> after long vowels or dipthongs (*erschraken, Pauke*).

(iii) Distribution

The plosive [k] occurs initially before vowels and [r], [l] and [n]: *Kalk, Kreis, klein, Knie*. Medially and finally it appears after short and long vowels and diphthongs: *Brücke, Laken, streiken; Glück, erschrak, Streik*.

(iv) Similarity with English sounds

As with [p] the palato-velar plosive [k] is pronounced with aspiration as in English *kin, can*.

(v) Major variants

In South Germany, Austria and Switzerland [k], like [p] and [t], is pronounced with little or no aspiration. In Central and Upper German dialects, including Swabian and Central Bavarian, it is weakened to a lenis [g̊], often merging with it in the *binnendeutsche Konsonantenschwächung* (internal German consonant weakening).

4.4.1.6 The voiced palato-velar plosive [g]

(i) Articulation

The voiced palato-velar plosive [g] show the same variation in exact place of articulation as the voiceless [k]. There is a palatal stop in *gießen, Gänse, Gürtel, gönnen* through a more central stop in *ganz* to a clear velar stop in *Gurke, golden*. However, in contrast with [k] the vocal cords vibrate immediately before the release of the occlusion. There is thus no voice onset time (Fig. 4.8). The volume of air passing out from the vocal cords and the lungs is relatively small and the muscles are less active than in the case of [k]. The lips take on the features of the following vowel: rounded before front and back rounded vowels, spread before unrounded vowels. The sound is also referred to as lenis in contrast with the fortis [k]. In voiceless contexts this lenis sound is also devoiced, transcribed [g̊].

(ii) Spelling

The voiced alveolar plosive [g] is usually spelt <g> initially (*gehen, Gnade*) and medially after long vowels and diphthongs (*Wagen, steigen*), with <gg> used medially after short vowels (*Roggen*).

(iii) Distribution

The voiced alveolar [g] occurs initially before vowels: *Gast, gähnen*; and [r], [l] and [n]: *Gras, Glas, Gnade.* It occurs medially and finally after long vowels and diphthongs: *biegen, neigen*; and less frequently after short vowels: *Egge, schmuggeln.*

(iv) Similarity with English sounds

It is very similar to the <g> in English *get, bigger.*

(v) Major variants

In South Germany, Austria and Switzerland [g] is a voiceless lenis [g̊] but sometimes it is even weakened to a palatal or a velar fricative medially between vowels. In the Cologne area and Berlin, initial [g] becomes [j] in the prefix *ge-* and other words, e.g. the colloquial abbreviation, originally from Berlin, *jwd: janz* (= *ganz*) *weit draußen.*

4.4.2 Fricatives

4.4.2.1 The voiceless labio-dental fricative [f]

(i) Articulation

The active articulator involved is the lower lip, which approaches the upper alveolar ridge and produces a narrowing through which the air-stream is forced rapidly out of the oral cavity. The tongue, since it is not actively involved in the articulation of this fricative, remains flat in the lower part of the oral cavity but the tongue tip approaches the lower alveolar ridge (Fig. 4.9). The vocal cords are not vibrating and the nasal cavity is sealed off by the raising of the velum. The voiceless [f] is always longer than the voiced [v], especially medially between vowels.

(ii) Spelling

The voiceless labio-dental fricative [f] is usually spelt <f> or <v> word-initially: *Fahne, Vogel.* Before consonants it is usually spelt <f>:

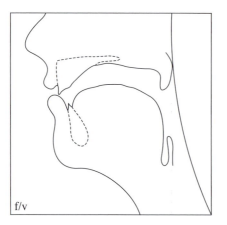

f/v

Figure 4.9   Articulation of [f] and [v]

fließen, fragen. Medially and finally after long vowels and diphthongs it is
spelt <f>: *schlafen, kaufen, Schlaf*; and <ff> after short vowels: *schaffen,
Schiff.* In Latin or Greek loans it is also spelt <ph>: *Phase, Philologie.*

(iii) Distribution

The fricative [f] occurs initially before vowels, [l] and [r]: *faul, Feld,
Fleisch, Frost.* Medially and finally it occurs after short and long vowels
and diphthongs: *Affe, schlafen, Seife, schlaff, Schlaf, reif.*

(iv) Similarity to English sounds

The fricative [f] is similar to the sounds in English *fan, offer.*

(v) Major variants

There are no major variants.

4.4.2.2 The voiced labio-dental fricative [v]

(i) Articulation

This is the same as for [f] except that the vocal cords are vibrating
(Fig. 4.9).

(ii) Spelling

The voiced labio-dental fricative [v] is usually spelt <w> word-initially:
Wein. Medially it is spelt <w> in a few words (*Möwe*) and <v> in loan
words: *Initiative, Salve, Kurve.*

(iii) Distribution

The fricative [v] occurs initially before vowels (*was, Wespe*) and in a few
words before [r]: *Wrack.* Medially it occurs only after long vowels: *Löwe.*
It does not occur finally.

(iv) Similarity to English sounds

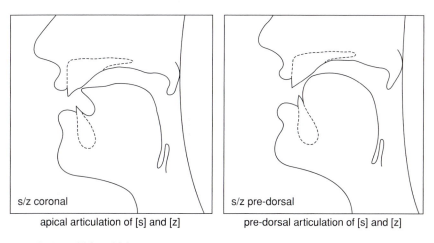

s/z coronal   s/z pre-dorsal

apical articulation of [s] and [z]   pre-dorsal articulation of [s] and [z]

Figure 4.10   Articulation of [s] and [z]

It is similar to the sound in English *very, ever*.
(v) Major variants
   The voiced labio-dental fricative [v] is also bilabial in south Germany, Austria and Switzerland.

4.4.2.3 The voiceless alveolar fricative [s]

(i) Articulation
   The active articulator is the tongue, which approaches the upper alveolar ridge. The blade of the tongue narrows the opening between the alveolar ridge and itself. The tip (apex) of the tongue is usually turned down. The back (dorsum) of the tongue presses against the side teeth and creates a groove over which the air-stream is forced out through the gap between the alveolar ridge and the blade of the tongue (Fig. 4.10). The vocal cords are usually not vibrating and the nasal cavity is sealed off by the raising of the velum.
(ii) Spelling
   The voiceless alveolar fricative [s] is usually spelt <s> word-initially, mostly in loan words: *Safe, Set, Sushi*. Medially after a short vowel and finally it is spelt <ss>: *müssen, Kuss*. Before consonants it is spelt <s>: *Post, bist*. After long vowels and diphthongs it is spelt <ß>: *stoßen, schmeißen*. Final [s] is spelt according to the medial consonant in inflected forms. This is either <ß> (*Fuß, Füße*) or <s> (*las, lasen;* <-s-> = [z]).
(iii) Distribution

The fricative [s] occurs initially before vowels, mostly in loan words: *Safe, Sample, surfen*. Medially and finally it occurs after short and long vowels and diphthongs: *müssen, Muße, außer, Fluss, Fuß, aus*.

(iv) Similarity to English sounds

It is similar to the sounds in English *save, missing*.

(v) Major variants

There are no major variants.

4.4.2.4 The voiced alveolar fricative [z]

(i) Articulation

This fricative is formed in the same way as [s] except that the vocal cords are vibrating (Fig. 4.10). In initial position before a vowel the voicing of the vocal cords may start halfway through the articulation of the sound.

(ii) Spelling

The voiced alveolar fricative [z] is spelt <s> word-initially before vowels (*sieben, suchen*) and medially after long vowels (*diese, Rose*). The spelling <s> in final position is always pronounced [s].

(iii) Distribution

The fricative [z] occurs initially before vowels: *sagen, Seele, Sohn*. Medially it only occurs after long vowels and diphthongs: *Vase, lesen, leise, Pause*.

(iv) Similarity to English sounds

It is similar to the sounds in English *zoo, easy, busy*.

(v) Major variants

In south Germany, Austria and Switzerland [z] is voiceless, or at least fortis.

4.4.2.5 The voiceless post-alveolar fricative [ʃ]

(i) Articulation

The blade of the tongue forms a constriction (narrowing) between itself and the front part of the hard palate. This place of articulation is also labelled pre-palatal or alveo-palatal. The tip of the tongue may be facing up or down. The back (dorsum) of the tongue is raised and the sides rest against the side teeth. The air-stream is forced rapidly along a wide groove, wider than that for [s], and out through the gap created between the blade of the tongue and the front part of the hard palate (Fig. 4.11).

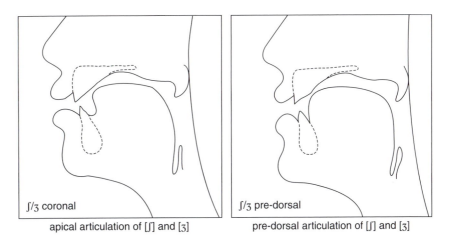

ʃ/ʒ coronal

apical articulation of [ʃ] and [ʒ]

ʃ/ʒ pre-dorsal

pre-dorsal articulation of [ʃ] and [ʒ]

Figure 4.11   Articulation of [ʃ] and [ʒ]

The vocal cords do not vibrate and the nasal cavity is sealed off by the raised velum. The lips are often rounded and fronted, especially before front rounded vowels.

(ii) Spelling

The voiceless post-alveolar fricative [ʃ] is spelt <sch> word-initially before vowels and the sonorants [m n l r] (*schon, schmal, schnell, Schlamm, Schrift*), as well as medially and finally after short vowels and diphthongs (long vowels are infrequent) and the sonorants: *waschen, Busch, ramschen* 'to buy up', *wünschen, fälschen, Kirsche*. Word-initially before the plosives [p] and [t] it is spelt <s>: *Spinne, Stadt*.

(iii) Distribution

The fricative [ʃ] occurs initially before vowels (*scharf, Schere, scheinen*), before [p t] (*spenden, stehen*) and [m n l r] (*Schmerz, Schnabel, Schlange, schreiben*). Medially and finally it occurs after short vowels and diphthongs (*mischen, Gemisch, tauschen, Tausch*) and infrequently after long vowels (*wuschen, wusch*).

(iv) Similarity to English sounds

It is similar to the sounds in English *shine, washing, wish*.

(v) Major variants

There are no major variants.

4.4.2.6 The voiced post-alveolar fricative [ʒ]

(i) Articulation

This fricative is formed in the same way as [ʃ] except that the vocal cords are vibrating (Fig. 4.11).

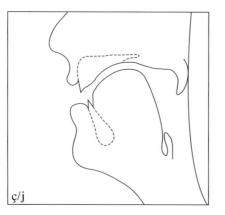

Figure 4.12   Articulation of [ç] and [j]

(ii) Spelling
The voiced post-alveolar fricative [ʒ] is usually spelt <j> word-initially before back vowels (*Jalousie, Journalist*) and <g> before front vowels (*genieren, Giro*). Medially it is spelt <g>: *Etage, Rage.*

(iii) Distribution
The fricative [ʒ] occurs initially before vowels: *Jargon.* Medially it only occurs after long vowels: *Garage, Loge.* It does not occur finally.

(iv) Similarity to English sounds
It is similar to the sound in English *rouge, vision.*

(v) Major variants
In colloquial speech the voiced fricative [ʒ] is often devoiced and merges with [ʃ].

4.4.2.7 The voiceless palatal fricative [ç]

The phonemic status of [ç] and [x] will be discussed in 5.4.1.1.

(i) Articulation
The voiceless palatal fricative [ç] is formed by the front of the tongue being raised to approach the hard palate. The edges of the tongue are in contact with the upper molars, the tongue forms a slightly rounded slit and its tip touches the upper alveolar ridge. The air is expelled through this opening, creating friction. The lips assume the position of the preceding vowel (Fig. 4.12). The vocal cords are not vibrating.

(ii) Spelling
The voiceless palatal fricative [ç] is usually spelt <ch>, in all positions in the word: *Chemie, stechen, dich.*

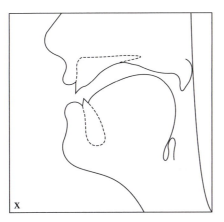

x

Figure 4.13   Articulation of [x]

(iii) Distribution

The voiceless palatal fricative [ç] occurs word-initially before vowels (*Chemie*), medially and finally after both short and long front vowels as well as diphthongs with a front second component: *sicher, riechen, bleichen, reich.*

(iv) Similarity to English sounds

It does not occur in RP but represents the final <ch> in Scots *nicht* 'night'.

(v) Major variants

In parts of the Rhineland [ç] is pronounced further forward in the mouth and merges with [ʃ]. This has also been noted around Leipzig. In Switzerland and Tyrol the voiceless palatal fricative [ç] is replaced by the velar fricative [x].

4.4.2.8 The voiceless velar fricative [x]

(i) Articulation

The voiceless velar fricative [x] is formed by raising the back of the tongue towards the soft palate. The edges of the tongue are in contact with the back upper molars. The tip of the tongue is pointing downwards and touches the upper alveolar ridge. Through the narrowing between the soft palate and dorsum of the tongue the air is expelled, creating friction. The vocal cords are not vibrating (Fig. 4.13). The lips assume the position of the preceding vowel.

(ii) Spelling

The voiceless palatal fricative [x] is usually spelt <ch> in all positions in the word: *kochen, doch.*

(iii) Distribution

The voiceless palatal fricative [x] occurs word initially (*Chassidismus*), medially and finally after both short and long back vowels as well as diphthongs with a back second component: *machen, buchen, rauchen.*

(iv) Similarity to English sounds

It does not occur in RP but represents the final <ch> in Scots *loch*, and <gh> in Irish *lough.*

(v) Major variants

The velar fricative in some regions merges with the uvular fricative [R] in some contexts.

4.4.2.9 The voiced palatal fricative [j]

(i) Articulation

This fricative is formed by the front part of the back (dorsum) of the tongue approaching the alveolar ridge below the hard palate. The sides of the tongue rest against the upper teeth forcing the air-stream through the gap between the tongue and the teeth. The tongue is further forward than for [ʃ] and [ʒ]. It is similar to that for the articulation of [i]. The body of the tongue is slightly rounded but not, as in the case of [ʃ] and [ʒ], grooved. There is less friction than in the case of [ç] and sometimes it can be regarded as an approximant (Fig. 4.12). The position of the lips varies according to the following vowel. The vocal cords are vibrating. The nasal cavity is sealed off by the raised velum.

(ii) Spelling

The voiced palatal fricative [j] is always spelt <j>: *Jahr, Koje.*

(iii) Distribution

The fricative [j] occurs initially before vowels (*jung*) and medially after long vowels: *Boje, Kajak.*

(iv) Similarity to English sounds

It is similar to the initial sound in English *yes, yet*, but with more friction.

(v) Major variants

There are no major variants.

4.4.3 Affricates

The phonemic status of the affricates (whether they are unitary phonemes or consonant clusters) will be treated in 5.4.1.2.

4.4.3.1 The labial affricate [pf]

(i) Articulation

The affricate [pf] is produced by a bilabial closure as for the plosive [p]. This is slowly released, resulting in a narrowing between the top teeth and lower lip, producing the labio-dental [f]. The vocal cords are not vibrating.

(ii) Spelling

The labial affricate is spelt <pf>: *Pfanne, stopfen, Kopf.*

(iii) Distribution

It occurs initially before vowels (*Pfingsten, Pfund*) and medially and finally only after short vowels: *Stapfe, Zopf.*

(iv) Similarity to English sounds

The labial affricate [pf] does not occur in English except across word and morpheme boundaries such as in *cupful.*

(v) Major variants

In north and east Germany it is often reduced to a fricative [f]. Pronunciations such as *Kopp* for *Kopf* are lexical borrowings from Low German dialect rather than pronunciation variants.

4.4.3.2 The alveolar affricate [ts]

(i) Articulation

The alveolar affricate [ts] is produced by a closure of the tongue tip or blade with the alveolar ridge. This is then slowly released, resulting in a narrowing between the tongue and the alveolar ridge, producing the alveolar fricative [s]. The vocal cords are not vibrating.

(ii) Spelling

The alveolar affricate [ts] is spelt <z> initially (*ziehen, Zinn, Zeit*) and medially and finally after diphthongs (*reizen, Reiz*), and <tz> medially and finally after short vowels (*sitzen, Schmutz*).

(iii) Distribution

The alveolar affricate [ts] occurs initially before vowels (*Zeichen, Zug*) and medially and finally, chiefly after short vowels and diphthongs: *setzen, Gesetz, Geiz, Kreuz.*

(iv) Similarity to English sounds

The alveolar affricate is similar to the consonant cluster <ts> in English *bits.*

(v) Major variants

The alveolar affricate is sometimes reduced to a voiceless alveolar fricative [s] in north Germany.

4.4.3.3 The post-alveolar affricate [tʃ]

(i) Articulation

The post-alveolar affricate [tʃ] is produced by a closure of the tongue tip or blade with the alveolar ridge. This is then slowly released, resulting in a narrowing, between the blade of the tongue and the front part of the hard palate, producing the post-alveolar fricative [ʃ]. The vocal cords are not vibrating.

(ii) Spelling

The post-alveolar affricate is spelt <tsch>: *tschüss, Putsch, deutsch*.

(iii) Distribution

The post-alveolar affricate [tʃ] occurs initially before vowels (*Tscheche, tschilpen*), medially and finally after vowels (*quetschen* 'to squash', *knutschen, Deutsche, Quatsch, deutsch*).

(iv) Similarity to English sounds

The post-alveolar affricate [tʃ] is similar to the sounds spelt <ch, tch> in English: *choose, ditch, riches*.

(v) Major variants

There are no major variants.

4.4.4 Nasals

There is a group of sounds whose articulation involves not only an occlusion at some point in the oral cavity before the release of the air-stream, but also a lowering of the velum so that the latter is also released through the nasal cavity as well. The vocal cords generally vibrate and so in German all the nasals are voiced. We will refer to them simply as nasals although their fuller name is nasal plosives.

4.4.4.1 The labial nasal [m]

(i) Articulation

The bilabial nasal [m] is produced by making a closure with both lips. The velum is lowered. When the closure of the lips is released the air is expelled both through the mouth and the nasal cavity. There is no great build-up of pressure in the oral cavity as in the case of the oral plosives. The vocal cords are vibrating. The tongue assumes the position of the preceding or following vowel (Fig. 4.14). The lips are rounded before rounded vowels and spread before unrounded vowels.

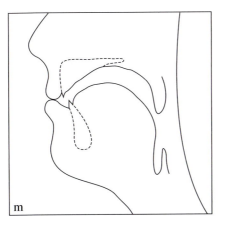

Figure 4.14   Articulation of [m]

(ii) Spelling

The nasal [m] is spelt <m> (*mit, Name*) and <mm> after short vowels (*sammeln, Kamm*).

(iii) Distribution

The bilabial nasal occurs initially before vowels (*Mond, Mund*) and medially and finally after short and long vowels and diphthongs: *Flamme, Dame, räumen, Damm, Kram, Raum.*

(iv) Similarity to English sounds

It is similar to the sounds in English *mid, name, swimming.*

(v) Major variants

There are no major variants.

4.4.4.2 The alveolar nasal [n]

(i) Articulation

The alveolar nasal [n] is produced by making a closure in the oral cavity with the blade (or tip) of the tongue and the centre of the alveolar ridge. The velum is lowered. When the closure is released the air is expelled both through the mouth and the nasal cavity (Fig. 4.15). There is no great build-up of pressure in the oral cavity as in the case of the oral plosives. The vocal cords are vibrating. The tongue assumes the position of the preceding or following vowel. The lips are rounded before rounded vowels and spread before unrounded vowels.

(ii) Spelling

The alveolar nasal is spelt <n>: *Nase, ohne,* and in the particles *an, in.* After short vowels it is otherwise spelt <nn>: *binnen, kann.*

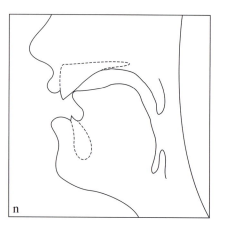

n

Figure 4.15   Articulation of [n]

(iii) Distribution

The alveolar nasal occurs initially, medially and finally after vowels: *nun*, *beginnen*, *rann*.

(iv) Similarity to English sounds

It is similar to the sounds in English *now*, *winner*, *son*.

(v) Major variants

When <n> appears before the labio-dental voiceless fricative [f] in *Senf*, *Fünf*, it usually becomes a labio-dental nasal [ɱ], also spelt <m> in *Triumph*. *DAW*, *WDA* and *Siebs* have tended to ignore this.

4.4.4.3 The palato-velar nasal [ŋ]

(i) Articulation

The velar nasal [ŋ] is produced by making a closure with the back of the tongue raised up against the soft palate. The place of the closure depends on the nature of the preceding vowel. The velum is lowered. When the closure is released the air is expelled both through the mouth and the nasal cavity (Fig. 4.16). There is no great build-up of pressure in the oral cavity as in the case of the oral plosives. The vocal cords are vibrating. The tongue assumes the position of the preceding vowel. The lips are rounded after rounded vowels and spread after unrounded vowels.

(ii) Spelling

The palato-velar nasal is spelt <ng>: *fangen*, *Klang*.

(iii) Distribution

The palato-velar nasal only occurs medially and finally after short vowels: *singen*, *lang*.

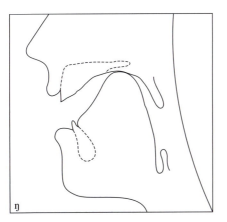

Figure 4.16   Articulation of [ŋ]

(iv) Similarity to English sounds

It is similar to the sounds in English *singer, song.* There must be no following plosive as in English *finger, longer.*

(v) Major variants

In north German colloquial speech the palato-velar nasal is sometimes devoiced and appears as the cluster [ŋk], *ging.*

4.4.5 Other consonants

4.4.5.1 The lateral [l]

(i) Articulation

The alveolar lateral [l] is produced by making a closure between the blade (or tip) of the tongue and the centre of the alveolar ridge. The edges of the tongue are in contact with the upper teeth but create a gap on both sides of the tongue through which the air-stream flows. The velum closes off the oral cavity. The dorsum (back) of the tongue is low in the mouth (Fig. 4.17). The vocal cords are not vibrating. The position of the lips depends on the preceding or following vowel.

(ii) Spelling

The alveolar lateral is spelt <l> (*laut, Meile*) and <ll> after short vowels (*bellen, Ball*).

(iii) Distribution

It appears initially before vowels (*Liebe, Laune*) and medially and finally after short and long vowels and diphthongs: *völlig, Mühle, teilen, voll, Stuhl, Teil.*

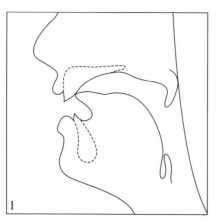

Figure 4.17   Articulation of [l]

(iv) Similarity to English sounds

The alveolar lateral is similar to the English sounds in *look, truly* but not like the 'dark' or velarized [ɫ] word-finally in *ball, little.*

(v) Major variants

In Cologne there is a postvocalic velarized [ɫ]. In Central Bavarian and the Swiss German dialect of Berne postvocalic [l] is vocalized.

4.4.5.2 The *r*-sounds

(i) Articulation

The articulation of the *r*-sounds is rather complex. *Siebs* originally only allowed a tongue-trill [r] but from 1933 the uvular trill was also allowed. However, in colloquial speech there was much more variation. In initial position before a vowel as in *reiten* the *r* is pronounced in careful speech as a trill (*der Vibrant, -en*), or roll (the rapid vibration of one articulator against another). The trill either involves the tongue tip which is tapped quickly two or three times against the alveolar ridge, or the uvula (*das Zäpfchen*), which is tapped two or three times against the back of the throat. The first of these articulations is called an apical or dental roll or trill (*das Zungenspitzen-r*) and the second is called the uvular roll or trill (*das Zäpchen-r*) (see Figs. 4.2 and 4.3). These articulations are symbolized [r] and [R] respectively. In colloquial informal pronunciation these rolls or trills lose their roll or trill character and become alveolar or uvular fricatives. Sometimes they are produced with little or no friction and can be called frictionless continuants, or approximants (*der Approximant, -en*), symbolized by writing the *r*

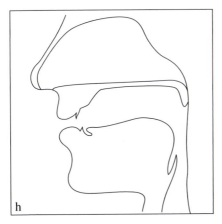

Figure 4.18   Articulation of [h]

symbols upside down, e.g. [ɹ], [ʁ]. Some idea of the variety of *r*-sounds
that are to be found in German is described in Wiese (2003) and for
European languages in Göschel (1971).

(ii) Spelling

The [r] sounds are spelt <r> (*rar, Rand, rühren*) and <rr> after short
vowels (*irren, Herr*).

(iii) Distribution

The sound [r] occurs initially before vowels (*reich, Risiko*), medially
(*Herren, sparen*) and finally (*bar, Bier, Wirrwarr*).

(iv) Similarity to English sounds

The alveolar or uvular variants do not occur in RP. Scots trilled [r] is
suitable for prevocalic pronunciation. In parts of Tyneside there is also a
uvular trilled [R]. Moulton (1962: 35–40) deals in detail with American
speakers' problem with German *r*-sounds.

(v) Major variants

Apart from the alveolar and uvular variants the other major variant is
the vocalization of [-er] to [ɐ] and of [r] after a long vowel, both
word-finally (*Uhr* [uːɐ]) and before a consonant (*Bart* [baːɐt]). Both
vocalizations are now sanctioned in *DAW*.

4.4.5.3 The glottal fricative [h]

(i) Articulation

The glottal fricative [h] is a unique sound. It is produced by a narrowing
in the glottis of the vocal cords as the air-stream passes through them.
There is no vibration of the vocal cords (Fig. 4.18). The tongue and the

lips in the oral cavity are always modified according to the articulation of the following vowels. The nasal cavity is sealed off by the raising of the velum.

(ii) Spelling

The glottal fricative is spelt <h>: *Hand, hinter.*

(iii) Distribution

It only occurs initially before vowels: *Henne, Hund, Haus.* The letter <h> medially between vowels is not pronounced (*sehen, Ruhe, siehe*), except in very formal reading style.

(iv) Similarity to English sounds

It is similar to the sounds in English *hen, house.*

(v) Major variants

There are no major variants.

QUESTIONS

1   Which of the following sounds are voiceless: [d, n, t, k, ʃ, z, m, x, l, p]?

2   Give the IPA symbols for the consonants represented by the following articulatory descriptions:

  (i)   voiced labio-dental fricative
  (ii) voiceless alveolar stop
  (iii) uvular trill
  (iv) voiced palato-velar
  (v)   voiceless post-alveolar
  (vi) velar nasal

3   How does the behaviour of the vocal cords differ in the production of [t] and [d]?

4   Which of the following sounds are fricatives: [p, f, g, s, n, b, z, x, m, ʒ]? What characterizes a fricative?

5   Transcribe the following words in the IPA transcription: *still, korrekt, Sprache, Verstand, groß, Frechheit, Lachkrampf, Stumpfsinn, Gesangverein, ordnungsgemäß.*

6   Which of the following sounds are alveolar: [m, s, ŋ, ç, n, p, b, ʃ, z, k]?

7   Give articulatory descriptions for the sounds represented by the following phonetic symbols: [ŋ, ç, ʃ, t, k, R, h, v, m, b].

8 Outline the differences between the two main types of *r*-sounds in German.

9 Transcribe the following passage about Kiel in IPA script back into standard German orthography:

ki:l ɪst, ʊm ɛs glaiç tsu: zɑ:gən, ainə ʃtat de:ɐ ge:gənvart. de:ɐ frɛmdə vɪrt hi:ɐ nu:ɐ ve:nɪgə tsoiknɪsə i:rɐ zi:bən jɛ:rɪgən fɛrgaŋənhait fɪndən. das tsɛntrʊm di:zɐ altən rezidɛnts de:ɐ ʃle:svɪçɔlstainɪʃən hɛrtsø:gə, di: grɑ:f ɑ:dɔlf de:ɐ fi:ɐtə tsvœlfhʊndɛttsvaiʊntfɪrtsɪç grʏndətə, vʊrdə ɪm kri:k tsɛrʃlɑ:gən. mɪt i:m fɛrʃvant das ʊnɔrganiʃə gəvir de:ɐ ʃtrɑ:sənʃlʊxtən, das ɪm lɛtstən fɪrtəl dɛs fo:rɪgən jɑ:rhʊndɛts dʊrç das rapi:də anvaksən als hɑ:fən de:ɐ raiçsmari:nə de:n altən mɑ:lərɪʃən ʃtatkɛrn y:bɐvu:xɐt hatə, zo: das man nu:ɐ nɔx ve:nɪç fɔn de:ɐ naty:ɐlɪçən ʃø:nhait de:ɐ aintsɪçartɪgən lɑ:gə an ainɐ de:ɐ anmu:tɪçstən bʊxtən de:ɐ ɔstze: spy:ɐtə.

10 Transcribe the following passage into IPA script:

Seit mehr als 900 Jahren weiß man von der Burg Hohentübingen. Die Universität, die die Stadt in aller Welt berühmt gemacht hat, wurde vor über 500 Jahren im Jahre 1477 gegründet. Die berühmte Stadtsilhouette bietet im wesentlichen noch den Anblick, den der Maler und Kupferstecher Merian im 17. Jahrhundert hatte. Die vielen krummen, bergauf- und bergab laufenden Gassen und ihre eng aneinanderstehenden Fachwerkhäuser haben der Stadt ein mittelalterliches Aussehen bewahrt: erhaltene Vergangenheit auf Schritt und Tritt, sehr zum Entzücken der Besucher. Maler, Fotografen und Amateurfilmer finden hier viele Motive. Die moderne Stadt ist auf den Höhen am Stadtrand entstanden. Die Naturwissenschaften der Universität, in denen für die Welt von morgen geforscht wird, fanden hier ein neues Quartier. Eine ihrer Leistungen ist der Botanische Garten, weit über Deutschlands Grenzen hinaus berühmt.

5 Sounds in contrast

5.1 Phonemes and allophones

The number of sounds that the organs of speech can produce is infinite. The utterance of every sound every time it is articulated is slightly different. Phoneticians want to describe pronunciation in as much detail as possible. However, as soon as the learner or linguist starts to study the sounds of a particular language then what becomes important is not simply how sounds are pronounced but which sound differences are made to distinguish words. In practice, therefore, only a limited number of distinctive sounds is used in each language. In German the difference in meaning between *Tier* 'animal' and *dir* 'you (dat.)' is carried solely by the difference between a voiceless alveolar plosive [t] and a voiced alveolar plosive [d] (cf. Engl. *town* vs *down*). Sound differences in a language that distinguish between the meanings of words are termed phonemic, and the sounds which carry this difference are called phonemes. Thus in German and English the plosives [t] and [d] are phonemes and the difference between them, the presence or absence of voice, is phonemic. What is important is not that they are alveolar plosives, but that one is voiceless, [t], and one voiced, [d].

As phonemes the sounds are written between slant lines /t/, /d/. They are said to form a phonemic opposition. There are many pairs of words in German which are distinguished solely by a difference of voice: *Paar* : *bar*; *Taten* : *Daten*; *Kasse* : *Gasse*; *fein* : *Wein*. Words such as these that differ only in one phoneme from each other are known as minimal pairs. The easiest way of establishing the phonemic system of a language is by using minimal pairs, but contrasts in a similar environment, e.g. before vowels (*Pass* : *Bus*), are considered to be sufficient if minimal pairs are not available.

Phonetic differences that are not phonemic are termed allophonic. Phonemic and allophonic features differ from language to language. In German the difference between the voiceless alveolar fricative [s] and its voiced counterpart [z] is phonemic (/s/ *reißen* : /z/ *reisen*), but in Spanish the difference is purely allophonic. A voiceless [s] appears initially, (*sol* 'sun') and medially (*casa*), but a voiced fricative, [z], appears before other voiced sounds: *asno* 'ass', *mismo/a* 'same'.

A definition of the phoneme has proved very difficult to formulate but there are two suggestions that may be helpful. Daniel Jones (1967: 7–12) regarded the phoneme as a family of sounds which are never in contrast with each other and which are phonetically similar. The Prague School is associated with Nikolai Trubetzoy (1890–1938) whose seminal work, *Grundzüge der Phonologie* (Foundations of Phonology) was published posthumously in 1939. He regarded the phoneme as an abstraction consisting of a bundle of distinctive, or phonemic, features that occur together. The phoneme /p/ in German, for instance, has certain distinctive features: it is a plosive – it contrasts with fricatives (*Pein* : *fein*); it is labial – it contrasts with other plosives at different points of articulation (*passen* : *Tassen* : *Kassen*); it is voiceless – it contrasts with voiced plosives (*packen* : *Backen*). The German phoneme is thus an abstract unit consisting of three distinctive features: (1) voice, (2) point of articulation, e.g. labial, and (3) manner of articulation, e.g. plosive. The allophones of a phoneme show other, non-distinctive or purely phonetic features (e.g. aspiration initially before a vowel) in addition to the three distinctive features. The voiceless palato-velar stop /k/, for example, has different allophones, whose place of articulation depends on the position of the following vowel. Thus in the words *Kinder, kennen, Kanne, konnte, Kunde* the /k/ is pronounced from palatal to uvular. This approach regards the phoneme as an abstraction that is realized by its allophones in the speech chain. Another important member of the Prague School, Roman Jakobson (1896–1982), found his way to the USA and continued to elaborate this notion of distinctive features. Through his work with Morris Halle it became of fundamental importance in generative phonology.

There is a considerable number of studies that have applied the phoneme to the description of German: Moulton (1962), Philipp (1970), Werner (1972), Keller (1978: 553–8), Kohler (1995: 152–74), Meinhold and Stock (1982: 79–170), Benware (1986: Chapter 4), Wiese (1996), Boase-Beier and Lodge (2003: Chapter 5) and Fox (2005: Chapter 2). We will be making use of these studies in our description.

5.1.1 Phonemic opposition

In addition to distinctive features the Prague school emphasized the notion of opposition. Trubetzkoy (1939) recognized different types of opposition.

The two principal types are bilateral and multilateral. Bilateral (or one-dimensional) oppositions are those formed between two phonemes, usually differentiated by one distinctive feature, thus in German /p/ : /b/ (*Pein* : *Bein*) is a bilateral opposition since not only are they distinguished solely by the feature of voice but no other phonemes are characterized by the features of plosiveness and labiality. Multilateral oppositions are those that consist of more than one feature occurring in other phonemes, thus in German in the opposition /p/ : /t/ the features they share of voicelessness and plosiveness also occur in /k/.

Within these divisions there are five sub-types:

(1) Proportional oppositions. /p/ : /b/ is characterized by the feature of voiced versus voicelessness. This kind of opposition is repeated by the pairs /t/ : /d/ and /k/ : /g/.

(2) Isolated oppositions: no other oppositions are distinguished by these combinations of features, e.g. /p/ : /ʃ/ or /r/ : /l/.

(3) Privative oppositions: these oppositions are characterized by the presence or absence of a feature, thus in the opposition /m/ : /b/, the former is nasal and the latter non-nasal.

(4) Gradual oppositions: these are degrees of difference within a continuum. The difference between high, mid and low in vowel heights is usually cited as an example of this.

(5) Equipollent: these oppositions are separated by several distinctive features, e.g. /p/ : /x/ or /f/ : /k/. In effect it comprises those oppositions that are neither privative nor gradual.

Related to this classification is the distinction by Martinet (1955: 69f.) between a series and an order. A series such as /p t k/ shares distinctive features, in this case voicelessness and plosiveness, whereas the members of an order such as /p b m/ share the distinctive feature of labiality but are distinguished in different ways, i.e. /p/ is a voiceless stop, /b/ is a voiced stop and /m/ is a nasal. Building on the suggestion of a Viennese dialectologist Anton Pfalz (1885–1958), a phonological series was designated as a *Reihe* and because very often in sound changes all the members of a series are affected together this type of change was called *Reihenschritt* (series change). As we shall see in the historical development of German, the shifting of Germanic *p, t, k* to affricates and fricatives or the diphthongization of MHG long *î, iu* and *û* are changes of series (for more details see Chapter 12).

5.1.2 Peripheral sounds

In our description of the phonemes of German and the oppositions they enter into we encounter some sounds that seem to have a very restricted distribution.

The glottal fricative /h/ only occurs before vowels; voiced pre-palatal fricative /ʒ/ only occurs initially before vowels and medially after long vowels. Similarly the velar nasal /ŋ/ normally only occurs medially and finally after vowels. The phonemes /h/ and /ŋ/ are native phonemes whereas /ʒ/ occurs in foreign words. The voiced labio-dental fricative /v/ occurs only in a few words medially between vowels and also before initial /r/ in Low German: *Wrack* 'wreck', *wringen* 'to wring (of washing)'. Similarly, the occurrence of short vowels before medial /b d g/ is also due to Low German borrowings: *Robbe* 'seal', *Kladde* 'exercise book', *Egge* 'harrow'. It is rather difficult to find a principled reason to divide off peripheral phonemes and infrequent distribution from a putative core phonemic system. In our description we will simply comment on the infrequency and origin of certain sounds and their distribution. Those sounds that are definitely due to borrowing, such as nasal vowels, will be dealt with in Chapter 8.

5.2 The vowel phonemes

One of the aims of phonemic phonology is to set up an inventory of the distinctive phonological units, i.e. phonemes of a language. Disagreements have arisen among linguists who differ in their phonemic analysis in three main ways:

(1) What is the status of a sound: is it a phoneme or an allophone?
(2) Are complex segments such as diphthongs or affricates one unitary phoneme, which will increase the phonemic inventory, or are they simply combinations of other phonemes?
(3) Which distinctive feature distinguishes phonemes?

Problems in the analysis of vowels feature in this section, those concerning consonants in 5.4.

In our analysis, which follows traditional lines in recognizing vowel length as being phonemic, there are seven short, lax vowels: /i/ *bitten*, /y/ *Bütten*, /u/ *Butter*, /ɛ/ *Betten*, /ø/ *Götter*, /o/ *Lotto*, /a/ *Ratte*; and eight long, tense vowels: /i:/ *bieten*, /y:/ *Güte*, /u:/ *gute*, /e:/ *beten*, /ɛ:/ *Räte*, /ø:/ *löten*, /o:/ *Boten*, /a:/ *baten*. German has three diphthongs, all falling, that is having the stress on the first component: [ai] *mein*, [au] *auch*, [oi] *euch*.

The main features which serve to differentiate vowel phonemes are vowel length, lip rounding, front/backness and tongue height. Vowel length is phonemic before all intervocalic consonants except /ŋ/ and the affricate /pf/, where only short vowels occur, and /j/, /z/ and /ʒ/ where only long vowels occur. Apart from this general restriction there are also some accidental 'gaps' where certain vowels do not appear before certain consonants.

5.2.1 Problems of phonemic analysis of the vowels

5.2.1.1 The feature of vowel length

The maximum number of phonemes occurs in stressed position, typically in disyllabic words such as *biete* or *bitte*, comprising one stressed syllable containing a vowel followed by a consonant, followed by an unstressed vowel. Apart from the word-initial consonants this pattern can be symbolized as VCv, where V = any stressed vowel, C = any consonant and v = an unstressed vowel. There are three types of vowel-like items that occur for V: (1) short, lax vowels, e.g. *bitte*, (2) long, tense vowels, e.g. *biete*, and (3) diphthongs, e.g. *leite*. The short vowels also differ in quality from the long vowels, being more open, or lax, i.e. their tongue height is slightly lower than that of their long counterparts (see 3.1). Since the long vowels, with the sole exception of /ɛ:/, are both long and tense, is the phonemic feature that separates the two groups quantity or quality? Should the opposition *biete* vs *bitte* be labelled /i:/ vs /i/, showing quantity as phonemic, or /i/ vs /ɪ/, showing quality as phonemic? As there is already one vowel, /ɛ:/, which, although long is not automatically close, or tense, and, in addition, short [a] and long [ɑ:] do not differ in quality in the same way, then it would seem that it is preferable, as many linguists do, to take length as being the distinctive phonemic feature, at least for the standard. The problem is compounded by the fact that /ɛ:/ does not occur in all colloquial varieties of German. Thus one could say the length is phonemic in varieties containing /ɛ:/, but quality is phonemic in other varieties. For a number of different analyses, see: Jones (1967: §§ 105, 525, 63), Philipp (1970: 22–41), Werner (1972: 24–30), Keller (1978: 553–5), Meinhold and Stock (1982: 88–90), Benware (1986: 50f.), Wiese (1996: 277–80), Fox (2005: 30–3).

5.2.1.2 The special status of /ɛ:/

The half-open, low-mid vowel /ɛ:/ is the only long vowel that is open or lax. All the others (except /ɑ:/) are close and tense. It means that the long vowels distinguish four tongue heights whereas the short vowels only distinguish three (see Figs. 3.3 and 3.11). In colloquial varieties in north Germany it tends to be replaced by /e:/. What holds the phoneme together is that it is always spelt <ä>. For more details see 12.6.5.1 and Moulton (1961: 34f.), Werner (1972: 30–2) and Russ (1982: 154–9).

5.2.1.3 The phonemic status of the diphthongs – unitary phonemes or vowel + glide

Since the diphthongs seem to contain two components, are they to be regarded as unit phonemes /ai/ etc., or as clusters of a vowel plus a semi-vowel, /a/ + /j/?

The question is complicated by the fact that it is not clear which phoneme forms the second component. Phonetically the second component shows a wide variability of pronunciation. In the case of the diphthong in *mein* is it /i/, /j/ or even /e/? What are the second components of the diphthongs in *auch* and *euch*? If we give weight to the phonetic unity of the sound (it is produced with a single articulatory movement) then the diphthongs are clearly unit phonemes. This is the position we will adopt here. For more discussion see Werner (1972: 32–5), Keller (1978: 555), Benware (1986: 49), Wiese (1996: 159–62), Fox (2005: 43–6).

5.2.1.4 The vowels in unstressed syllables

The range of vowels in unstressed syllables differs in two points from that in stressed syllables: (1) there is no distinction between long and short vowels, and (2) the vowel [ə] only occurs in unstressed position. There is also a phonemic contrast between /ə/ and /ɐ/ in unstressed syllables, e.g. *bitte* : *bitter*. From one point of view this phonemic opposition is simply limited to unstressed syllables. A complication is that /ɐ/ can be regarded as the realization of the phoneme sequence /ər/. Building on this idea, Fox (2005: 47f.) views [ɐ] in parallel to the unstressed sequences [əm ən əl] which become a single syllabic sound when the [ə] is elided [m̩ n̩ l̩]. [ɐ] would be the syllabic sound for [ər].

Through loan words there is in NHG a full range of unstressed vowels, but phonetically the long vowels of stressed syllables show short, close allophones when unstressed. The following alternations illustrate this: ['] shows that the next vowel bears the stress: *Mo'tif* > *moti'vieren*; *'leben* > *le'bendig*; *'Drama* > *dra'matisch*; *'Motor* > *Mo'toren*; *'Muse* > *Mu'seum*; *A'syl* > *Asy'lant*. In the pronunciation of some speakers these shortened vowels become open and merge with the 'ordinary' short vowels [ɪ ɛ a ɔ œ ʊ ʏ]. According to pronunciation dictionaries some speakers distinguish in unstressed syllables between [o] and [ɔ] (*Ko'lonne* vs *Ko'llekte*), as well as [e] and [ɛ] (*Me'nage* vs *trai'nieren*) but it seems unclear as to how far this reflects actual usage. In general, however, these differences are determined by the number of following consonants. Before a single consonant the close vowel tends to occur: [to'taːl, te'noːr], but before a consonant cluster the open vowel occurs: [kɔm'pliːtsə, tɛn'dɛnts] (*Komplize*, *Tendenz*). Open vowels also occur frequently before /r/: [tɛ'rasə] (*Terrasse*).

Those linguists who regard quality and not quantity as being one of the main distinctive features of the stressed vowel system point to this continued presence of qualitative distinctions among unstressed vowels as supporting their argument. However, since nearly all the words involved are of foreign origin and vary in their pronunciation the whole basis for arguing this is rather uncertain.

The most frequent unstressed vowel in word-final position in modern German is [ə], spelt <e>, e.g. *bitte.* Other vowels do occur, but mostly in foreign words: *Sofa, Pony, Auto, Zulu.* Since [ə] is restricted to unstressed position it is possible to regard it simply as an allophone of stressed short /ɛ/. However, contrasts such as *'Moslem, 'Totem* (with [ɛ] in unstressed position) vs *Amen, Namen* (with [ə]) seem to show the two sounds in contrast and leave unresolved the phonemic status of [ə]. For further discussion see Werner (1972: 35–9 and 57f.), Keller (1978: 555f.), Meinhold and Stock (1982: 91), Benware (1986: 45–7), Wiese (1996: 252–8), Fox (2005: 46–8).

5.3 Oppositions between vowels

5.3.1 Opposition between long (tense) vowels and short (lax) vowels

In the following sections examples of the opposition between short (lax) vowels and long (tense) vowels will be illustrated before intervocalic consonants, voiceless and voiced obstruents, nasals and liquids. Not all possible occurrences are to be found. There are certain systematic gaps in distribution:

(1) the opposition does not occur before the velar nasal /ŋ/, where only short vowels occur;

(2) the opposition does not occur before the labial affricate /pf/, where only short vowels occur;

(3) the opposition does not occur before voiced fricatives, where only long vowels occur;

(4) the opposition is infrequent before the other affricates, /ts/ and /tʃ/, where mostly short vowels occur;

(5) the opposition is also infrequent before the voiceless post-alveolar fricative /ʃ/, where only /iː/ : /i/, /oː/ : /o/, /uː/ : /u/ and /yː/ : /y/ show contrasts, but the examples of long vowels are quite rare.

All these restrictions are understandable in that the affricates can be considered consonant clusters and /ŋ/ and /ʃ/ were originally the consonant clusters [ŋg] and [sk]. The lack of the contrast before voiced fricatives reflects the low frequency of short vowels before voiced obstruents in general, for example, /y/ : /yː/ only occurs before intervocalic /g/. The lack of the opposition /ɛ/ : /ɛː/ before intervocalic /p/ is of an accidental nature and we may still find examples.

5.3.1.1 /i/ : /iː/

(1) Before voiceless plosives: *Lippe, bitte, schicken* : *piepen, bieten, quieken* 'to squeak'
(2) Before voiced plosives: *kribbeln* 'to tickle', *Widder* 'ram', *Riggung* 'rigging' : *lieben, Lieder, kriegen*
(3) Before voiceless fricatives: *Schiffe, wissen, wischen, wichen* : *schliefen, gießen, Nische, riechen*
(4) Before nasals: *Zimmer, binnen* : *ziemen, dienen*
(5) Before liquids: *Willen, irren* : *spielen, frieren*

5.3.1.2 /ɛ/ : /ɛː/

(1) Before voiceless plosives: *Steppe, Wette, lecken* : *Räte, häkeln* 'to crotchet'
(2) Before voiced plosives: *Ebbe, verheddern* 'to get muddled up', *Egge* 'harrow' : *Säbel, prägen, gnädig*
(3) Before voiceless fricatives: *treffen, messen, Rechen* : *Käfig, mäßig, Gespräche*
(4) Before nasals: *Lämmer, rennen* : *schämen, gähnen*
(5) Before liquids: *Keller, sperren* : *wählen, gären*

5.3.1.3 /ɛ/ : /eː/

(1) Before voiceless plosives: *Teppich, Betten, strecken* : *Reepe* 'ropes', *beten, Ekel*
(2) Before voiced plosives: *Ebbe, fleddern* 'to plunder', *eggen* : *geben, reden, legen*
(3) Before voiceless fricatives: *äffen* 'to imitate' : *Hefe*
(4) Before nasals: *kämmen, nennen* : *nehmen, lehnen*
(5) Before liquids: *Quelle, zerren* : *fehlen, lehren*

5.3.1.4 /o/ : /oː/

(1) Before voiceless plosives: *stoppen, Motte, locken* : *Opa, Brote, Koker* 'worker in a coking plant'
(2) Before voiced plosives: *Robbe, Modder* 'mud', *Roggen* : *loben, Mode, Woge*
(3) Before voiceless fricatives: *hoffen, Rosse, Gosche* 'mouth (vulgar)', *lochen* : *Ofen, Soße, koscher, malochen* 'to graft, work hard'
(4) Before nasals: *Sommer, Sonne* : *Koma, Krone*
(5) Before liquids: *Wolle, dorren* : *Sohle, bohren*

5.3.1.5 /u/ : /u:/

(1) Before voiceless plosives: *struppig, Butter, spucken* : *Lupe, bluten, spuken* 'to haunt'
(2) Before voiced plosives: *rubbeln, buddeln, schmuggeln* : *Grube, luden, schlugen*
(3) Before voiceless fricatives: *muffig, Busse, pfuschen, bruchig* : *rufen, Buße, wuschen, suchen*
(4) Before nasals: *Rummel, Brunnen* : *Puma, Wune* 'hole in the ice'
(5) Before liquids: *Gully, murren* : *Schule, fuhren*

5.3.1.6 /a/ : /a:/

(1) Before voiceless plosives: *Klappe, Ratte, packen* : *Stapel* 'pile', *raten, Laken* 'sheet'
(2) Before voiced plosives: *Krabbe, Kladde, Bagger* 'excavator' : *Gabel, laden, lagen*
(3) Before voiceless fricatives: *schaffen, lassen, Sache* : *Hafen* 'to hoist', *spaßen, Sprache*
(4) Before nasals: *Hammer, Tannen* : *Samen, Fahnen*
(5) Before liquids: *fallen, harren* 'to wait' : *malen, Haare*

5.3.1.7 /ø/ : /ø:/

(1) Before voiceless plosives: *klöppeln* 'to make fine lace', *Götter, Böcke* : *Köper* 'twill cloth', *töten, blöken*
(2) Before voiced plosives: the opposition does not occur
(3) Before voiceless fricatives: *öffentlich* : *Öfen* (otherwise the opposition does not occur)
(4) Before nasals: *sömmern, können* : *Ströme, Söhne*
(5) Before liquids: *Hölle, dörren* : *Höhle, hören*

5.3.1.8 /y/ : /y:/

(1) Before voiceless plosives: *üppig, schütten, pflücken* : *Rüpel* 'lout, yob', *Güte, Küken*
(2) Before voiced plosives: *flügge* 'fully-fledged' : *lügen*
(3) Before voiceless fricatives: *süffig, Küsse, Büsche, Brüche* : *prüfen, süßen, Rüsche* 'frill', *Bücher*
(4) Before nasals: *dümmer, dünner* : *rühmen, grünen*
(5) Before liquids: *füllen, Dürre* : *fühlen, spüren*

5.3.2 Oppositions between front and back vowels

5.3.2.1 High vowels /iː/ : /uː/

(1) Before voiceless plosives: *Kiepe* 'basket', *brieten, Spieker* 'ship's nail' : *Lupe, bruten, Luke* 'hatch, skylight'
(2) Before voiced plosives: opposition does not occur
(3) Before voiceless fricatives: *riefen, gießen, Nische, kriechen* : *Stufen, fußen, wuschen, buchen*
(4) Before voiced fricatives: *Biesen* : *Busen*
(5) Before nasals: *Mime, Schiene* : *Blume, Wune*
(6) Before liquids: *spielen, Tieren* : *spulen, Touren*

5.3.2.2 High vowels /i/ : /u/

(1) Before voiceless plosives: *Sippe, bitten, kicken* : *Suppe, Butte, gucken*
(2) Before voiced plosives: *bibbern, Widder, Riggung* : *schrubben, muddig* 'muddy', *meschugge* 'mad, insane'
(3) Before voiceless fricatives: *schiffen, Bissen, wischen, sicher* : *muffig, Busse, kuscheln, bruchig* 'boggy'
(4) Before voiced fricatives: opposition does not occur
(5) Before nasals: *stimmen, gewinnen* : *stumme, Brunnen*
(6) Before liquids: *stillen, irren*: *Bullen, surren*

5.3.2.3 Mid vowels /eː/ : /oː/

(1) Before voiceless plosives: *beten* : *Popel* 'snot', *Boten, pokern*
(2) Before voiced plosives: *leben, weder, segen* : *loben, Boden, Bogen*
(3) Before voiceless fricatives: *Hefe, Späße, dreeschen* 'to rain', *Gespräche* : *Pofel* 'rubbish', *große, koscher, Maloche* 'hard work'
(4) Before voiced fricatives: *lesen* : *losen*
(5) Before nasals: *Schemen* 'diagrams', *sehnen* : *verchromen, schonen*
(6) Before liquids: *fehlen, Meere* : *Fohlen, Moore*

5.3.2.4 Mid vowels /ɛ/ : /o/

(1) Before voiceless plosives: *Treppen, retten, lecken* : *stoppen, spotten, locken*
(2) Before voiced plosives: *Ebbe, pedden* 'to kick' (north German), *Egge* : *Robbe, Bodden* 'shallow bay', *Roggen*
(3) Before voiceless fricatives: *Pfeffer, besser, dreschen, Becher* : *Koffer, Bosse, erloschen, gebrochen*

Cons.	/i/	/ɛ/	/a/	/o/	/u/	/y/	/ø/
/p/	Krippe	Steppe	Happen	stoppen	Suppe	üppig	Klöppel
/t/	Sitte	Wetter	Watte	stottern	Butter	Mütter	Götter
/k/	Wicken	wecken	backen	stocken	drucken	Rücken	Röcke
/b/	bibbern	Ebbe	Krabbe	Robbe	rubbeln		
/d/	Widder	fleddern		Bodden	buddeln		
/g/		Egge		Roggen	schmuggeln	flügge	
/f/	kniffen	Pfeffer	Affe	gesoffen	muffig	süffig	Schöffe
/s/	wissen	wessen	Wasser	Bosse	Busse	Küsse	Schlösser
/ʃ/	wischen	Esche	waschen	gedroschen	tuschen	Büsche	löschen
/ch/	wichen	stechen	lachen	pochen	bruchig	Sprüche	Löcher
/m/	Stimme	stemmen	Amme	kommen	bummeln	dümmer	frömmer
/n/	binnen	Sennen	Kannen	Sonnen	Brunnen	dünne	können
/ŋ/	singen	sengen	sangen	bongen	gesungen	Sprünge	
/l/	Wille	Welle	wallen	Wolle	Bulle	Füllen	völlig
/r/	irren	zerren	Karren	Schlorre	murren	Dürre	dörren

Figure 5.1   Oppositions of short vowels before single intervocalic consonants

(4) Before voiced fricatives: opposition does not occur

(5) Before nasals: *schwemmen, nennen* : *kommen, Nonnen*

(6) Before liquids: *Schwelle, Sperre* : *Stollen, verworren*

5.3.2.5 Low vowels /ɛ:/ : /a:/

(1) Before voiceless plosives: *Täter, häkeln* : *Taten, Haken*

(2) Before voiced plosives: *Säbel, Schädel, Jäger* : *Nabel, schaden, jagen*

(3) Before voiceless fricatives: *Käfer, Gefäßer, Gespräche* : *Hafen, saßen, Sprachen*

(4) Before voiced fricatives: *Käse* : *Vase*

(5) Before nasals: *lähmen, Zähne* : *Namen, mahnen*

(6) Before liquids: *schälen, Fähre* : *Schale, fahren*

5.3.3 Multilateral oppositions between vowels of different tongue heights

Among the short vowels three levels of tongue height are distinctive: high, mid and low. We will include seven vowel phonemes and represent the oppositions in Fig. 5.1.

5.3.4 Oppositions between front vowels with rounded and unrounded lips

5.3.4.1 /y/ : /i/

(1) Before voiceless plosives: *üppig, Mütter, Stücke* : *Rippe, Mitte, sticken*
(2) Before voiced plosives: *flügge* : *wriggen*
(3) Before voiceless fricatives: *süffig, müssen, Büsche, Sprüche* : *pfiffig, missen, zischen, strichen*
(4) Before voiced fricatives: opposition does not occur
(5) Before nasals: *Lümmel, verdünnen, Sprünge* : *Bimmel, binnen, springen*
(6) Before liquids: *füllen, Dürre* : *Willen, Irre*

5.3.4.2 /y:/ : /i:/

(1) Before voiceless plosives: *Typen, Mythen, Küken* : *Piepen, mieten, kieken*
(2) Before voiced plosives: *Schübe, Süden, lügen* : *schieben, sieden, liegen*
(3) Before voiceless fricatives: *Küfer* 'cooper', *Süße, Rüsche, Bücher* : *Kiefer, spießig, Nische, riechen*
(4) Before voiced fricatives: *Drüse* : *Riese*
(5) Before nasals: *rühmen, Bühnen* : *Riemen, Bienen*
(6) Before liquids: *fühlen, spüren* : *fielen, zieren*

5.3.4.3 /ø/ : /ɛ/

(1) Before voiceless plosives: *Klöppel* 'clapper; bobbin', *Götter, Höcker* : *Treppe, Betten, Hecke*
(2) Before voiced plosives: opposition does not occur
(3) Before voiceless fricatives: *Löffel, Schlösser, löschen, Löcher* : *treffen, besser, Esche, Becher*
(4) Before voiced fricatives: opposition does not occur
(5) Before nasals: *schwömme, können* : *schwemmen, kennen*
(6) Before liquids: *Hölle, Dörre* 'dryness' : *Helle, Sperre*

5.3.4.4 /ø:/ : /e:/

(1) Before voiceless plosives: *Göpel* 'treadmill', *töten, pökeln* : *Fete, Ekel*
(2) Before voiced plosives: *Möbel, spröde, Vögel* : *Nebel, edel, fegen*
(3) Before voiceless fricatives: *Höfe, Blöße* : *Hefe, mäßig*
(4) Before voiced fricatives: *Möwe, lösen* : *ewig, lesen*
(5) Before nasals: *Ströme, Söhne* : *Schemel, Sehne*
(6) Before liquids: *Höhlen, Möhre* : *hehlen* 'to conceal', *Meere*

5.4 The consonant phonemes

The consonant phonemes are distinguished by three main distinctive features: (1) voiced vs voiceless (or lenis/fortis); (2) place of articulation; and (3) manner of articulation.

In this section we are only dealing with single consonants – combinations of consonants, clusters, being described in Chapter 7. However, the affricates [pf ts tʃ] present a problem of analysis as to whether they are single phonemes, e.g. /pf/, /ts/, /tʃ/, or clusters, e.g. /p/ + /f/ etc., and their phonological status is discussed in 5.4.1.2.

5.4.1 Problems of phonemic analysis among the consonants

There are disagreements among linguists concerning the status of [x] and [ç] and whether the affricates should be analysed as unitary phonemes (monophonematic analysis) or as a sequence of two consonants (biphonematic analysis).

5.4.1.1 The status of [x] and [ç]

Phoneticians recognize that there is a phonetic difference between the voiceless velar fricative [x] and the voiceless palatal fricative [ç]. Kohler (1995: 160f.) adds a uvular [χ]. There is, however, disagreement about their phonemic status. For the most part they are in complementary distribution with [x] occurring after low and back vowels and [ç] occurring after front vowels. In the words *tauchen* and *Tauchen* 'little rope' there is an apparent contrast of /x/ with /ç/. However this can easily be dealt with and their allophonic status confirmed if morphological information is allowed in the phonological analysis (something that many phonemic phonologists are unwilling to do: they wish to use only phonological criteria at the phonological level). In *Tauchen*, where [ç] occurred after a back vowel, it was in the initial position of the diminutive suffix. The description of the distribution of the allophones [x] and [ç] can therefore be framed as follows: 'The allophone [ç] appears after front vowels and initially in words (*Chemie*) or morphemes (*-chen*) and after /n 1 r/; the allophone [x] appears elsewhere, i.e. after low and back vowels.'

This question is still being aired. Griffen (1985: 53–72) argues that the variation in articulation lies chiefly in the vowel and need not be symbolized in the consonant. T. A. Hall (1992: 221–35) argues that both [ç] and [x] are produced by a rule of 'Dorsal fricative assimilation' which only operates within morphemes, thus in *tauchen* the [x] is within the morpheme *tauch-* while the [ç] of *-chen* in *Tauchen* belongs to a different morpheme.

For a survey of a variety of different analyses, see: Moulton (1962: 28–32), Jones (1967: §§ 230–2), Keller (1978: 557f.), Benware (1986: 49f.), Wiese (1996: 209–18), Fox (2005: 40–2).

5.4.1.2 The affricates: are they one phoneme or two?

Are the affricates [ts, pf] to be considered as single phonemes /ts/ and /pf/ (monophonematic solution), which would add to the inventory of phonemes, or are they combinations of distinct consonants, /t/ + /s/ and /p/ + /f/ (biphonematic solution) like /t/ + /r/ etc.? Linguists are divided in their opinion and almost all analyses seem to use their own criteria (Werner 1972: 50–5). Several criteria seem, however, to point to the independent nature of the two parts of the affricates and thus to regarding them as clusters of two consonants. Firstly, the ability of the individual components of the affricates to occur on their own: the affricate /ts/ contrasts with /t/ and /s/ ([s] as a realization for initial *s* only occurs in South Germany and Austria), e.g. *zeigen, Teig, seinen*; /pf/ contrasts with /p/ and /f/, e.g. *Pfeife, Pein, fein*. Secondly, their ability, albeit limited, to reverse position. Of the theoretical combinations and their reversals, i.e. /ts st pf fp/, the sequences /ts/, /st/ and /pf/ occur as intervocalic and word-final clusters: *sitzen, Netz; beste, Nest; klopfen, Topf;* but not /fp/. A third pointer to the fact that both components have an independent nature is shown by the fact that both can be divided by a morpheme boundary: *rät + st, Ab + fall*. For these three reasons it will be assumed here that the affricates [pf] and [ts] are biphonematic, being clusters of /p/ + /f/ and /t/ + /s/. This will also affect the description of consonant clusters, describing the initial combinations of words such as *pflegen* and *Zweifel* as being composed of three consonants: /p/ + /f/ + /l/ and /t/ + /s/ + /v/.

For a discussion of different analyses, see: Keller (1978: 557f.), Kohler (1995: 166–8), Wiese (1996: 265–8) and Fox (2005: 46).

5.5 Phonemic oppositions among consonants

The consonant phonemes are distinguished by three main distinctive features: (1) voice, (2) place of articulation and (3) manner of articulation. These manifest themselves in the opposition between voiced and voiceless obstruents (lenis and fortis), between maximally five places of articulation (labial – alveolar – post-alveolar – palatal – palato-velar) and between two oppositions of manner of articulation between plosive and fricative and oral obstruent and nasal. We will give examples in all these three main categories, covering several different positions in the word and also before and after other sounds. We will thus see that the distribution of the sounds in opposition varies. For example, the opposition between voiced and voiceless obstruents does not occur in word-final position. The opposition is said to be neutralized.

The main positions of occurrences of the consonants in the word and before or after certain sounds are: (1) word-initially before vowels; (2) word-initially before sonorants /l r m n/; (3) word-initially after obstruents; (4) medially between vowels; (5) medially before sonorants /l r m n/; (6) medially before obstruents; (7) word-finally after vowels; (8) word-finally before or after sonorants /l r m n/; and (9) word-finally before or after obstruents. In collecting examples, Muthmann (1996) and the reverse dictionaries Mater (1965), Brückner and Sauter (1984), Muthmann (1988) and Lee (2005) were a great help.

5.5.1 The bilateral opposition between voiceless and voiced plosives

5.5.1.1 /p/ : /b/

(1) Word-initially before vowels: *Paar* : *bar*; *Pest* : *bestens*; *Piste* : *bist*; *Posse* : *Bosse*; *putzen* : *Butzen* '(apple) core'; *Pöbel* : *Böden*; *Püffe* : *Büffel*
(2) Word-initially before sonorants /l r m n/: *Pleite* : *Blei*; *Preis* : *breit*
(3) Word-initially after obstruents: opposition does not occur
(4) Medially between vowels: *Raupen* : *Tauben*; *piepen* : *blieben*; *Steppe* : *Ebbe*
(5) Medially before or after sonorants /l r m n/: *Welpe* 'pup, whelp' : *selber*; *Schärpe* 'scarf' : *Scherbe*; *Pumpe* : *Plombe*
(6) Medially before or after obstruents: *Wespe* : *Lesbe*
(7) Word-finally after vowels: opposition does not occur
(8) Word-finally before or after sonorants /l r m n/: opposition does not occur
(9) Word-finally before or after obstruents: opposition does not occur

5.5.1.2 /t/ : /d/

(1) Word-initially before vowels: *Taten* : *Daten*; *Teller* : *Delle* 'dent'; *Tier* : *dir*; *Torf* : *Dorf*; *tuten* : *duzen*; *Töne* : *Döner*; *tüfteln* 'to puzzle over' : *Düfte*
(2) Word-initially before sonorants /l r m n/: *treten* : *drehen*; *trüben* : *drüben*. The opposition does not occur before /l/.
(3) Word-initially after obstruents: opposition does not occur
(4) Medially between vowels: *leiten* : *leiden*; *bieten* : *Lieder*; *litten* : *Widder*

(5) Medially before or after sonorants /l r m n/: *halten* : *Halde* 'mound, heap'; *Härte* : *Herde*; *Ämter* : *Hemden*; *hinten* : *hindern*

(6) Medially before or after obstruents: opposition does not occur

(7) Word-finally after vowels: opposition does not occur

(8) Word-finally before or after sonorants /l r m n/: opposition does not occur

(9) Word-finally before or after obstruents: opposition does not occur

5.5.1.3 /k/ : /g/

(1) Word-initially before vowels: *Kabel* : *Gabel*; *Kern* : *gern*; *Kolben* 'butt (of rifle)' : *Gold*; *Kuss* : *Guss*; *können* : *gönnen*; *Küsse* : *Güsse*

(2) Word-initially before sonorants /l r m n/: *Klette* : *Glätte*; *Kränze* : *Grenze*; *kneten* 'to knead' : *gnädig*

(3) Word-initially after obstruents: opposition does not occur

(4) Medially between vowels: *Laken* : *Lagen*; *Ecke* : *Egge*

(5) Medially before sonorants /l r m n/: *Balken* : *Balgen* 'bellows'; *Erker* 'oriel, bay-window' : *Ärger*; *Schinken* : *Bingo*

(6) Medially before or after obstruents: opposition does not occur

(7) Word-finally after vowels: opposition does not occur

(8) Word-finally before or after sonorants /l r m n/: opposition does not occur

(9) Word-finally before or after obstruents: opposition does not occur

5.5.2 The bilateral opposition between voiceless and voiced fricatives

5.5.2.1 /f/ : /v/

(1) Word-initially before vowels: *Fall* : *Wall*; *Felder* : *Wälder*; *finden* : *winden*; *fort* : *Wort*; *Fund* : *wund* 'sore'; *fühlen* : *wühlen* 'to burrow, rummage'

(2) Word-initially before sonorants /l r m n/: *Frack* : *Wrack*. The opposition does not occur before /l/.

(3) Word-initially before or after obstruents: *Schwere* : *Sphäre*;

(4) Medially between vowels: *Ofen* : *stowen*

(5) Medially before or after sonorants /l r m n/: *Wölfe* : *Pulver*; *Larve* : *Kurve*

(6) Medially before or after obstruents: opposition does not occur

(7) Word-finally after vowels: opposition does not occur

(8) Word-finally before or after sonorants /l r m n/: opposition does not occur

(9) Word-finally before or after obstruents: opposition does not occur

5.5.2.2 /s/ : /z/

(1) Word-initially before vowels: *Sex* : *sechs*; *City* : *Sitte*
(2) Word-initially before sonorants /l r m n/: opposition does not occur
(3) Word-initially before or after obstruents: opposition does not occur
(4) Medially between vowels: *reißen* : *reisen*; *Hasen* : *hassen*
(5) Medially before or after sonorants /l r m n/: opposition does not occur
(6) Medially before obstruents: opposition does not occur
(7) Word-finally after vowels: opposition does not occur
(8) Word-finally before or after sonorants /l r m n/: opposition does not occur
(9) Word-finally before or after obstruents: opposition does not occur

5.5.2.3 /ʃ/ : /ʒ/

(1) Word-initially before vowels: *Schale* : *Jalousie*; *schier* : *Giro*
(2) Word-initially before sonorants /l r m n/: opposition does not occur
(3) Word-initially before or after obstruents: opposition does not occur
(4) Medially between vowels: *waschen* : *Page*
(5) Medially before or after sonorants /l r m n/: opposition does not occur
(6) Medially before obstruents: opposition does not occur
(7) Word-finally after vowels: opposition does not occur
(8) Word-finally before or after sonorants /l r m n/: opposition does not occur
(9) Word-finally before or after obstruents: opposition does not occur

5.5.3 Bilateral opposition: plosive : fricative

5.5.3.1 /p/ : /f/

(1) Word-initially before vowels: *Pate* : *Vater*; *Pudel* : *Fuder* 'cartload'; *Pein* : *fein*
(2) Word-initially before sonorants /l r m n/: *Plunder* : *Flunder*; *priesen* : *Friese* 'friezes'
(3) Word-initially before or after obstruents: *später* : *Sphäre*
(4) Medially between vowels: *Kneipe* : *Eifer*; *Lupe* : *rufen*; *kippen* : *kniffen*
(5) Medially before or after sonorants /l r m n/: *Stulpe* 'cuff' : *Hilfe*; *Zirpe* 'cicada' : *Schilfe*
(6) Medially before obstruents: opposition does not occur
(7) Word-finally after vowels: *Leib* : *reif*; *Hub* 'lifting' : *Ruf*; *Riff* 'reef' : *Tipp*
(8) Word-finally before or after sonorants /l r m n/: opposition does not occur

(9) Word-finally before or after obstruents: *Rezept* : *Saft*; *Schöps* 'mutton' : *betreffs* 'concerning'

5.5.3.2 /t/ : /s/

(1) Word-initially before vowels: *Tonne* : *Song*; *Tenne* : *Cent*
(2) Word-initially before sonorants /l r m n/: opposition does not occur
(3) Word-initially before or after obstruents: opposition does not occur
(4) Medially between vowels: *weiter* : *weißer*; *Bote* : *Soße*; *mitten* : *rissen*
(5) Medially before or after sonorants /l r m n/: opposition does not occur
(6) Medially before obstruents: opposition does not occur
(7) Word-finally after vowels: *weit* : *weiß*; *tot* : *Stoß*; *mit* : *bis*
(8) Word-finally before or after sonorants /l r m n/: *halt* : *Hals*; *Gurt* : *Kurs*; *Zimt* 'cinnamon' : *Sims* '(window)sill'; *Gans* : *Hand*; *bedingt* : *Dings*
(9) Word-finally before or after obstruents: *Delikt* : *Knicks*; *Markt* : *Murks* 'botch-up'; *Luft* : *behufs* 'concerning'

5.5.3.3 /k/ : /x–ç/

(1) Word-initially before vowels: *Kinn* : *Chi* 'Greek letter chi'; *Kenntnis* : *chemisch*; *Karte* : *Chanukka*; *kurz* : *Chuzpe*
(2) Word-initially before sonorants /l r m n/: *Klammer* : *Chlamys* 'cloak'; *kriechen* : *Chrysopras*
(3) Word-initially before or after obstruents: opposition does not occur
(4) Medially between vowels: *streiken* : *reichen*; *quieken* : *Griechen*; *Bäcker* : *Becher*; *Küken* : *Bücher*
(5) Medially before or after sonorants /l r m n/: *Falke* : *erdolchen*; *harken* : *schnarchen*; *Imke* : *Blümchen*; *trinken* : *tünchen*
(6) Medially before obstruents: opposition does not occur
(7) Word-finally after vowels: *Streik* : *Laich* 'spawn'; *Grammatik* : *zwanzig*; *Rock* : *roch*
(8) Word-finally before or after sonorants /l r m n/: *Volk* : *Dolch*; *Werk* : *Kelch*; *Fink* : *Mönch*
(9) Word-finally before or after obstruents: *direkt* : *zurecht*; *Dachs* 'badger' : *Dachs* (gen. of *Dach*)

5.5.3.4 /b/ : /v/

(1) Word-initially before vowels: *Bann* : *wann*; *Besen* : *Wesen*; *Biese* 'braid' : *Wiese*; *Bohnen* : *wohnen*; *Bucht* : *Wucht* 'force'; *Börse* : *Wörter*; *Bühne* : *wüten*

(2) Word-initially before sonorants /l r m n/: *bringen* : *wringen*

(3) Word-initially before or after obstruents: opposition does not occur

(4) Medially between vowels: *Gabe* : *Sklave*; *blubbern* : *Struwwel(peter)* 'shock-headed Peter'

(5) Medially before or after sonorants /l r m n/: *Schwalbe* : *Malve*; *Narbe* : *Arve* 'stone pine'

(6) Medially before obstruents: opposition does not occur

(7) Word-finally after vowels: opposition does not occur

(8) Word-finally before or after sonorants /l r m n/: opposition does not occur

(9) Word-finally before or after obstruents: opposition does not occur

5.5.3.5 /d/ : /z/

(1) Word-initially before vowels: *Dame* : *Samen*; *denken* : *senken*; *Dieb* : *Sieb*; *Donner* : *Sonne*; *Döner* : *Söhne*; *Dünen* : *sühnen*

(2) Word-initially before sonorants /l r m n/: opposition does not occur

(3) Word-initially before or after obstruents: opposition does not occur

(4) Medially between vowels: *seiden* : *reisen*; *wieder* : *Wiese*

(5) Medially before or after sonorants /l r m n/: *Bilder* : *Hülse*; *Hürde* : *Ferse*; *Fremden* : *Gemse*; *finden* : *Pinsel*

(6) Medially before obstruents: opposition does not occur

(7) Word-finally after vowels: opposition does not occur

(8) Word-finally before or after sonorants /l r m n/: opposition does not occur

(9) Word-finally before or after obstruents: opposition does not occur

5.5.3.6 /g/ : /j/

(1) Word-initially before vowels: *gar* : *Jahr*; *gären* : *jäten*; *Gockel* : *Joch*; *Gurke* : *jucken*

(2) Word-initially before sonorants /l r m n/: opposition does not occur

(3) Word-initially before or after obstruents: opposition does not occur

(4) Medially between vowels: *Bogen* : *Bojen* 'buoys'

(5) Medially before or after sonorants /l r m n/: opposition does not occur

(6) Medially before obstruents: opposition does not occur

(7) Word-finally after vowels: opposition does not occur

(8) Word-finally before or after sonorants /l r m n/: opposition does not occur

(9) Word-finally before or after obstruents: opposition does not occur

5.5.4 Nasal plosion vs oral plosion

5.5.4.1 /m/ : /b/

(1) Word-initially before vowels: *machen* : *backen*; *Menge* : *Bengel*; *mieten* : *bieten*; *morgen* : *borgen*; *Mutter* : *Butter*; *mögen* : *Bögen*; *müde* : *Bühne*
(2) Word-initially before sonorants /l r m n/: opposition does not occur
(3) Word-initially before or after obstruents: opposition does not occur
(4) Medially between vowels: *reimen* : *reiben*; *Rahmen* : *Raben*; *Robben* : *kommen*
(5) Medially before or after sonorants /l r m n/: *Halme* : *halbe*; *Arme* : *Farbe*
(6) Medially before obstruents: opposition does not occur
(7) Word-finally after vowels: opposition does not occur
(8) Word-finally before or after sonorants /l r m n/: opposition does not occur
(9) Word-finally before or after obstruents: opposition does not occur

5.5.4.2 /n/ : /d/

(1) Word-initially before vowels: *nass* : *dass*; *Nelke* : *denken*; *Nord* : *dort*; *Nutzen* : *Dutzend*; *nötig* : *dösig* 'dozy'; *Nüstern* 'nostrils' : *düster*
(2) Word-initially before sonorants /l r m n/: opposition does not occur
(3) Word-initially before or after obstruents: opposition does not occur
(4) Medially between vowels: *leiden* : *Leinen*; *Faden* : *Fahnen*; *Troddel* : *Wonne*
(5) Medially before or after sonorants /l r m n/: opposition does not occur
(6) Medially before obstruents: opposition does not occur
(7) Word-finally after vowels: opposition does not occur
(8) Word-finally before or after sonorants /l r m n/: opposition does not occur
(9) Word-finally before or after obstruents: opposition does not occur

5.5.4.3 /ŋ/ : /g/

(1) Word-initially before vowels: opposition does not occur
(2) Word-initially before sonorants /l r m n/: opposition does not occur
(3) Word-initially before or after obstruents: opposition does not occur
(4) Medially between vowels: *ringen* : *Riggung* 'rigging'
(5) Medially before or after sonorants /l r m n/: opposition does not occur
(6) Medially before obstruents: opposition does not occur
(7) Word-finally after vowels: opposition does not occur

(8) Word-finally before or after sonorants /l r m n/: opposition does not occur

(9) Word-finally before or after obstruents: opposition does not occur

5.5.5 Multilateral oppositions between places of articulation

5.5.5.1 Voiceless plosives: /p/ : /t/ : /k/

(1) Word-initially before vowels: *peilen* 'to sound, take bearings' : *teilen* : *keilen* 'to wedge'; *passen* : *Tassen* : *Kassen*; *picken* : *ticken* : *kicken*; *putzen* : *tuschen* 'to paint in watercolours' : *kuscheln*

(2) Word-initially before sonorants /l r m n/: *Pracht* : *Tracht* 'traditional dress' : *Kraft*; *Protz* 'swank' : *trotz* : *Kropf* 'crop (of a bird)'

(3) Word-initially before or after obstruents: *Spitze* : *Stift* : *Skizze*; *Spaten* : *Staat* : *Skat* 'card game'

(4) Medially between vowels: *Raupe* : *Laute* : *Pauke*; *Paten* : *Taten* : *Laken*; *Sippe* : *Sitte* : *nicken*

(5) Medially before or after sonorants /l r m n/: *Tulpe* : *Pulte* : *ulken* 'to joke'; *Zirpe* 'cicada' : *Hirte* : *Birke*

(6) Medially before or after obstruents: *Wespe* : *Weste* : *Freske*

(7) Word-finally after vowels: *Leib* : *leid* : *Streik*; *lieb* : *Lied* : *Fabrik*; *schlapp* : *satt* : *Sack*

(8) Word-finally before or after sonorants /l r m n/: *gelb* : *Geld* : *Kalk*; *herb* : *hart* : *stark*; (after a nasal) *Lump* : *fand* : *Tank*

(9) Word-finally before or after obstruents: opposition does not occur

5.5.5.2 Voiced plosives: /b/ : /d/ : /g/

(1) Word-initially before vowels: *baumeln* : *Daumen* : *Gaumen*; *Bann* : *dann* : *kann*; *bieten* : *dienen* : *gießen*

(2) Word-initially before sonorants /l r m n/: *breit* : *drei* : *gleich*

(3) Word-initially before or after obstruents: opposition does not occur

(4) Medially between vowels: *bleiben* : *beneiden* : *neigen*; *Reben* : *reden* : *Regen*; *Ebbe* : *verheddern* 'to get tangled up' : *Egge* 'harrow'

(5) Medially before or after sonorants /l r m n/: *Milbe* 'mite' : *Milde* : *tilgen*; *erben* : *werden* : *Ärger*

(6) Medially before obstruents: opposition does not occur

(7) Word-finally after vowels: opposition does not occur

(8) Word-finally before or after sonorants /l r m n/: opposition does not occur

(9) Word-finally before or after obstruents: opposition does not occur

5.5.5.3 Nasal plosives: /m/ : /n/ : /ŋ/

(1) Word-initially before vowels: opposition does not occur
(2) Word-initially before sonorants /l r m n/: opposition does not occur
(3) Word-initially before or after obstruents: opposition does not occur
(4) Medially between vowels: *schwimmen* : *sinnen* 'to meditate' : *singen*
(5) Medially before or after sonorants /l r m n/: opposition does not occur
(6) Medially before obstruents: *Bombe* : *fanden* : *Bingo*
(7) Word-finally after vowels: *Lamm* : *Mann* : *lang*
(8) Word-finally before or after sonorants /l r m n/: opposition does not occur
(9) Word-finally before or after obstruents: opposition does not occur

5.5.5.4 Voiceless fricatives: /f/ : /s/ : /ʃ/ : /x–ç/

(1) Word-initially before vowels: *finden* : *Single* : *schinden* 'to maltreat' : *Chirurg*; *Fest* : *Cent* : *Chef* : *chemisch*
(2) Word-initially before sonorants /l r m n/: opposition does not occur
(3) Word-initially before or after obstruents: opposition does not occur
(4) Medially between vowels: *reifen* : *reißen* : *heischen* : *reichen*; *taufen* : *draußen* : *rauschen* : *rauchen*; *rufen* : *fußen* : *wuschen* : *Buche*; *begriffen* : *wissen* : *wischen* : *sicher*
(5) Medially before or after sonorants /l r m n/: opposition does not occur
(6) Medially before obstruents: opposition does not occur
(7) Word-finally after vowels: *reif* : *weiß* : *Fleisch* : *reich*; *Ruf* : *Fuß* : *wusch* : *Buch*
(8) Word-finally before or after sonorants /l r m n/: *Wolf* : *Hals* : *falsch* : *Molch* 'salamander'; *Wurf* : *Vers* : *Marsch* : *Storch*; *fünf* : *uns* : *Wunsch* : *manch*
(9) Word-finally before or after obstruents: opposition does not occur

5.5.5.5 Voiced fricatives: /v/ : /z/ : /ʒ/ : /j/

(1) Word-initially before vowels: *Vene* : *Sehne* : *Genre* : *jene*
(2) Word-initially before sonorants /l r m n/: opposition does not occur
(3) Word-initially before or after obstruents: opposition does not occur
(4) Medially between vowels: *stowen* : *Dose* : *Loge* : *Koje* 'cabin'
(5) Medially before or after sonorants /l r m n/: opposition does not occur
(6) Medially before obstruents: opposition does not occur
(7) Word-finally after vowels: opposition does not occur
(8) Word-finally before or after sonorants /l r m n/: opposition does not occur
(9) Word-finally before or after obstruents: opposition does not occur

5.5.6 Oppositions with the lateral /l/ and trill or fricative /r/

5.5.6.1 /l/ : /r/

(1) Word-initially before vowels: *leise* : *Reise*; *lachen* : *Rachen*; *leben* : *Reben*; *Lippen* : *Rippen*; *Loch* : *roch*; *lutschen* : *rutschen*; *löten* 'to solder' : *Röte*; *Lücken* : *Rücken*

(2) Word-initially before sonorants /l r m n/: opposition does not occur

(3) Word-initially before or after obstruents: *Pleite* : *Breite*; *Blei* : *Brei*; *fließen* : *frieren*; *schlank* : *Schrank*

(4) Medially between vowels: *feurig* : *heulen*; *Wahlen* : *waren*; *Willen* : *Wirren*

(5) Medially before or after sonorants /l r m n/: opposition does not occur

(6) Medially before obstruents: opposition does not occur

(7) Word-finally after vowels: *Saal* : *rar*; *heil* : *Feier* ([ə] after a diphthong); *still* : *wirr*

(8) Word-finally before or after sonorants /l r m n/: opposition does not occur

(9) Word-finally before or after obstruents: opposition does not occur

5.5.6.2 /l/ : /d/

(1) Word-initially before vowels: *Lamm* : *Damm*; *lenken* : *denken*; *Licht* : *dicht*; *Loch* : *doch*; *lösen* : *dösen*; *Lücke* : *dürfen*; *Launen* : *Daunen*; *Leiche* : *Deiche*

(2) Word-initially before sonorants /l r m n/: opposition does not occur

(3) Word-initially before or after obstruents: opposition does not occur

(4) Medially between vowels: *mahlen* : *Nadel*; *wählen* : *Läden*; *wieder* : *Ziele*; *Sohle* : *roden*; *Schule* : *Bude*; *Höhle* : *blöde*; *Schüler* : *Süden*

(5) Medially before or after sonorants /l r m n/: *Erle* 'alder' : *Erde*

(6) Medially before obstruents: opposition does not occur

(7) Word-finally after vowels: opposition does not occur

(8) Word-finally before or after sonorants /l r m n/: opposition does not occur

(9) Word-finally before or after obstruents: opposition does not occur

5.5.6.3 /r/ : /d/

(1) Word-initially before vowels: *rein* : *dein*; *Raum* : *Daumen*; *rasch* : *Dach*; *rennen* : *denn*; *ringen* : *Dinge*; *Dock* : *Rock*; *dudeln* 'to hum, tootle' : *rudern*; *Röte* : *Dödel* 'simple person'; *Rübe* : *Dübel* 'dowel'

(2) Word-initially before sonorants /l r m n/: opposition does not occur

(3) Word-initially before or after obstruents: opposition does not occur

(4) Medially between vowels: *Waren* : *Waden*; *gären* : *Läden*; *Mieder* 'bodice' : *frieren*; *bohren* : *Boden*; *spuren* : *Bude*; *stören* : *Köder*; *führen* : *müde*

(5) Medially before or after sonorants /l r m n/: opposition does not occur

(6) Medially before obstruents: opposition does not occur

(7) Word-finally after vowels: opposition does not occur

(8) Word-finally before or after sonorants /l r m n/: opposition does not occur

(9) Word-finally before or after obstruents: opposition does not occur

5.5.6.4 /l/ : /t/

(1) Word-initially before vowels: *leicht* : *Teich*; *lau* : *Tau*; *lag* : *Tag*; *Lende* : *Tenne*; *lief* : *tief*; *loben* : *toben*; *Luch* 'swamp' : *Tuch*; *Löhne* : *Töne*; *Lücke* : *Tücke*

(2) Word-initially before sonorants /l r m n/: opposition does not occur

(3) Word-initially before or after obstruents: *Schlange* : *Stange*; *schleppen* : *Steppen*; *schlingen* : *stinken*; *Schloss* : *Stoß*; *Schluss* : *Stuss* 'nonsense'

(4) Medially between vowels: *schallen* : *Schatten*; *schälen* : *später*; *schielen* 'to squint' : *mieten*; *Sohle* : *Quote*; *Köhler* : *löten*; *Hülle* : *Hütte*; *Zeilen* : *Zeiten*; *jaulen* : *lauter*

(5) Medially before or after sonorants /l r m n/: *Kerle* : *Härte*

(6) Medially before obstruents: opposition does not occur

(7) Word-finally after vowels: *weil* : *weit*; *Maul* : *Maut* 'toll'; *Saal* : *Saat*; *hell* : *Bett*; *still* : *Schritt*; *Zoll* : *Gott*

(8) Word-finally before or after sonorants /l r m n/: opposition does not occur

(9) Word-finally before or after obstruents: opposition does not occur

5.5.6.5 /r/ : /x–ç/

(1) Word-initially before vowels: *rasch* : *Charisma*; *rennen* : *chemisch*; *Riese* : *Chi*; *rutschen* : *Chuzpe*

(2) Word-initially before sonorants /l r m n/: opposition does not occur

(3) Word-initially before or after obstruents: opposition does not occur

(4) Medially between vowels: *Karre* : *Kachel*; *ernähren* : *Gespräche*; *verdorren* : *kochen*; *spuren* : *suchen*; *dörren* : *Köche*; *führen* : *Bücher*

(5) Medially before or after sonorants /l r m n/: opposition does not occur

(6) Medially before obstruents: *Torte* : *Tochter*

(7) Word-finally after vowels: *Jahr* : *sprach*; *Rohr* : *hoch*; *Kur* : *Buch*

(8) Word-finally before or after sonorants /l r m n/: opposition does not occur

(9) Word-finally before or after obstruents: *Wart* : *Wacht*; *dort* : *Docht*

5.5.7 Multilateral oppositions: Affricates in opposition to their plosives and fricatives

5.5.7.1 /pf/ : /p/ : /f/

(1) Word-initially before vowels: *Pfanne* : *Panne* : *Fahne*

(2) Word-initially before sonorants /l r m n/: *Pflaume* : *Plan* : *Flamme*; *Pfriem* 'awl' : *prima* : *frieren*

(3) Word-initially before or after obstruents: opposition does not occur

(4) Medially between vowels: *Apfel* : *Mappe* : *Affe*

(5) Medially before or after sonorants /l r m n/: opposition does not occur

(6) Medially before obstruents: opposition does not occur

(7) Word-finally after vowels: *Kopf* : *Stopp* : *Stoff*

(8) Word-finally before or after sonorants /l r m n/: *Kampf* : *Lump* : *Triumph*

(9) Word-finally before or after obstruents: opposition does not occur

5.5.7.2 /ts/ : /t/ : /s/

(1) Word-initially before vowels: *Zopf* : *Topf* : *soft*

(2) Word-initially before sonorants /l r m n/: opposition does not occur

(3) Word-initially before or after obstruents: opposition does not occur

(4) Medially between vowels: *reizen* : *reiten* : *reißen*; *Mieze* 'pussy-cat' : *Miete* : *spießen*; *Spitze* : *Sitte* : *wissen*

(5) Medially before or after sonorants /l r m n/: opposition does not occur

(6) Medially before obstruents: opposition does not occur

(7) Word-finally after vowels: *Reiz* : *Streit* : *weiß*; *Blitz* : *Tritt* : *Biss*

(8) Word-finally before or after sonorants /l r m n/: *Holz* : *alt* : *als*; *schwarz* : *hart* : *Kurs*; *Tanz* : *Hand* : *Gans*

(9) Word-finally before or after obstruents: opposition does not occur

5.5.7.3 /tʃ/ : /t/ : /ʃ/

(1) Word-initially before vowels: *tschüss* : *tun* : *Schuh*

(2) Word-initially before sonorants /l r m n/: opposition does not occur

(3) Word-initially before or after obstruents: opposition does not occur

(4) Medially between vowels: *peitschen* : *gleiten* : *heischen* 'to demand'; *knutschen* 'to smooch': *Puten* : *wuschen*; *Pritschen* 'plank bed': *bitten* : *fischen*

(5) Medially before or after sonorants /l r m n/: opposition does not occur

(6) Medially before obstruents: opposition does not occur

(7) Word-finally after vowels: *Rutsch* : *Schutt* : *Busch*; *deutsch* : *zerstreut* :
     keusch

(8) Word-finally before or after sonorants /l r m n/: opposition does not
     occur

(9) Word-finally before or after obstruents: opposition does not occur

QUESTIONS

1 How useful is the difference between phoneme and allophone in language
       teaching and learning?

2 Discuss the phonemic status of /ɛː/.

3 Before which of the following sounds is there no contrast between short and
       long vowels: /ʃ t ŋ pf n ts p l/?

4 What is the phonemic status of [x] and [ç]?

5 What is the main phonemic difference between the stressed vowels in [biːtən]
       and [bɪtən]?

6 Where is there no contrast between voiced and voiceless plosives?

7 Which of the following fricatives do not occur frequently in word-initial
       position: [s v f ʃ ʒ x ç j]? Why might this be the case?

8 How far can it be maintained that [pf] and [ts] are consonant clusters rather
       than unitary phonemes?

9 Transcribe the following passage phonemically:

> Die deutsche Sprache hat mannigfache Abstufungen. Im allgemeinen aber
> unterscheidet man drei Hauptschichten: Als höchste Formstufe von
> überlandschaftlicher Gültigkeit haben wir die Hochsprache. Ihr gegenüber stehen
> als Grundschicht die Mundarten mit raumlich begrenztem Geltungsbereich.
> Dazwischen liegen die verschiedenen Formen der Umgangssprache.

10 What are the main difficulties facing an English language-speaking learner in
        mastering the phonemes of German?

6 Sounds and spelling

6.0 General principles

Up to now our discussion of the pronunciation of the sounds of German has mostly used the IPA as well as giving examples in spelling. This has given us a more detailed description of the pronunciation of the individual sounds. In this chapter we want to examine the relationship between the sounds of German that we have established and their orthographic representation. English has long been renowned for the difficulties of its spelling system but German also provides many difficulties for those learning to read and write and connect the spelling system and the sounds they stand for, not only for foreign learners but also for native learners. German like English is written with an alphabetic writing system, with separate orthographic symbols for vowels and consonants. This makes it different from languages such as Hindi or Japanese (in its Katakana syllabary) where each syllable, consonant plus vowel, is given a separate symbol. These are called syllabic scripts. In Chinese, on the other hand, each morpheme or word is given a separate sign. This is known as a logographic script (Crystal 1987: 197–203).

The ideal situation in alphabetic writing systems is usually considered to be that one symbol should stand for each sound, or rather for each distinctive sound or phoneme. In Chapter 5 we dealt with the phonemic analysis of German and some of its problems. In this chapter we will assume a basic phonemic system that will reflect a 'broad' phonetic description of German. Alphabets are said to be more or less 'phonemic' according to the degree in which they match up to this principle of one letter for one distinctive sound. The important relationship is therefore between the letter, or grapheme, and the distinctive sound (*Phonem-Graphem-Beziehung*). This is the phonemic principle (6.1). There are also other principles that influence the choice of letters in the orthography: the morphophonemic principle (6.2) and the homonymy principle (6.3). There are other principles enumerated by Augst (1984: 66–87) and Nerius (2001: 326ff.), including the lexical and grammatical principles. We shall be concerned chiefly with sound–letter correspondences and ignore other orthographic conventions that do not reflect pronunciation such as the use of capital and lower-case letters and writing of orthographic words as one item or two.

6.1 The phonemic principle (*phonematisches Prinzip*)

The phonemic principle states that one symbol or letter or grapheme should represent one sound or phoneme. Theoretically and ideally it should be the case that one phoneme should only be represented by one letter. When we apply this criterion to German we find in fact that there are only three phonemes that fulfil this criterion: /j/ (*jung*, *Koje* 'bunk'); /h/ (*Haar*); and /z/, which is written *s* (*sein*, *Sinn*, *lesen*). Conversely, one letter should only represent one phoneme. However, this relationship is not adhered to in several ways. The phonemic principle can be broken in several ways.

6.1.1 One phoneme is represented by more than one letter

Firstly, the simplest case is when a phoneme is represented by a cluster or sequence of two or more letters, e.g. /ʃ/ is spelt *sch* (*schon*, *waschen*, *Wunsch*) except before *p* (*spät*) and *t* (*Stein*); /x–ç/ is represented by the digraph (a cluster of two letters) *ch* (*dich*, *Dach*, *Sache*) and /ŋ/ is spelt with the digraph *ng* (*lang*, *länger*).

6.1.2 Predictable variation of letters for a phoneme

Secondly, a phoneme may be spelt by several different letters but these are in complementary distribution, i.e. one is used in one position in the word, or before a certain letter, and the other is used in a different position or before a different letter. As we have seen, the phoneme /ʃ/ is spelt *sch* in all positions except before *p* and *t* at the beginning of words when it is written *s*, e.g. *schon*, *schreiben*, *schlimm*, *schnell*, *schwamm*, but *stehen*, *sparen*. The plosives /p t k b d g/, the nasals /m n/ and the liquids /l r/ are spelt double medially after a short vowel before unstressed -*e*: *Rippe*, *Sitte*, *Robbe* 'seal', *Kladde* 'rough book', *Roggen*, *schwimmen*, *sinnen*, *füllen*, *irren*. This also happens to the plosive /k/ but instead of the expected *kk*, the 'double sign' is *ck*: *Lücke*. Also under the heading of predictability of letters could come the use of *q* before *u* in the cluster *qu* for *k*: *Quelle*, *Qualität*, *Quittung* (the *u* is pronounced as a voiced [v]).

6.1.3 Random variation of letters for a phoneme

Thirdly, a phoneme may be spelt by several different letters but the distribution of the letters is largely random. The sign *v* is used initially for /f/ in some words (*Vater, Vogel*), but *f* is used as well: *Fall, Fohlen*. For medial /f/, *ff* occurs after short vowels (*Schiffe*), and *f* after long vowels and diphthongs (*liefen, Schleife*), following the normal doubling rule. In the one word *Frevel* 'outrage', *v* is used for medial /f/. Before initial /l r/ *f* is used (*fließen, fressen*) but with the exception of the one word *Vließ* 'fleece' where *v* is used. For initial and medial /v/ the letter *w* is used (*Wein, wo, Möwe*), but *v* occurs in foreign words: *Vase, vage, brave* (inflected form). After /l, r/ only *v* occurs: *Malve, Pulver, Salve*. In Greek loan words the phoneme /f/ is written *ph*: *Physik, Orthographie, Apostroph*. The overlap in the use of the letter *v* for both /f/ and /v/ leads often to uncertainty in the pronunciation of *v* in non-initial position. In names such as *David, Eva, Sievers,* or *Nerven* the *v* is sometimes pronounced as /f/ and sometimes as /v/.

These random inconsistencies of spelling are due in part to the historical evolution of German spelling over the centuries and also to the introduction of foreign words. The chief offenders in this are learned words from Greek containing *ph, th* and *rh*: *physisch, theoretisch, rhythmisch*. The digraph *ph* is used for /f/, as we have seen, *th* for /t/ and *rh* for /r/. It has been suggested over the years that in common foreign words *ph, th, rh* should be replaced by *f, t, r*, i.e. *fysisch, teoretisch, rytmisch*. In the new spelling reform of 1998 *f* for *ph* is allowed in a large number of words: *Foto, Telefon*.

The phoneme /k/ initially is usually rendered by *k* (*kann, Kind*), but in foreign words it is rendered by *c* (*Café, Curry, Code*), *kh* (*Khaki*) and *ch* (*Charakter*). In South Germany *ch* before *i* and *e* renders /k/ (*Chemie, Chirurg, China*), but in North Germany and the standard pronunciation the *ch* in these words is pronounced like the *ch* in *ich*, [ç]. The digraph *ch* is also used in some French loan words for the phoneme /ʃ/: *Chef, Champignon, Chance*.

The spelling of vowels from Greek does not present many difficulties except that for the long /y:/ the letter *y* is used, e.g. *Mythos, physisch*, whereas in German words *ü* (*über*) or *üh* (*Bühne*) is used. Loans from French and English show many different combinations of vowel signs for vowel phonemes. The digraph *ou* occurs in French loans for /u:/: *Cousine, Routine*. The digraph *eu* is used for /ø:/ in the endings *-eur, -euse* for agentive nouns from verbs in *-ieren* (*frisieren, Friseur, Friseuse; massieren, Masseur, Masseuse*), although there is the variant form *-ör, -öse*. For an unstressed /i/ at the end of English words *y* is used: *Rowdy, Party, Pony, Teddy*. The diphthong /ai/ is spelt *ei*, but also *ai* in some words: *Kaiser, Haifisch, Mai, Kai, Mais*. Some names are spelt with *ey* (*Speyer*) and *ay* (*Karl May, Bayern*). An orthographic distinction is made between *bayerisch* 'belonging to Bavaria' and *bairisch* 'belonging to the Bavarian dialect'. In the foreign words *Linotype* and *Nylon* the diphthong /ai/ is spelt *y*. The diphthong /au/ is spelt *au* in German words (*glauben, faul, laut*) but in some foreign words it is also spelt *ou* (*Couch, foul*) and *ow* (*Clown, Rowdy*). French nasal vowels are rendered by exactly the same spelling as in French (*Fonds, Teint, Chance, Bonbon*), but are pronounced in a different way. For more details of the spelling of foreign words see Chapter 8.

6.1.4 A cluster of phonemes is represented by one letter

Fourthly, a cluster of phonemes can be represented by a single letter. This is the exact opposite of our first group of examples (6.1.1), where one phoneme was represented by two or more letters. This is not frequent in German but can be exemplified by the use of the letter *x* for /ks/: *Hexe* and in loans such as *mixen*. Another, more important, example is the use of *z* initially for /ts/: *Zeit, Zins, Zug*. This, of course, assumes that we are regarding /ts/ as comprising two phonemes and not a unitary phoneme (see 5.4.1.2). The single letter <z> also occurs medially after long vowels and diphthongs (*duzen, siezen, Brezel, reizen*), but it is written *tz* after short vowels (*sitzen, Ketzer*), and *zz* in Italian loans (*Pizza*).

The distribution of length signs is not entirely random. The letter *e* only appears after *i*, and only *o, e* and *a* can be doubled. The letters *i* and *y* are mostly used in foreign words: *Mine, Tiger, Maschine; Mythos, physisch, zynisch*. The length sign *h* is used before *l, m, n, r*, (*kahl, nahm, Lohn, wahr*), and only exceptionally before other consonants: *Fehde* 'feud', *Naht*, and in the inflected forms of verbs whose stems ends in the letter *h*, e.g. *nähen, du nähst, er näht*. The signs *ü* and *i* do not appear in monosyllables in word-final position alone but always followed by *h* (*früh*), or, in the case of *i*, by *e* (*sie*). Although the doubled vowels do not usually appear in open syllables, the important exceptions are: plural forms *Aale, Haare, Paare, Staaten; Beeren, Beeten; Boote, Moose*; and words such as *Waage, Seele, verheeren*. In these examples the doubling of the letters to show vowel length is unnecessary since the occurrence of a vowel letter before a single medial consonant shows that the former is long. Similarly the length sign *h* is used unnecessarily in the following examples since the vowel is long by position: *lehnen, stehlen, nehmen, lehren*. Before medial and final /x/, spelt *ch*, the spelling does not show whether the preceding vowel is short or long: *Rache* (short), *Sprache* (long); *Koch* (short), *hoch* (long). Long vowels are also designated with one letter in closed syllables if the vowel alternates with a long vowel in an open syllable in inflected forms: *Tag, Tages; legt, gelegt, legen*. Before consonant clusters there is no way of telling from the orthography whether a vowel is short or long since it will always be written with a single letter: *Herd* (long), *Herz* (short); *düster* (long), *Küste* (short).

6.2 The morphophonemic principle (*Stammprinzip*)

In a language like German with many words or stems appearing in several inflected forms, often with a different pronunciation, the orthographic unity of the word or stem is maintained by writing the different inflected word forms the same way. This is typically the case when the differences in pronunciation are automatically conditioned by the phonetic environment.

We will illustrate this principle with three examples. Firstly, in final position in German only voiceless obstruents occur, and thus in any stem with a medial voiced obstruent, this will automatically be changed to a voiceless obstruent when it appears in word-final position, e.g. /ta:gəs/ gen. but /ta:k/ nom./acc. Such an automatic alternation is designated morphophonemic. In normalized Middle High German (MHG) texts this alternation and similar ones, affecting *b* and *p*, *d* and *t*, were shown directly in spelling: MHG *tages, tac, wîbes, wîp; todes, tot.* Although this is fully consistent with the principle of one letter for each phoneme wherever it occurs, in NHG, however, this principle has been overruled by the morphophonemic principle of maintaining the orthographic unity of words and stems. In German this is also called *Schemakonstanz.* Thus we have NHG *Tages, Weibes, Todes* and the nom./acc. forms *Tag, Weib, Tod.* This also occurs in English words, e.g. *nation, national* where the first vowel *a* is pronounced differently in each word. The uninflected words *ab* and *ob*, as well as *irgend, ihr seid* have their final consonant written *b* and *d* although they have no medial forms with *b* or *d*. This morphophonemic principle affects the fricatives *s* (*lesen*, voiced; *las*, voiceless) and *v* (*brave*, voiced; *brav*, voiceless). It is also used in word formation: *tödlich, todmüde* and *Todfeind* are derived from *Tod, Todes*, but only in the latter is <d> pronounced [d]. In the other forms [t] occurs.

A second example of this principle is the use of double consonants after vowels to show that the preceding vowels are short. These orthographic double consonants are retained in inflected forms before consonantal endings to maintain the unity of the morpheme. Thus we have the following forms for plosives: *pp* (*kippen, er kippt(e), kipp!*); *tt* (*wir schnitten, er schnitt, glatter, glatt*); *ck* (*blicken, er blickt, die Blicke, der Blick*); and for fricatives except [s]: *ff* (*wir pfiffen, er pfiff*); for nasals: *mm* (*glimmen, es glimmt, glomm*); *nn* (*rinnen, er rinnt, er rann*); for liquids: *ll* (*sollen, er soll, ihr sollt*); *rr* (*irren, er irrt, irr!*).

In the case of [s] the 1998 spelling reform has removed an orthographic alternation after a short vowel of medial <ss> and final <ß>: *müssen – muß;*

wissen – wußte. This alternation has now been abolished and only <ss> is used: *müssen – muss; wissen – wusste.* The sign <ß> is now only used after long vowels.

There are exceptions to this rule. In the case of medial double consonants before unstressed syllables the double consonant in the inflected form corresponds to a single one in word-final position: *nn* (*Königinnen*, pl.; *Königin*, sg.); *ss* (*Hindernisse, Hindernis; Atlasse, Atlas*). The following words are also exceptions, showing an alternation of a single letter in an uninflected form and a double consonant in the inflected forms: *der Atlas, des Atlasses* (pl. is *Atlanten*); *der Gros, Grosse* 'a gross'; and *der Bus, Busse*, although in this last case this may be due to the longer form *Omnibus, Omnibusse.*

A third example of the morphophonemic principle is the relationship between the letters *ä* and *e* which are both used for the short phoneme /ɛ/. If the word containing /ɛ/ has an inflected form or related word containing *a* then it is written <ä>. This can be in inflection (sg. *Gast*, pl. *Gäste*); comparison of adjectives (*schwach, schwächer, am schwächsten*); second and third person singular present of strong verbs (*fallen, du fällst, er fällt*); subjunctive of strong verbs, and some irregular verbs (*fand, fände; brachte, brächte;* but note the subjunctive of verbs like *nennen* which are written with *e, nennte,* and not with *ä!*); and in word formation (*arm, ärmlich; Fass, Fässchen; krank, kränklich; kalt, Kälte; Kraft, kräftig*). In some cases homonyms are distinguished through the use of *e* and *ä* (see 6.3). Several words, previously written with <e>, now appear with <ä> in the 1998 Reform, e.g. *behände, überschwänglich.*

Also affected by the morphophonemic principle is the spelling of the diphthong /oi/. This is spelt *äu* if it results from mutation of *au: gläubig,* from *glauben;* pl. *Häuser,* sg. *Haus; du läufst, er läuft,* from *laufen.* Otherwise it is spelt *eu* in German words: *Freund, Freude.* Again several words previously written with <eu> now appear with <äu> in the 1998 Reform, e.g. *Schnäuze, verbläuen.* A few words are still spelt with *äu* although their connection with a related word with *au* is tenuous or now non-existent: *Knäuel, Säule, läutern* (originally related to *lauter*), *räudig, räuspern, sträuben.*

6.3 The homonymy principle

The third principle is one where the use of spelling differences signals a difference in meaning, not reflecting a difference in pronunciation.

This is known is the homonymy principle, writing words differently that are pronounced the same because they are different in meaning, e.g. *malen* 'to paint' and *mahlen* 'to grind'. This principle is the opposite of the morphophonemic principle and is carried out irregularly. The examples are often limited to a small set of words. In German it is mostly letters used for vowels that are affected, the only exception to this being the distinction between the definite article and relative pronoun *das* 'the, that' and the conjunction *dass* 'that'.

Vowel length signs are sometimes used to distinguish homonyms: <i> : <ie>, *wider* 'against', *wieder* 'again'; *das Lid* 'eye-lid', *das Lied* 'song'; *die Mine* 'mine, re-fill', *die Miene* 'air, countenance'; *der Stil* 'style', *der Stiel* 'stick'; <a> : <ah>, *das Mal* 'time, occasion', *das Mahl* 'meal'; *malen* 'to paint', *mahlen* 'to grind'; <o> : <oh>, *die Dole* 'drain, culvert', *die Dohle* 'jackdaw'; *die Sole* 'salt water', *die Sohle* 'sole'; <ee> : <eh>, *das Meer* 'sea', *mehr* 'more'; *leeren* 'to empty', *lehren* 'to teach'.

The usual digraph for /ai/ is *ei* but *ai* is used to distinguish between homonyms: *das Laib* 'loaf', *der Leib* 'body'; *die Saite* 'string of an instrument', *die Seite* 'side'; *die Waise* 'orphan', *die Weise* 'way, manner'; *schwaigen* 'to make cheese', *schweigen* 'to be silent'.

The letters <e> and <ä> are also used with this principle to distinguish between: *die Blässe* 'paleness', *die Blesse* 'blaze, white spot'; *die Äsche* 'grayling (fish)', *die Esche* 'ash (tree)'; *die Färse* 'heifer', *die Ferse* 'heel'; *die Lärche* 'larch', *die Lerche* 'lark'; *die Stärke* 'strength', *die Sterke* (North German) 'heifer'; *rächen* 'to avenge', *rechen* 'to rake'; *schlämmen* 'to dredge', *schlemmen* 'to carouse'.

It is difficult to see where the application of this principle stops. Are such cases as *seid* '(you pl.) are' and *seit* 'since' or *statt* 'instead of' and *Stadt* 'town', or even *viel* 'much' and *fiel* 'fell' covered by it? At best it should be limited to distinction between words of the same word class otherwise examples might simply be due to chance.

6.4 Spelling of individual phonemes

The spelling that will be used is to be found in *DR* 24 (2006).

In giving examples of spellings we will try to give as complete a description as possible of the letters before all medial and final consonantal signs. Only a selection of consonant clusters will be given. Names will be taken into account as they often contain some interesting idiosyncratic spellings but coverage of them does not aim at completeness.

6.4.1 Short vowels in stressed syllables

In disyllabic words short vowels are followed by double consonant signs, e.g. *bitten*, or the digraphs *ck* and *ng* or consonant clusters. Although *x* is a single letter it functions as a consonant cluster since it is pronounced [ks] and only short vowels occur in front of it. In monosyllables, short vowels mostly occur before double consonants (*Brett*), except in some uninflected words (*ab, von, bis*), English loans (*fit, top*) and some other exceptions (*Gas*).

Both short and long vowels can occur before *ch, tz, sch* and *tsch*, although not in the case of every vowel. Also before *r* + alveolar stops both short and long vowels occur.

Short vowels are always spelt with a single letter. We will give examples of their distribution: (1) before double consonants (*ck* represents *kk*, the latter only appearing in loan words); (2) before the digraphs *ck, ng* and *pf*; (3) before consonant clusters; (4) before *x*; (5) before *ch, tz* (*zz* in loans), *sch* and *tsch*; (6) in monosyllables; and (7) in affixes.

6.4.1.1 Short /a/

Short /a/ is spelt <a>: (1) *knabbern, Lappen, Kladde, Ratte, Flagge, schaffen, lassen, lammen, rannen, fallen, starren* (2) *packen, sangen, stapfen* (3) *Wald, Rand, Dachs* (4) *faxen, lax* (5) *wachen, Spatzen, waschen, watscheln* (6) In monosyllables, sometimes before a single consonant – *an, das, hat, man* – and sometimes before a double consonant: *dann, dass*. Monosyllables with other inflected forms mostly have double consonants – *schlapp, schlaff, Pass, Lamm, rann* – but note the exceptions: *As, Gas, Tram*. (7) Prefixes: *a-/an-* (*asozial, analphabetisch*), *ab-* (*abnehmen*), *an-* (*annehmen*), *anti-* (*Antikörper*); suffixes: *-ant* (*arrogant*), *-anz* (*Arroganz*), *-haft* (*lebhaft*), *-schaft* (*Landschaft*).

6.4.1.2 Short /ɛ/

Short /ɛ/ is spelt (i) <e>: (1) *Steppen, Ebbe, verheddern, retten, Egge, treffen, essen, klemmen, rennen, stellen, sperren* (2) *wecken, Enge, Schnepfe* (3) *Pelz, Held* (4) *Hexe* (5) *sprechen, setzen, Esche, fletschen* (6) In monosyllables before double consonants in uninflected forms – *denn, wenn, des, wes* (but *dessen, wessen*); in words with inflected forms – *Brett, Treff, kess, Fell, Herr*; exception before a single consonant, *Ges* 'G flat'. (7) Prefixes: *ent-* (*entgleisen*), *er-* (*erzählen*), *Erz-* (*Erzbischof*), *ex-* (*Ex-Kanzler*), *ver-* (*vergessen*), *zer-* (*zerstören*); suffixes: *-el* (*Deckel*), *-ell* (*aktuell*), *-ent* (*kompetent*), *-enz* (*Kompetenz*).

(ii) <ä> in words which have a related word with <a> as the stem vowel: *Gast – Gäste; waschen – Wäsche; kalt – Kälte; backen – Bäcker*.

(iii) Spelling in loan words: <a> in recent English loans, *Camping, Fan, trampen*.

6.4.1.3 Short /ɪ/

Short /ɪ/ is spelt <i>: (1) *Rippe, kribbeln, bitten, Widder, Riggung, Schiffe, wissen, Zimmer, binnen, Willen, irren* (2) *wickeln, singen, Gipfel* (3) *Wirt, Birke* (4) *mixen, Pixel* (5) *sicher, sitzen* (*zz* in loans: *Pizza*), *wischen, zwitschern* (6) In uninflected monosyllables – *mit, in, bin, hin, bis*; exceptions, *Bim* 'tram' (colloquial Austrian); in monosyllables with inflected forms – *Tipp, Kitt* 'putty', *schlimm, Sinn, still, wirr*, but the English loan *fit*. (7) Prefixes: *miss-* (*Missbrauch*), *dis-* (*Disharmonie*), *mini-* (*Minirock*); suffixes: *-icht* (*töricht*), *-ig* (*milchig*), *-in* (*Chefin*), *-isch* (*kindisch*), *-ist* (*Komponist*), *-lich* (*väterlich*), *-ling* (*Setzling* 'seedling'), *-nis* (*Ereignis*).

6.4.1.4 Short open /o/

Short open /o/ is spelt <o>: (1) *stoppen, Robbe, Motte, Modder, Roggen, hoffen, genossen, Sommer, Sonne, sollen, verworren* (2) *locken, bongen, stopfen* (3) *Holz, Onkel, Post* (4) *boxen* (5) *lochen, glotzen, Broschen* (6) In some uninflected words – *von, ob*; with inflected forms – *Stopp*; with a single consonant, English loan *top*. (7) Prefixes: *ob-* (*Obhut*), *top-* (*topfit*).

6.4.1.5 Short open /ʊ/

Short open /ʊ/ is spelt <u>: (1) *struppig, schrubben, Mutter, Schmuddel, schmuggeln, muffig, Busse, Rummel, Brunnen, Stulle, murren* (2) *schlucken, gesungen, rupfen* (3) *Luft, Verlust* (4) *juxen* (5) *bruchig, Butze, kuscheln* (6) In uninflected monosyllabic words such as *um, und*, and before double consonants in *Schutt, Muff, dumm, Null*; exception, *Bus*, pl. *Busse*. (7) Prefix: *un-* (*unmöglich*); suffix: *-ung* (*Vergebung*).

6.4.1.6 Short open /ʏ/

Short open /ʏ/ is spelt <ü>: (1) *üppig, flügge, Hütte, müssen, verdünnen, dümmer, füllen, Dürre* (2) *pflücken, düngen, hüpfen* (3) *Hüfte, rüsten, stülpen* (4) *Büxen* (5) *Sprüche, nützen, Büsche* (6), (7) /ʏ/ does not occur in uninflected monosyllables and affixes.

It is also spelt <y> in loan words before consonant clusters: *Ypsilon, Mystik, Rhythmus*.

6.4.1.7 Short open /œ/

Short open /œ/ is spelt <ö>: (1) *klöppeln, spöttisch, Löffel, frömmeln, können, Hölle, dörren* (2) *Böcke, schröpfen* (3) *Mönch, Töchter, Stöpsel* (4) no form with *x* (5) *Löcher, Götzen, Böschung* (6), (7) /œ/ does not occur in uninflected monosyllables and affixes.

6.4.2 Long vowels

One of the most complicated areas in German spelling is the designation of vowel length. As we have seen, the short vowels in German are written with one symbol each. The quantity of long vowels, however, is shown in several ways. Firstly, in disyllabic words one letter may be followed by a single consonant: *geben, raten*. Secondly, the vowel letter itself may be doubled: *Saal, Boot*. Thirdly, it may be followed by *h* – *Stahl, lahm* – and, fourthly, in the case of /i:/ by *e*: *lieben, Lied*. These ways of designating long vowels are not used equally for all long vowels. Figure 6.1 shows how they are distributed:

Phoneme	Spelling	Examples
/i:/	i, ih, ie, ieh	Bibel, ihn, sieben, sieht
/u:/	u, uh	Stube, Stuhl
/y:/	ü, üh, y	lügen, früh, physisch
/o:/	o, oo, oh	loben, Boot, Sohn
/ø:/	ö, öh	hören, Höhle
/e:/	e, ee, eh	geben, See, Lehrer
/ɛ:/	ä, äh	Käse, Nähte
/a:/	a, aa, ah	baden, Saal, Sahne

Figure 6.1   Orthographic designation of long vowels

During the course of the history of German there have been many attempts to render vowel length by orthographic means. The resulting complicated system has resisted all attempts to reform it. This means that there is usually one main spelling for each long vowel, the others being exceptions.

Long vowels are very often followed by single consonant signs. The sign *ß* is treated as a single consonant sign since it is pronounced as a single consonant, [s]. Long vowels do not occur before the digraphs *ck*, *ng* and *pf* but both short and long vowels can occur before *ch*, *tz*, *sch* and *tsch*, although not in the case of every vowel. Also both short and long vowels occur before *r* + alveolar plosives. We will describe their spelling according to the main and subsidiary spellings, then their distribution (1) in open syllables before single consonants; (2) before *ch, tz, sch* and *tsch*; (3) before other consonant clusters; (4) in monosyllables; and (5) in affixes.

6.4.2.1 Long /ɑ:/

Long /ɑ:/ is usually spelt <a>, particularly in open syllables, but is also spelt <ah>, particularly before nasals and liquids (*Rahmen, nahm, Bahn, kahl, fahren*) and <aa> as in *Aal, Staat*.

Examples of the spellings <a, ah, aa>: (1) in open syllables before a single consonant: *Stapel, Gabel, Taten, laden, Laken, sagen, Hafen, braver, Maßen, Hasen, nahmen, Sahne, Aale, Haare*; (2) before *ch, tz, tsch: Sprache, Akazie, Bratsche, watscheln* (examples lacking before *sch*); (3) before other consonant clusters: *Jagd, Magd*; (4) in monosyllables: *gab, Bad, Tag, Schlaf, las, lahm, Kahn, Aas, Saal*; (5) in suffixes: *-abel* (*invariabel*), *-at* (*Telefonat*), *-bar* (*lesbar*), *-maßen* (*gewissermaßen*), *-sal* (*Mühsal*), *-sam* (*mühsam*).

Homonyms distinguished by <a>, <ah> and <aa> are: *malen – mahlen; Mal – Mahl; der Nachname – die Nachnahme; der Wal – die Wahl; Wagen – Waagen*.

6.4.2.2 Long /e:/

Long /e:/ is usually spelt <e>, particularly in open syllables (*Leben*), but is also spelt <eh>, particularly before nasals and liquids (*nehmen, sehnen, fehlen, lehren*; exceptionally *eh* occurs before *d* in *Fehde*), and <ee> as in *leer, See*.

Examples of the spellings <e, eh, ee>: (1) in open syllables: *Epen, geben, treten, reden, ekel, fegen, Hefe, ewig, lesen, Schemel, denen, selig, scheren, leeren*; (2) before /ts/: *Brezel*; long /e:/ is lacking before *ch, sch* and *tsch*; (3) before two or more consonants, mostly *r* + consonant: *wert, Herd, zuerst*, but also *Krebs, nebst, stets*; (4) in monosyllables: *Beet, Weg*; and in the pronouns *den(en), wem, wen*; (5) only in the suffix *-wesen*.

Homonyms distinguished by <e>, <eh> and <ee> are: *Meltau* 'honeydew' – *Mehltau* 'mildew'; *leeren – lehren; mehr – Meer*.

6.4.2.3 Long open /ɛ:/

Long open /ɛ:/ is usually spelt <ä>, particularly in open syllables (*Bären*), but it is also spelt <äh>, particularly before nasals and liquids: *ähnlich, gefährlich*. It never occurs doubled, thus *Pärchen*, not **Päärchen*.

Examples of the spellings <ä, äh>: (1) in open syllables: *Säbel, später, gnädig, häkeln, Jäger, Häfen, Späße, Käse, schämen, erwähnen, Täler, wäre,* or before *th* or *ph*: *Äther*; or before final *r*: *Bär*; (2) before *ch, Gespräche*; /ts/, *Rätsel*; *tsch, tätscheln*; examples lacking before *sch*; (3) before other consonant clusters: *Bärte, Gebärde,* or a syllable-final consonant followed by the suffix *-chen* (*Mädchen, Märchen*) or *-lich* (*dämlich, zärtlich*); (4) in monosyllables: *Bär, nächst, schräg, spät*; (5) in the suffixes *-är* (*illusionär, Millionär*), *-ität* (*Formalität*), *-gemäß* (*ordnungsgemäß*), *-mäßig* (*vorschriftsmäßig*).

There appear to be no homonyms distinguished by <ä> and <äh>.

6.4.2.4 Long /iː/

Long /iː/ is spelt usually spelt <ie> (*sieben, Glied*), but it is also spelt <i>, particularly in open syllables (*Bibel, Igel*), and also <ih>, particularly before nasals and liquids in pronouns: *ihm, ihn, ihr*. It is also spelt <ieh> in *Vieh* and the second and third person singular *siehst, sieht* from *sehen,* and *ziehst, zieht* from *ziehen*. It is spelt <y> in a few loan words from Greek and French (*Zylinder*), and <ee> in a few English loan words such as *Jeep, Spleen, Tweed*.

Examples of <ie, i ih>: (1) before single consonants in open and closed syllables: *piepen, Liebe(n), bieten, Titel, Lied(er), Pike, quieken, kriegen, Igel, Brief(e), sprießen, niesen, Riemen, dienen, Bier(e), zielen*; (2) before *ch, kriechen*; /ts/, *siezen*; *sch, Nische*; and *tsch, quietschen*; (3) before other consonant clusters: *ihrzen, Biester*; (4) in monosyllables, especially in pronouns: <ih> in *ihn, ihnen, ihm, ihr* and *ihr(e)* but <i> in *mir, wir, dir* and also <ie> in *hier, Tier, sie, Sie*; (5) in the stressed foreign suffixes, *-ie* (*Partie, Geografie*), *-ieren* (*spionieren*), *-ik* (also occurs unstressed) (*Republik*), *-iv* (*depressiv*), and also in the final stressed syllables of *Berlin, Paris*.

Homonyms distinguished by <ie> and <i> are: *wieder – wider*; *Lied – Lid*; *Stiel – Stil*; *Miene – Mine*.

6.4.2.5 Long /oː/

Long /oː/ is usually spelt <o> in open syllables (*loben, Ofen, Bote, so, wo*) and before *ph* (*Philosoph*), and in closed syllables (*grob, groß, Not*); and <oh>, particularly before nasals and liquids: *Bohnen, empfohlen, gestohlen, bohren*. It is also spelt <oo> in *Boote, Moor, moorig, Moos, moosig*.

Some minor spellings are <oe, oi> in some names (*Itzhoe, Soest, Voigt*), <ow> in place-names of Slavonic origin (*Pankow, Treptow*), or personal names (*Schadow, Bülow*) and <oa> in English loan words (*Toast, Goal*).

Examples of the spellings <o, oh, oo>: (1) in open syllables: *Oper, loben, geboten, Mode, Koker, gezogen, Ofen, stowen, Soße, Rose, verchromen, Bohne, Kohle, bohren*; (2) before *ch, malochen* (also short); /ts/, *Lotse*; *sch, koscher*; long /o:/ is lacking before *tsch*; (3) before other consonant clusters: *Mond, Ostern, Vogt, Obst*; (4) in monosyllables: *Lob, Boot*; (5) in the suffixes *-ion* (*Nation*), *-ios* (*kurios*), *-los* (*farblos*).

Homonyms distinguished by <o>, <oh> and <oo>: *Boote – Bote*; *Mohr – Moor*; *Sole – Sohle*; *Dole – Dohle*.

6.4.2.6 Long close /u:/

Long close /u:/ is usually spelt <u> in open and closed syllables before a single consonant: *rufen, Rute, Luke, tun, Spur*. It is also spelt <uh>, particularly before nasals and liquids, in *Kuh, Ruhm, Huhn, Buhle, Uhr(en)*. It is never doubled, except in surnames (*Huuck*).

Examples of the spellings <u, uh>: (1) in open syllables: *Lupe, Bube, bluten, luden, spuken, Tugend, Stufen, Buße, Busen, Puma, Wune, Schule, fuhren*; (2) before *ch, fluchen*; /ts/, *duzen*; *sch, wuschen*; and *tsch, knutschen*; (3) before other consonant clusters: *Geburt, Wuchs, Husten*; (4) in monosyllables: *Schub, Wut, klug, Spuk*; (5) in the prefix *ur-* (*Urgroßvater*).

6.4.2.7 Long close /ø:/

Long close /ø:/ is usually spelt <ö> in open and closed syllables before a single consonant: *Bö, töten, Größe, hören, krönen, Öl, schön*. It also occurs in some French loan words, e.g. *Likör*.

It is also spelt <öh>, particularly before nasals and liquids: *Söhne, Röhre, Höhle*. In French loan words it occurs as <eu>: *Malheur, Milieu*. A minority spelling is <oe> in names such as *Goethe, Schroeder, Goedecke*.

Examples of the spellings <ö, öh>: (1) in open syllables: *Köper, Döbel, töten, blöde, blöken, Bögen, Höfe, Möwe, Größe, lösen, Ströme, Söhne, Höhle, stören*; (2) before /ts/, *Flöze* (examples lacking before *ch, sch* and *tsch*); (3) before other consonant clusters: *höchstens, trösten*; (4) in monosyllables: *höchst*; (5) in the suffixes *-ös* (*seriös*) and *-eur/-euse*: *Fritteuse, Masseur, Masseuse, Souffleur, Souffleuse* (some words are now mainly spelt *-ör*, e.g. *Frisör*).

A homonymic pair distinguished by <ö> and <öh> is: *Fön – Föhn*.

6.4.2.8 Long close /y:/

Long close /y:/ is usually spelt <ü> in open and closed syllables before a single consonant (*betrüben, Süden, betrügen, prüfen, Gemüse, grünen, spüren, schwül*) and <üh>, particularly before nasals and liquids (*Mühle, führen, rühmen*). It is spelt <y> in Latin and Greek loan words: *Analyse, Asyl, Hybris, Mythos, Oxyd*. There is a minority spelling of <ui> in a few names: *Duisburg, Duisdorf, Juist* (an East Frisian island).

Examples of the spellings <ü, üh>: (1) in open syllables: *trübe, Güte, Süden, Küken, lügen, prüfen, grüßen, Drüse, Tücher, rühmen, Sühne, fühlen, spüren*; (2) before *ch, Bücher; sch, Rüsche*; examples are lacking before /ts/ and *tsch*; (3) before other consonant clusters: *düster, Wüste*; (4) in monosyllables: *grün, kühl, Tür*; (5) it does not occur in any affixes.

6.4.3 Diphthongs

German has three falling diphthongs: /ai/, /au/ and /oi/. A fourth diphthong /ui/ is a rising diphthong and only appears in the interjection *pfui!*

6.4.3.1 The falling diphthong /ai/

The falling diphthong /ai/ is spelt <ei> in most cases in open and closed syllables: *bei, reiben, Weib, Reigen, Zweig, reiten, kleiden, Kleid, reisen, reißen, weiß, reifen, Reif, reichen, Reich, kreischen, Fleisch, reimen, Reim, reinigen, rein, Reihen*. It occurs in the prefix *ein-* (*einreichen*) and the suffixes *-lei* (*allerlei*), *-lein* (*Bächlein*).

It is spelt <ai> in a limited number of words: *Bai, Baier, Hai, Hain, Kaiser, Kai, Laie, Laich, Mai, Rain, Anrainer*. It is used to distinguish homophones in <ei>: *Laib* (*Leib*), *Waise* (*Weise*), *Saite* (*Seite*).

Minority spellings for /ai/ are <ey> in some names, (*Nordeney, Meyer, Heyne*) and also <ay> in some names, notably *Bayern, Mayer* (a variant of *Meier*), *Haydn*. The spelling <y> for /ai/ only occurs in *Nylon*.

6.4.3.2 The falling diphthong /au/

The falling diphthong /au/ is spelt <au> in most cases in open and closed syllables: *Bau, Haube, taub, Raupe, plaudern, Laute, Auge, Pauke, kaufen, Knauf, Haus, draußen, Strauß, rauchen, Rauch, rauschen, Tausch, Daumen, Raum, Daune, Zaun*. It occurs in the prefix *aus-* (*ausgehen*).

Minority spellings are <ow> (*Clown, down, Rowdy*) and <ou> (*Couch*), in loan words from English.

6.4.3.3 The falling diphthong /ɔi/

The falling diphthong /ɔi/ is spelt <eu> in most cases in open and closed syllables in native and Greek loan words: *Efeu, Freude, Leute, Teufel, Schleuse, Seuche, Rheuma, Scheune, Eule, Euro.*

The spelling <äu> is used in words that have a morphologically related form with <au> as a stem vowel: *Häuser* (*Haus*), *Verkäufer* (*verkaufen*), *äugeln* (*Auge*).

Minority spellings are <oi> in loan words – *Boiler* (English), *Loipe* (Norwegian) – and in place names (*Hoisdorf*), and <oy> in personal names (*Lloyd*).

6.4.4 Consonants

The description of the spelling of the consonants varies from cases such as [j], always spelt <j>, to the complicated variation with [ts], spelt <z, tz, zz, ts>. The main headings that will be used to describe the spelling of the individual sounds are: (1) word-initially before vowels; (2) word-initially before sonorants; (3) medially between vowels and after sonorants; (4) word-finally after vowels and sonorants; (5) in consonant clusters with obstruents. Only those contexts that contain examples will be cited.

6.4.4.1 The labial affricate /pf/

The labial affricate /pf/ is always spelt <pf>: (1) word-initially before vowels: *Pferd, Pfirsich*; (2) word-initially before sonorants: *Pfriem* 'awl', *Pflanze*; (3) medially after short vowels (*klopfen*) and sonorants (*kämpfen, Karpfen*); (4) word-finally after short vowels and sonorants: *Topf, Dampf.*

6.4.4.2 The alveolar affricate /ts/

The alveolar affricate /ts/ is spelt <z>, <tz>, <zz>, <ts> and <c>: <z> is written (1) word-initially before vowels (*Zahn, Zeichen*); (2) word-initially before /v/: *Zwang, zwischen, Zweifel*; (3) medially and finally after long vowels and diphthongs (*Brezel, duzen, Weizen, Flöz* 'mining stratum', *Geiz*) and after sonorants (*Pilze, Kerze, Pelz, Schwarz*), and after /ch/ in *jauchzen*. It is written <tz> medially and finally after short vowels: *Katze, sitzen, putzen, Satz, Putz*. The spelling <zz> occurs in Italian and French loans (*Pizza, Razzia*) and in the place-name *Nizza* 'Nice'. The spelling <ts> only occurs in *Lotse, Rätsel* and *Tsetsefliege*. The letter <c> is pronounced [ts] in spelling words and in alphabetisms (*CD*, *PC*), abbreviations (*CDU*, *CSU*), as well as in the words *Cäsar*, *Celsius* (both from names).

6.4.4.3 The alveo-palatal affricate /tʃ/

The alveo-palatal affricate /tʃ/ is mostly spelt <tsch>: (1) word-initially before vowels: *Tscheche*, *tschüss*; (2) medially and finally after short vowels (*Kutsche*, *rutschen*, *Quatsch*), long vowels (*Bratsche* 'viola', *knutschen* 'to smooch', *Tratsch* 'gossip') and diphthongs (*Peitsche*, *Deutsche*). In English loans it is spelt <ch> in initial position before vowels (*Chat*, *checken*, *Chip*) and <tch> medially (*catchen*) and finally (*Match*, *Sketch*). The word *Ketchup* has the alternative spelling *Ketschup*. The spelling <c> occurs in the Italian loans *Cello*, *Cembalo* 'harpsichord'.

6.4.4.4 The voiceless labial stop /p/

The voiceless labial stop /p/ is spelt <p>, <pp> and <b>: <p> is written (1) word-initially before vowels: *Pass*, *pochen*, *Pute*; (2) word-initially before sonorants: *Plan*, *Probe*; (3) medially after long vowels (*dopen*, *hupen*, *Typen*), diphthongs (*Kneipe*, *Raupe*, *Loipe* 'cross-country ski run'), and sonorants (*Tulpe*, *Schärpe*, *Lampe*); (4) word-finally after long vowels (*Mikroskop*, *Prinzip*), diphthongs and sonorants (*Alp*, *Gezirp* 'chirping', *Vamp*); (5) in other consonant clusters with obstruents, initially or medially, <p> is also used: *Sprache*, *Splitter*, *Wespe*. After short vowels <pp> is written medially (*Lappen*, *Treppen*, *Puppen*) and finally (*knapp*, *Trupp*). In word-final position after long vowels, diphthongs and sonorants /p/ is also written <b>, if the stem plosive alternates with a medial <b>: *grob – grobe*; *Dieb*, *Lob*, *Staub*; *gelb*, *Korb*. In English loans final <b> is also used after a short vowel: *Job*, *Mob*, *Snob*. <b> is also used in the particles *ab*, *ob*. In medial consonant clusters with obstruents /p/ is also spelt <b>: *Erbse*, *Kebse* 'concubines', *Krebs*, *hübsch*.

6.4.4.5 The voiced labial stop /b/

The voiced labial stop /b/ is spelt <b> and <bb>: <b> is written (1) word-initially before vowels: *bar*, *Bett*, *Bild*; (2) word-initally before sonorants: *Blei*, *breit*; (3) intervocalically after long vowels and diphthongs: *leben*, *Diebe*, *Bube*, *Taube*, *Räuber*. It is spelt <bb> intervocalically after short vowels: *Ebbe*, *Mobbing* 'workplace bullying'.

6.4.4.6 The voiceless alveolar stop /t/

The voiceless alveolar stop /t/ is spelt <t>, <tt>, <th>, <d> and <dt>: <t> is written (1) word-initially before vowels: *Tasse, Tochter, Tür*; (2) word-initially before /r/: *treiben*; (3) medially after long vowels (*mieten, Stute* 'mare', *Tüte*), diphthongs (*reiten, Raute* 'lozenge', *deuten*) and after sonorants (*wollte, Torte, Kante*); (4) word-finally after long vowels (*Saat, tot*), diphthongs (*weit*) and sonorants (*alt, Art, Amt, Argument*); (5) in other consonant clusters with obstruents, initially or medially: *Streit, Geschäfte, Weste*. After short vowels <tt> is written medially (*Mitte, Betten, Mutter*), and finally (*Brett, Schnitt*). In English loans final <t> is also used after a short vowel: *Jet, Set*. <t> is also used in the particle *mit*. In Greek loans /t/ is spelt <th>: *Thema, Ether, Ethnologie*. In word-final position after long vowels, diphthongs and sonorants /t/ is also written <d>, if the stem plosive alternates with a medial <d>: *Kleid – Kleider; Rad, Lied, Süd; Gold, Herd, Hand*. The spelling <dt> is used for final /t/ in *Stadt, verwandt*.

6.4.4.7 The voiced alveolar stop /d/

The voiced alveolar stop /d/ is spelt <d> and <dd>: <d> is written (1) word-initially before vowels (*Dank, denn, dich*); (2) word-initally before /r/ (*drei*); (3) intervocalically after long vowels and diphthongs: *Leder, müde, leiden, Räude* 'mange'. It is spelt <dd> intervocalically after short vowels: *Kladde, jiddisch*.

6.4.4.8 The voiceless palato-velar stop /k/

The voiceless palato-velar stop /k/ is spelt <k>, <ck>, <ch>, <c> and <g>: <k> is written (1) word-initially before vowels: *Kasse, kochen, Kuchen*; (2) word-initially before sonorants: *Knie, Klasse, Krone*; (3) medially after long vowels (*Laken*), diphthongs (*Rauke* 'rocket (salad)'), and sonorants (*Wolke, Birke, Imker* 'bee-keeper', *denken*); (4) word-finally after long vowels (*Geblök* 'bleating', *reziprok*), diphthongs (*Klamauk*) and sonorants (*Kalk, Werk, Dank*); (5) in other consonant clusters with obstruents, initially or medially: *Skala, Sklave, Skrupel, Freske*.

After short vowels <ck> is written medially (*lecken, Brücke*) and finally (*Blick, Glück*). Word-initially in loans /k/ is written <ch> in Graeco-Latin words (*Charakter, Chaos, Chor, Chlor, Christ*) and <c> in French and English words (*Café, Coup, Couch, Clown, Crew, Cursor*). /k/ is also written <ch> before <s> within native morphemes: *Dachs, Lachs, wachsen*. In the loan words *Khaki, Khan,* /k/ is written <kh>. In word-final position after long vowels, diphthongs and sonorants /k/ is also written <g>, if the stem plosive alternates with a medial <g>: *Tag – Tage; Trog, Flug; Erfolg, Berg.* In English loans final <g> is also used after a short vowel for /k/: *Blog, Logbuch, Smog.* In medial consonant clusters with obstruents /k/ is also spelt <g>: *sagte.*

6.4.4.9 The voiced palato-velar stop /g/

The voiced palato-velar stop /g/ is spelt <g>, <gg> and <gh>: <g> is written (1) word-initially before vowels: *gar, Gäste, gilt;* (2) word-initally before sonorants: *gleich, Greis, Gnade;* (3) intervocalically after long vowels and diphthongs: *regen, Riegel, Jugend, taugen, erzeugen.* It is spelt <gg> intervocalically after short vowels: *Egge, joggen.* In the Italian loans *Ghetto, Spaghetti,* and the Turkish loan *Joghurt,* <gh> occurs, but they also have alternative forms with <g>.

6.4.4.10 The voiceless labio-dental fricative /f/

The voiceless labio-dental fricative /f/ is spelt <f>, <ff>, <v> and <ph>: (1) word-initially before vowels <f>, <v> and <ph> all occur, but <f> predominates among native words (*fallen, Vogel*) and <ph> occurs exclusively in Graeco-Latin words (*Philosophie, Phonetik*); (2) word-initially before sonorants, <f> is the main sign (*Flagge, fragen*), but <ph> occurs in a very few forms (*Phlegma, Phlox, Phrase*) and <v> in the one word *Vließ* 'fleece'; (3) medially and finally after long vowels and diphthongs <f> occurs: *Schafe, Schleife, Schaf, reif.* One exception, spelt with <v>, is *Frevel* 'heinous deed'; (4) medially and finally after short vowels <ff> occurs: *schaffen, Schiffe, schlaff, Treff;* (5) in consonant clusters with obstruents <ff> is written after short vowels (*betreffs* 'concerning'), and <f> after long vowels (*behufs* 'with a view to'). In the case of several word families of loans there are alternative forms with <f> or <ph>, the latter being the older form: *Foto – Photo; Telefon – Telephon; Grafik – Graphik; Fantasie – Phantasie.*

6.4.4.11 The voiced labio-dental fricative /v/

The voiced labio-dental fricative /v/ is spelt <w> and <v>: <w> occurs (1) word-initially before vowels: *was, warum, Wolke, Wurm;* (2) word-initially before /r/ in a very few words: *Wrack, wringen* 'to wring'; (3) medially after long vowels in a small list of words: *Löwe, Möwe.* In loan words <v> is used (1) word-initially before vowels: *Vakuum, variabel, vegetarisch, violett,*

Volleyball, Vulkan; (2) medially after long vowels (*brave*) and sonorants (*Pulver, Salve, Larve*). In many instances the pronunciation of loan words written with <v> varies between [v] and [f]: *Vers, Vesper, November, Initiative, nerven.*

6.4.4.12 The voiceless alveolar fricative /s/

The voiceless alveolar fricative /s/ is spelt <s>, <c> (mostly in loan words), <ss> and <ß>: (1) <s> and <c> word-initially before vowels: *Safe, surfen, City, Cent*; (2) medially and finally after short vowels, <ss> occurs: *Wasser, wissen; Fluss, Pass, muss*; (3) medially and finally after long vowels and diphthongs, <ß> is used: *Straße, Größe, Füße, beißen, außer*. In recent loans <s> occurs in consonant clusters with obstruents (*Sponsoring, Star, Splitting, Spray, Stretch*), often with an alternative pronunciation [ʃ]. There is a semantic and grammatical difference between the conjunction *dass* and the article/relative pronoun *das*. The final <s> is also the product of the devoicing of a medial voiced /z/: *las – lasen.*

6.4.4.13 The voiced alveolar fricative /z/

The voiced alveolar fricative /z/ is spelt <s>: (1) word-initially before vowels: *Sonne, Summe*; (2) medially after long vowels (*Rasen, Riese, Rose*), diphthongs (*Reise, tausend, Reuse* 'fish trap'), and sonorants (*Hülse* 'husk, pod', *Ferse* 'heel', *Gämse* 'chamois', *Binse*).

6.4.4.14 The voiceless alveo-palatal fricative /ʃ/

The voiceless alveo-palatal fricative /ʃ/ is written <sch>, <s> and <ch>: (1) word-initially before vowels: *Schatten, schön, Schiene, Schuh*; (2) word-initially before sonorants: *schlagen, schreiben, Schmerz, Schnee*; (3) medially between vowels (*wischen*) and after sonorants (*fälschen*, Kirsche); (4) word-finally after vowels (*wusch*) and sonorants (*falsch, Hirsch, Wunsch*); (5) in consonant clusters with obstruents: *Gischt* (only example).

6.4.4.15 The voiceless palato-velar fricative /ç–x/

The voiceless palato-velar fricative /ç–x/ is spelt <ch>: (1) word-initially before vowels: *Chirurg, Chuzpe*; (2) word-initially before sonorants: *Chrysalide* 'chrysalis'; (3) medially and finally after short vowels (*brechen, sicher, frech, Spruch*), long vowels (*Sprache, Bücher*), diphthongs (*streichen, brauchen, reich, Lauch* 'leek') and sonorants (*milchig, Lerche, Mönche, Milch, Storch, Mönch*).

6.4.4.16 The voiced alveo-palatal fricative /ʒ/

The voiced alveo-palatal fricative /ʒ/ is spelt <j> or <g>: (1) word-initially before vowels: *Jalousie, Genie*; (2) <g> medially after long vowels: *Page, Loge*.

6.4.4.17 The voiced palatal fricative /j/

The voiced palatal fricative /j/ is spelt <j>: (1) word-initially before vowels: *Januar, Jugend*; (2) medially after long vowels: *Boje, Koje*. In some loan words it is spelt <y>: *Yacht, Yak, Yo-Yo*.

6.4.4.18 The labial nasal /m/

The labial nasal /m/ is spelt <m> and <mm>. <m> occurs: (1) word-initially before vowels: *man, melken, Milch, müssen*; (2) medially and finally after long vowels and diphthongs and sonorants: *lähmen, kamen, lahm, kam, leimen, Leim, baumeln, kaum, Arme, arm, Halme, Halm*; (3) in consonant clusters with obstruents: *kämpfen, Bombe, Pumpe, Beamte, Imker, bumsen* 'to thump'. Medially and finally after short vowels <mm> occurs: *schwimmen, kommen, Schwamm, Kamm*.

6.4.4.19 The alveolar nasal /n/

The alveolar nasal /n/ is spelt <n> and <nn>. <n> occurs: (1) word-initially before vowels: *nun, Nelken, niedrig, Nüsse*; (2) medially and finally after long vowels and diphthongs: *mahnen, Zonen, Wahn, Tran* 'fish oil', *weinen, kein, Daunen, kaum*; (3) in consonant clusters with obstruents: *winzig, Kinder, hinter, Linsen*. Medially and finally after short vowels <nn> occurs: *nennen, Sonne, Sinn, dann*.

6.4.4.20 The velar nasal /ŋ/

The velar nasal /ŋ/ is spelt <ng> and <n>. It is spelt <ng> medially after short vowels: *bringen*. It is spelt <n> in consonant clusters with palato-velar plosives (*denken, Banken*) and in a few words before /g/ (*Tango, Bingo, Bongo*).

6.4.4.21 The lateral /l/

The lateral /l/ is spelt <l> and <ll>. <l> occurs: (1) word-initially before vowels: *los, leben, Liebe*; (2) medially and finally after long vowels and diphthongs: *malen, Täler, Seele, Mühle, Saal, Tal, Seil, Maul*; (3) in consonant clusters with obstruents: *Pelze, Stülpe, Kolben* 'piston', *selten, golden, Balken, tilgen, Hilfe, Kelche, falsche, Halse*. Medially and finally after short vowels <ll> occurs: *bellen, Pille, Ball, toll*.

6.4.4.22 The /r/ phoneme

The /r/ phoneme is spelt <r> and <rr>. <r> occurs: (1) word-initially before vowels: *Reis, rennen, Riss, Ruß* 'soot'; (2) medially and finally after long vowels and diphthongs: *sparen, gebären, bar, Paar, feurig, Feuer, bäuerisch, Bauer*; (3) in consonant clusters with obstruents: *scherzen, Schärpe, Kerbe* 'notch', *Karte, Marder* 'marten', *Kerker, Ärger, Bursche*. Medially and finally after short vowels <rr> occurs: *Karren, Sperren, Herr, Narr*.

6.4.4.23 The glottal fricative /h/

The glottal fricative /h/ is spelt <h>: (1) word-initially before vowels: *Haar, Henne, Hirsch, Hut*. Although it is written medially in *sehen, leihen*, it is not pronounced. <h> also occurs as a marker of vowel length (see Fig. 6.1).

6.5 Spelling reform

Having reviewed the general principles of orthographic representation and described the spelling of the phonemes of present-day German, revised in 1998, we will look at the development of German spelling. We can see how some of the problems highlighted in the nineteenth century have only partially been dealt with and some have yet to find a solution. We will restrict our remarks to what changes have affected the sound–letter correspondences and not deal with matters such as capitalization and writing items together or apart. We have drawn on a number of works, including Scheuringer (1996) and Johnson (2005).

6.5.1 Spelling reform up to 1901

Although a large amount of agreement in orthographic usage had been achieved by the beginning of the nineteenth century, particularly in printed works, there were still fluctuations and uncertainties in the use of many forms. Orthographic usage in letters and hand-written documents fluctuated more than on the printed page. The gradual introduction of compulsory primary education from 1763 served rather to aggravate the situation since there was no central authority that could be appealed to in matters of orthography.

Konrad Duden (1829–1911), whose name has since become the trademark for orthographic reference works published by the *Dudenverlag*, characterized the situation as follows: 'Nicht zwei Lehrer derselben Schule und nicht zwei Korrektoren derselben Offizin waren in allen Stücken über die Rechtschreibung einig, und eine Autorität, die man hätte anrufen können, gab es nicht' ('No two teachers at the same school nor two copy editors of the same publishers agreed about everything regarding orthography, and there was no authority that could be called upon'; quoted in Nerius 1975: 61). An informative biography of Konrad Duden is Wurzel (1985).

However, the political climate changed drastically in 1870–71 with the creation of the German Empire. The unifying force of the newly created empire seems to have acted as a spur to those who wanted reform and unification of German orthography. Schlaefer (1984) is an excellent collection of primary sources on the history of German spelling in the nineteenth century. The discussion on orthography led to the first Orthographic Conference, called by the Prussian Education Minister Adalbert Falk (1827–1900), and held in the new capital of the German Empire, Berlin, during 4–15 January 1876.

There were fourteen participants, of whom the most influential were Rudolf von Raumer (1815–76), from Erlangen, who prepared a paper 'Regeln und Wörterverzeichnis für die deutsche Orthographie' ('Rules and word list for German orthography'); Wilhelm Wilmanns (1842–1911), a Professor of German at Greifswald, later Bonn; and Konrad Duden, a headteacher. Von Raumer's draft was debated and his suggestions were worked into the final orthographic rules that the conference passed in its session, although in some cases the conference suggested more radical changes than his. Von Raumer was an advocate of the phonetic principle for orthography, as against the historical principle of Jacob Grimm (1785–1863) and Karl Weinhold: 'Schreib wie es die geschichtliche Entwicklung des Neuhochdeutschen verlangt' ('Write as the historical development of German demands'; Schlaefer 1984: 18). The main recommendations of the conference were as follows (*Konferenz* 1876: 133–52):

(1) Only to designate vowel length for *i* and *e*. Thus modern German *Bahn, Sohn, Bühne, Stuhl* were to be written *Ban, Son, Büne, Stul*. In certain words the vowel length was to be shown in the case of *a, o, ü, ö, u* if confusion with a short vowel would result, e.g. *fahnden – fanden; Ruhm – Rum*. In other words the homonymy principle was brought into play.

(2) In final and initial position *th* should be abolished in native words. Earlier *Thal, Rath* would now become *Tal, Rat*. The abolition is expressed by merely stating where *th* can occur (*Konferenz* 1876: 139): 'th kann in

deutschen Wörtern nur durch Zusammensetzung entstehen, z.B. Rathaus'.

(3) Medial and final *dt* in certain words was also to be abolished: *Brodt, Erndte, gescheidt, todt* become *Brot, Ernte, gescheit, tot*; but it was to be retained in *Stadt, beredt, bewandt* and *verwandt*. Possibly in the last three the *t* gives the word a pseudo-participial shape.

(4) The nominal suffix *-nis* was to be written *-nis* and not *-niß*.

(5) Nouns and other parts of speech used as nouns should be written with initial capital letters.

(6) Assimilated loans were to be adapted to German orthography (*Konferenz* 1876: 147): 'Fremdwörter, welche in ihrem Lautstande sich der deutschen Sprache anbequemt haben, folgen, je früher sie aufgenommen und je gangbarer sie sind, um so mehr der deutschen Orthographie.'

Thus in foreign words with *c* (the cause of most problems here) it was recommended that before *a, o, u* or a consonant it be replaced by *k* (*Kasse, Kolonie, Kur, Klasse, Akt*) and before *e* and *i* by *z* (*Zelle, Zirkel*). The conference, however, allowed considerable fluctuation between *z* and *c*. Initial *ph, th* were to be retained in loans: *Philosoph, Theater* (*Thee* was still regarded as a loan for orthographic purposes).

The recommendations of the conference were widely regarded as a compromise. Many of them had passed by only small majorities, and others had many exceptions. None of the authorities accepted them. Four years later they had become dead history. Instead of furthering unity in orthographic usage the conference led to each authority going its own way. From 1879 to 1884 spelling primers were published in Bavaria, Prussia, Saxony, Baden, Württemberg and Mecklenburg. The most important of these were the Bavarian (1879) and Prussian (1880) books. Wilmanns, who together with Konrad Duden was responsible for the Prussian book, stressed the similarities between the two books. In 1880 Duden also produced his own orthographic work: *Vollständiges Orthographisches Wörterbuch für die Schule: Nach den neuen preußischen, bayerischen und sächsischen Regeln* (Duden 1880). It was soon in great demand and by the following year had run through five impressions, to be followed by a second edition in 1882.

The orthography of Duden's work and the efforts of Wilmann's received a major set-back when Otto von Bismarck (1815–98), the Chancellor, forbade the use of this so-called Puttkamersche Orthographie (after Robert Puttkamer (1828–94), the Prussian Education Minister 1879–88, who was Bismark's brother-in-law!) by civil servants and in official publications of the empire. It was not until 1901, when a second orthographic conference was held in Berlin, attended also by delegates from Austria, that there was a change in atmosphere. The recommendations of this second conference, which were more of an agreement on administrative details rather than a discussion of the reform of the system, were ratified for official use by the German *Bundesrat* (the Upper House) on 18 December 1902 for use in all official publications from 1 January 1903. The *Bundesrat* (the Federal Cabinet) in Switzerland accepted the orthography on 18 July 1902, having already agreed to follow Duden in 1892, and the Austrian government also followed suit. The normative book was the seventh edition of Duden's *Orthographisches Wörterbuch*. The wish of 1880 had become a reality.

The main recommendations of the orthographic conference of 1901 were: (1) the abolition of *th* in native words, e.g. *Thür* > *Tür*; (2) the assimilation of *c* in most loans to either *k* (*Caffee* > *Kaffee*) or *z* (*Cigarre* > *Zigarre*); and (3) the alteration of individual words, e.g. *todt* to *tot, sämmtlich* to *sämtlich*. The spelling of 1903 was used up until after 1945, when various scholars and bodies started to clamour for its revision.

The seventh edition of Konrad Duden's *Orthographisches Wörterbuch* contained the sub-title *Nach den für Deutschland, Österreich und die Schweiz gültigen amtlichen Regeln*. In his foreword Konrad Duden said that he regarded his dictionary as only being an intermediate stage (*Zwischenziel*) and hinted that more spelling reforms might be needed but that no one need worry about when they would come about. The successor of the *Orthographisches Wörterbuch* is the *Duden Rechtschreibung*, which was published in a separate edition in Leipzig between 1951 and 1985 and appeared in its twenty-fourth edition in 2006. Sauer (1988) traces the development of the *Duden* up to just before re-unification. The spelling system set out in both volumes was no different from that of the seventh edition of 1902, except that roman is now used instead of Gothic. In 1991 the twentieth edition was published for a united Germany and the twenty-first edition in 1996 introduced the new spelling system for German that had been agreed in 1994. The long road from 1901 to 1996 will be detailed in the next section.

6.5.2 Spelling reform 1901 to 1996

The 1901 orthographic system had had its critics from the beginning and there were continual moves for spelling reform. Mostly these were lone voices but pressure groups such as the Swiss *Bund für vereinfachte rechtschreibung*, founded in 1924, and similar societies in Germany and Austria, always kept interest in spelling reform alive. There were radical suggestions by teachers in Leipzig in 1931 and by printers in Erfurt in 1933 but nothing came of them.

However, any decisive moves could only come from all the German-speaking countries taking common steps. After 1933 this proved impossible, although it has been suggested that in 1941 a simplified spelling system was put forward but in the confusion of the times nothing came of it. Thus it was not till after 1945 that common discussions of spelling reform could get under way again. Enthusiasm was great and interested parties from the Federal Republic of Germany (including, however, such East German scholars as Theodor Frings, Ruth Klappenbach and Wolfgang Steinitz), Austria and Switzerland formed the *Arbeitsgemeinschaft für Sprachpflege*, which discussed ways of reforming the spelling of German. On 16 May 1954 they produced their suggestions, *Empfehlungen zur Erneuerung der deutschen Rechtschreibung*, at a conference in Stuttgart, whence the name *Stuttgarter Empfehlungen*. The recommendations were accepted unanimously by all members of the working party and were submitted to the authorities in the Federal Republic of Germany, Austria and Switzerland (*Stuttgarter Empfehlungen* 1955).

Among the suggestions was that there should be a uniformity in consonant clusters. This would mean replacing *tz* by *z* (*spitzen* > *spizen*) and *ß* would become *ss*. In the case of the creation of consonant clusters with three members the same the three would be reduced to two, e.g. *Schiffahrt*, but if the word was divided at the end of a line, the third consonant would re-appear, e.g. *Schiff-/fahrt*. Also suggested was that orthographic variants should be dispensed with and only one form allowed. This would affect the assimilation of foreign words to the German spelling system since this produced the most alternative spelling forms. Thus *ph, th, rh* should be replaced by *f, t, r* and short unstressed *y* by *i*. The sequence *ti*, if pronounced [tsi], should be spelt *zi*, e.g. *Sensazion* instead of *Sensation*. The replacement of *c* by *z* and *k*, *eu* by *ö* and other substitutions in loan words should continue.

The designation of vowel length was also examined and it was suggested that the length marker *h* could be dispensed with after vowels other than *e*, with the exceptions of the pronouns *ihm, ihn*. It was also suggested that *ie* should be replaced by *i* except before *ss*.

The result of the publication of these recommendations was that in 1956 the Minister of the Interior and the Permanent Conference of Education Ministers of the *Länder* of the Federal Republic of Germany set up the *Arbeitskreis für Rechtschreibregelung* to look into spelling reform. In October 1958 the working party produced their recommendations, which became known as the *Wiesbadener Empfehlungen*. The text was published as *Empfehlungen* (1959) and is reprinted in Drewitz and Reuter (1974: 139–64). They made six major recommendations, all of which were also to be found in the *Stuttgarter Empfehlungen*. For phoneme–letter correspondences it was again suggested that no variant spellings should be allowed. In addition the spelling of foreign words should be made to fit the German spelling system as far as possible. More radical points, such as the simplification of consonant clusters, e.g. *tz* to *z*, replacement of *ß* by *ss* and any changes in designation of vowel length, were not on the agenda.

The *Wiesbadener Empfehlungen* were unsuccessful. However, interest in reform was still maintained throughout the 1970s and 1980s by scholars and laypeople in the different German-speaking countries. In 1973 the *internationaler arbeitskreis für deutsche rechtschreibung* with its headquarters in Tuttlingen was founded. The pace quickened up after Dieter Nerius became head of the research group *Orthographie* in the GDR Academy of Sciences and a *Kommission für Rechtschreibfragen* was established by the Institut für deutsche Sprache in Mannheim headed by Wolfgang Mentrup. Starting in 1978 with a conference in Vienna, scholars representing all the German-speaking countries worked together in the late 1970s and throughout the 1980s to produce sets of rules for different areas of German orthography: use of capital and lower-case letters, syllabification of words at the end of lines, punctuation, words written separately or together, the use of *s/ss/ß*, and foreign words (Kommission für Rechtschreibfragen 1985). In Vienna in 1986 these were officially recognized as being the areas where the rules of spelling had become too complicated since 1901.

In February 1987 the commission was officially asked by the Permanent Conference of Education Ministers of the *Länder* of the Federal Republic of Germany to prepare suggestions for reforming the German spelling system for all areas except the use of capital and lower-case letters. This omission, or rather postponement, since a suggestion for reform was envisaged at a later date, was because the commission and the *Gesellschaft für deutsche Sprache* agreed to differ on their suggestions in Vienna in 1986.

In October 1988 the commission was able to submit their suggestions for the five areas to the Permanent Conference of Education Ministers (Kommission für Rechtschreibfragen 1989). Among them were suggestions concerning three main areas of phoneme–letter relationships: (1) the doubling of vowels, except for *ee*, should be abolished, e.g. *Haar > Har, Boot > Bot*; (2) *ai* should be replaced by *ei* in nine words, e.g. *Meis < Mais*; and (3) *ä* should be replaced by *e* in a small number of words, e.g. *demmern < dämmern*. Where there is a need to distinguish between homonyms the oppositions *ai : ei* and *ä : e* remained. The following, rather nonsensical, sentence, which is written according to the suggested rules, illustrated the proposed changes:

Der Keiser streubt sich gegen die Statsgeschäfte und fängt liber im Mor Ale.

According to the traditional orthography it is:

Der Kaiser sträubt sich gegen die Staatsgeschäfte und fängt lieber im Moore Aale. ('The Emperor shows reluctance for affairs of state and would rather catch eels in the marsh!')

These suggestions did not feature in the *Stuttgarter Empfehlungen*. Another proposal was that both foreign and nativized forms (*chic*, *schick*) would be allowed to co-exist for about ten years, after which one would be omitted. It might be either the foreign or the nativized form.

The Permanent Conference of Education Ministers in Germany reacted swiftly, but negatively, rejecting the recommendations in 1990. Predictably the proposal changing the designation of long vowels, which changed the 'look' of words considerably, seemed to have caused most upset among journalists and the public.

Nothing daunted, the scholars submitted further recommendations in 1992 (*Internationaler Arbeitskreis für Orthographie* 1992) including the following for the phoneme–letter relationship: (1) *ä* should be substituted for *e* in several words, e.g. *überschwänglich*; (2) following the principle of uniform shape for morphemes (*Schemakonstanz*), the following changes were proposed: *nummerieren*, cf. *Nummer*; *platzieren*, cf. *Platz*; *Ass*, cf. *Asse*; and *fitt*, cf. *Fitter*; (3) the alternation of *ss* and *ß* was regulated to allow *ß* only after long vowels and diphthongs (*weiß*, *gießen*). The sequence *ss* thus gains ground, being allowed to occur word- and morpheme-finally after a short vowel: *wisst*, *müsst*; *Kuss*, *Fluss*; (4) sequences of three consonants were allowed (*Schifffahrt*) and *h* introduced before *-heit* (*Rohheit*).

These proposals formed the basis of the 'new' spelling system but it was not until the Vienna Conference of 1994 that they were finally agreed. After a long and wearisome campaign they were accepted in 1998 with a transition period until 2005. This new spelling system as set out in *Duden Rechtschreibung* 2006 is the one that has formed the basis of this chapter. Basically the most farreaching change has been the regulation of the use of *ß* only after long vowels and diphthongs regardless of its position in the word. There is a good account in Johnson (2005: 45–86) and a useful summary by Heller (1996).

QUESTIONS

1   Explain and illustrate the morphophonemic principle with reference to German orthography.

2   Describe the use of the letters used to spell /ʃ/. How far is their usage predictable?

3   How are the letters <e> and <ä> used for short /ɛ/?

4   What role does the doubling of consonant letters play in German orthography?

5   Illustrate some of the problems for spelling caused by the introduction of foreign words into German.

6   How far is the orthographic use of <v> and <f> in German predictable?

7   How might the spelling of long vowels be regulated for German in the future?

8   How has the use of <ss> and <ß> changed in the latest reform of German spelling? What principle does this change of usage illustrate?

9   Compare and contrast the strengths and weaknesses of German and English spelling.

10   What are the most difficult aspects of spelling for foreign learners of German?

7 Distribution of vowels and consonants

7.0 Introduction

In Chapter 5 we dealt with the phonemic differences between sounds, emphasizing the notion of contrasts between phonemes at particular positions in the word. This paradigmatic approach to phonology shows that before medial /t/ there are contrasts for all the short vowel phonemes in German, whereas the complementary syntagmatic approach puts the emphasis on the sequence of sounds and which sounds co-occur with other sounds: in other words, what makes up syllables in German. Some phoneticians believe that the syllable only belongs in phonology but many believe there is also an articulatory basis for it. The native speaker listening to a string of sounds can usually divide them quite easily into different syllables. They can perceive that there are differences in the prominence given to certain sounds.

7.1 The structure of the syllable: Vowels and consonants

In previous chapters we have used the term syllable in an undefined way to designate that part of a word that does or does not bear stress, e.g. stressed and unstressed syllables. Here we want to attempt to examine syllabic structure in more detail. The most suitable kind of word to start with is the monosyllable. To describe its structure we need general symbols such as C, standing for any consonant, and V, for any vowel. This distinction between vowels and consonants is fundamental for the syllable. A simple monosyllable consists of an initial element, a nucleus and a releasing element. Thus the word *Tisch* [tiʃ] can be symbolized CVC. A more complex word such as *Spruch* [ʃprux] could be symbolized CCCVC. The concept of the syllable as a phonological unit is based partly on the assumption that some speech sounds are more sonorous, emitting more 'noise' than others. A scale of sonority can be set up among

vowels	a, e, o, u, i
sonorants	r, l, m, n
voiced fricatives	v, z, ʒ, j
voiceless fricatives	f, s, ʃ, ç, x
voiced plosives	b, d, g
voiceless plosives	p, t, k

Figure 7.1   The Sonority Scale

speech sounds ranging from the low vowel [a] to the voiceless plosives [p, t, k] as can be seen from Fig. 7.1. The first sounds in the groups are the most sonorous.

In the structure of words those sounds that are most sonorous, the vowels, make up the peak, or nucleus, of the syllable and they are preceded or followed by sounds that are less sonorous. Thus in *dort* the vowel is followed by a sonorant and a voiceless plosive, in *Treff* the vowel is preceded by a sonorant and a voiceless plosive. From the peak of the vowel the syllable descends through a sonorant to a voiceless plosive or from a voiceless plosive it ascends through a sonorant to the peak. This is reflected in the phonotactics of the pre- and postvocalic consonant clusters in German.

Using the conventions of C and V (V covering both short and long vowels and diphthongs) we can illustrate which sort of words form monosyllables in German. The minimum word consists simply of the diphthong [ai]: *Ei*. Words that begin with a vowel can be followed by one, two, three or at most four consonants: VC *in*, VCC *und*, VCCC *Angst*, VCCCC *Ernst*. Words that begin with a single consonant can have up to four consonants after the vocalic nucleus V: CV *du*, CVC *Dach*, CVCC *Geld*, CVCCC *Kunst*, CVCCCC *selbst*. Words that begin with two consonants seem to only have up to three consonants after the vocalic nucleus V: CCV *frei*, CCVC *Traum*, CCVCC *Trunk*, CCVCCC *Knirps*. The maximum number of consonants that a word can begin with is three but after V in these words the maximum number of consonants is only two: CCCV *Spreu* 'chaff', CCCVC *Sprung*, CCCVCC *Strand*. In our treatment we have ignored for the moment the difference in the nucleus between short and long vowels and diphthongs. We have also assumed that the affricates [pf] and [ts] are unit phonemes, representing only one C place in a word, e.g. *Pferd* is symbolized CVCC. These examples bring us to a formula for monosyllables in German: (C)(C)(C)V(C)(C)(C)(C). There has to be a vocalic nucleus preceded by up to three consonants and followed by up to four consonants (with a maximum five consonants in total).

7.2 Phonotactics

Phonotactics describes the phonological structure of permissible words in a language. Although we have established that German words may begin with one, two or three consonants, we have not ascertained what the set of possible consonant clusters might be. We shall try to answer the question of why *Blick* is a permissible German word, **Dlick* is not. Most phonotactic descriptions deal with consonant combinations, the permissible vowel structures being handled simply as distribution. Discussions and illustrations of the phonotactics of German are: Philipp (1970/1974: Chapter 3); Meinhold and Stock (1982: Chapter 3); Benware (1986: Chapter 7). Theoretical linguistic studies are Vennemann (1982: 261–305) and Smith (2003: 147–224).

7.2.1 Initial consonant clusters

German words occur with either one, two or three consonants in initial position before a stressed vowel: *baten, braten, sprachen*. If we use C for consonant then the initial structure of these three possibilities can be symbolized C, CC, CCC. This can be reduced to the formula $C^1C^2C^3$. We can then be more specific about the nature of each of these consonants and how they co-occur with each other. If three consonants occur then C^1 must be [ʃ] and C^3 must be /1/ or /r/, whereas C^2 may be either /p/ or /t /: *Splitter, Sprache, Strafe*. If C^3 is /1/ then C^2 must be /p/, in other words /ʃtl/ is not an admissible cluster in German (and also in English). Of the three admissible clusters /ʃtr, ʃpr, ʃpl/ the first two occur frequently but there are not many examples of /ʃpl/: *Spleen, spleißen*. Since we have assumed a phonemic analysis of the affricates [pf, ts] as unit phonemes /pf/ and /ts/, then we do not have initial CCC clusters in *Pflaume* /pfl/, *Pfropf* /pfr/ and *zwei* /tsv/ but only CC clusters. Other CCC clusters occur in initial position but only in very few words: /skl, skr/, *Sklave, Skrupel* (all loan words).

In initial clusters of two consonants (C^1C^2), C^1 can comprise a larger number of members /p b t d k g f ʃ/ whereas C^2 comprises only /1 r m n v/ in native words. The permissible combinations of the two groups can be shown in Fig. 7.2, with + marking the occurrence of a particular combination. We have excluded the clusters with affricates.

Examples: /ʃm/ *schmal*; /kn/ *Knie*, /gn/ *Gnade*, /ʃn/ *schnell*; /pl/ *Platz*, /bl/ *blasen*, /kl/ *klein*, /gl/ *glatt*, /fl/ *Fluss*, /ʃl/ *Schlange*; /pr/ *Preis*, /br/ *Bremse*, /tr/ *träge*, /dr/ *drei*, /kr/ *Kreis*, /gr/ *grau*, /fr/ *Frost*, /ʃr/ *schreiben*; /kv/ <qu> *Quelle*, /ʃv/ *schwer*; /ʃp/ *sparen*, /ʃt/ *stehen*; /tʃ/ *tschüss*.

C²=	m	n	l	r	v	p	t	ʃ
C¹= p			+	+				
b			+	+				
t				+				+
d				+				
k		+	+	+	+			
g		+	+	+				
f			+	+				
ʃ	+	+	+	+	+	+	+	

Figure 7.2   Combinations of CC initial clusters

Other possible clusters appear mostly in foreign words (/pn/ *Pneumatik*, /ps/ *Psychologie*, /ks/ *Xylophon*, /sf/ *Sphäre*), names (/pʃ/ *Pschorr(bräu)*) or Low German words: /vr/ *Wrack*. Through the borrowing of chiefly English, but also French words, consonant clusters with /s/ as C¹ have been introduced into German. Before /t/ and /p/ older loans have substituted /ʃ/ for /s/ (*Streik*, *Sport*), but in many recent loans both /ʃ/ and /s/ occur in variation (*Star, Stil, Spot, spontan*). Besides /st sp/ where the pronunciation of /s/ can vary with /ʃ/ there is also a group of clusters where the pronunciation of /s/ is always [s]: /sk/ *Skat, Skala*; /sm/ *smart*; /sn/ *Snack*; /sl/ *Slum*. The sonorants /m n l r/ always appear nearest the vowel in a consonant cluster. In prevocalic clusters they follow the obstruent whereas in postvocalic clusters they precede the obstruent, e.g. *Schlaf* vs *falsch*, giving a mirror image of /ʃl/ vs /lʃ/.

7.2.2 Final consonant clusters

Of the eighteen initial CC clusters in German in Fig. 7.2 that contain a sonorant, eleven also occur (reversed) in word-final position: /lp/ *Kalb*, /rp/ *Korb*, /rt/ *Art*, /lk/ *Kalk*, /rk/ *Werk*, /lf/ *elf*, /rf/ *Dorf*, /mʃ/ *Ramsch*, /nʃ/ *Wunsch*, /lʃ/ *falsch*, /rʃ/ *Dorsch*. In addition there are other word-final clusters comprising sonorants which do not occur in initial position, nor do their mirror images, e.g. /lx-ç/ *Milch*, /lt/ *mild*, /ls/ *Hals*; /ŋk/ *Bank*; /rs/ *Kurs*, /rx-ç/ *durch*. Altogether there are forty-four word-final CC consonant clusters in German. Figure 7.3 shows their occurrence. Those that are infrequent are bracketed, (+).

Examples: /pt/ *bleibt*, /ps/ *Krebs*, /pʃ/ *hübsch*; /tʃ/ *Matsch*; /kt/ *Takt*, /ks/ *Dachs*, /kʃ/ *tücksch*; /ft/ *Luft*, /fs/ *Treffs*; /st/ *Lust*, /sk/ *brüsk*; /ʃt / *Gischt*; /xt/ *recht*; /mp/ *Camp*, /mt/ *Amt*, /ms/ *Sims*, /mʃ/ *Ramsch*; /nt/ *Land*, /nf/ *Senf*, /ns/ *Gans*, /nʃ/ *Wunsch*, /nx-ç/ *Mönch*; /ŋt/ *hängt*, /ŋk/ *Bank*, /ŋs/ *längs*; /lp/ *halb*, /lt/ *Geld*, /lk/ *Kalk*, /lf/ *Golf*, /ls/ *Hals*, /lʃ/ *falsch*, /lx-ç/ *Milch*, /lm/ *Helm*, /ln/

C¹= \ C²=	p	t	k	f	s	ʃ	x–ç	m	n	l
p		+			+	+				
t							+			
k		+			+	(+)				
f		+			+					
s		+	(+)							
ʃ		(+)								
x–ç		+								
m	(+)	+			+	+				
n		+		+	+	+	+			
ŋ		+	+		(+)					
l	+	+	+	+	+	+	+	+	(+)	
r	+	+	+	+	(+)	+	+	+	+	+

Figure 7.3   Final CC clusters in German

Köln; /rp/ *Korb*, /rt/ *Bart*, /rk/ *Park*, /rf/ *Torf*, /rs/ *Kurs*, /rʃ/ *Hirsch*, /rx-ç/ *durch*, /rm/ *Lärm*, /rn/ *Stern*, /rl/ *Kerl*.

There are also clusters with the affricates /pf/ and /ts/: /mpf/ *Kampf*, /nts/ *ganz*, /lts/ *Pelz*, /rts/ *Herz*, /x-çts/ *lechzen* 'to pant' and (/tst/ *jetzt*).

Combinations of CCC clusters in word-final position are more frequent than CC clusters: thirty-four end in /t/, e.g. *Fürst*, *Wulst*, thirty in /s/ (*Knirps*, *Murks*, *Rülps*) and two in /ʃ/. Groups of four consonants can occur but the final consonant(s) are phonetically alveolar obstruents, mostly representing an inflectional ending: /s/ for the gen. sg. (*Markts*), /st/ for the second person (*rülpst*) or /t/ for the third person verbal ending (*kämpft*). There are even a small number of groups of five consonants (*kämpfst*, *Herbsts*), where the final consonant is always part of the inflectional ending. There is thus more freedom of combination among consonants after stressed vowels than before them. One constant feature is that /r/ and /l/ are always nearest the vowel.

7.2.3 Medial consonant clusters

The initial and final consonant clusters have been illustrated with reference to monosyllables. If we extend our pattern of words to disyllabic structures such as *bitte*, then we find that there are consonant clusters that occur before the unstressed vowel: *winden*, *folgen*.

There are over fifty different such combinations of consonants. We will group them according to their first consonant. Those that are infrequent will be put in brackets.

	$C^2=$	p	t	k	f	v	s	ʃ
$C^1=$	p		+				+	(+)
	t					(+)		+
	k	+					+	
	f	+						
	s	+	+	(+)				
	x–ç	+						

Figure 7.4   Medial CC obstruent clusters

Among the consonant clusters consisting of a sonorant and an obstruent, the sonorant always comes first. The few cases of sonorant + sonorant are /rm/, /rn/, /rl/ and /lm/, /ln/. Examples:

/r/ + obstruent: /rp/ *Schärpe*, /rb/ *Scherbe*, /rt/ *Härte*, /rd/ *Herde*, /rk/ *Erker*, /rg/ *Ärger*, (/rf/ *Larve*), (/rv/ *Kurve*), /rz/ *Verse*, /rʃ/ *Kirsche*, /rx-ç/ *Kirche*, /rm/ *Schirme*, /rn/ *lernen*, /rl/ *Kerle*.

/l/ + obstruent: /lp/ *Welpe*, /lb/ *selber*, /lt/ *halten*, /ld/ *Halde*, /lk/ *Nelke*, /lg/ *folgen*, /lf/ *Wölfe*, /lv/ *Pulver*, /lz/ *Pinsel*, /lʃ/ *fälschen*, /lx-ç/ *milchig*, /lm/ *Helme*, (/ln/ *Kellner*).

/m/ + obstruent: /mp/ *Pumpe*, (/mb/ *Bombe*), /mf/ *Triumphe*, (/mt/ *Ämter*), /md/ *Hemden*, (/mk/ *Imker*), /mz/ *Gemse*.

/n/ + obstruent: /nt/ *Winter*, /nd/ *winden*, /nz/ *Gänse*, /nʃ/ *wünschen*, /nx-ç/ *Fenchel* 'fennel'.

/ŋ/ + obstruent: /ŋk/ *trinken*, (/ŋg/ *Bingo*).

The consonant clusters consisting of two obstruents show more flexibility of position in that several obstruents can appear as first or second consonant, e.g. /ps/ and /sp/. Figure 7.4 shows these combinations.

Examples: /pt/ *Häupter*, /ps/ *knipsen*, (/pʃ/ *hübscher*); (/tv/ *Witwe*), /tʃ/ *kitschig*; /kt/ *Akte*, /ks/ *knicksen*; /ft/ *Lüfte*; /sp/ *Wespe*, /st/ *lustig*, (/sk/ *Maske*); /x-çt/ *wichtig*.

Altogether there are fifty-seven medial CC clusters in NHG.

There are also clusters with affricates /pf/ and /ts/: /mpf/ *kämpfen*, /nts/ *schwänzen*, /lts/ *schmelzen*, /rts/ *schwärzen*.

7.3 The hierarchical structure of the syllable

Growing out of generative phonology have come several developments of phonological theory. These are generally referred to by prefacing 'phonology' with a qualifying epithet, e.g. autosegmental phonology, dependency

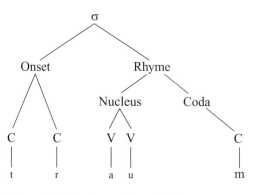

Figure 7.5   Hierarchical structure of the syllable

phonology, dynamic phonology, lexical phonology, natural phonology, natural generative phonology and metrical phonology. They are not quite as diverse as their names suggest and share a number of common features, notably an interest in the syllable. A survey of their methods of description and theoretical terminology is provided by Carr (1993: 157–304). We will show how they have attempted to shed light on the syllabic structure of German.

Using the information we have gained about the combination of consonants a hierarchical structure of the syllable can be constructed in the form of a tree diagram (see Fig. 7.5), comprising three parts. There is the onset, /tr/, the nucleus, /au/, and the coda, /m/. The nucleus and the coda can further be combined to form the rhyme.

One of the goals of syllabic phonology is to set up a pattern or template for the words of a language. More traditional approaches do this by listing the patterns of words with consonant clusters that occur in the language (see 7.1). Syllabic phonology does this by setting up a template for the syllable structure of words in a language, i.e. summarizing in the form of a tree diagram all the possible structures. Figure 7.6 attempts to do this for German, based on the information in 7.1.

The only part of the template which is obligatory is V^1, V^2, e.g. *Ei*. As we have seen, the consonants are optional but restrictions are placed on the types of consonants occurring in the different slots in the template (see Figs. 7.2, 7.3 and 7.4). When the onset is CCC, C^1 is always [ʃ, s], C^2 is an obstruent and C^3 a sonorant, e.g. [ʃpl, ʃpr, ʃtr]. Where C^2 and C^3 occur together, then C^2 is always an obstruent and C^3 a sonorant (see Fig. 7.2). Non-frequent clusters in foreign words will be excluded. The consonants C^4 and C^5 in word-final position are largely the mirror image of C^2, C^3, with C^4 being a sonorant and C^5 an obstruent (see Fig. 7.3). However, there are exceptions to which we will

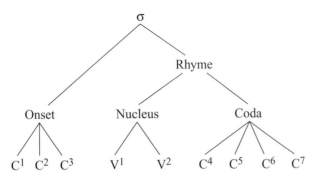

Figure 7.6   Syllable template in tree diagram form

return. In the case of C^6 and C^7, the obstruent is always an alveolar, usually an inflectional ending.

7.3.1 Analysis of consonant clusters

This hierarchical approach to syllabic phonology has been based on the sonority scale and the occurrence of [ʃ, s] in C^1 position and [s, t] in C^6, C^7 position are violations of this scale, as are C^4, C^5 clusters such as [pt, ps, pʃ, kt] etc. (see Figs. 7.2 and 7.3). Suggestions to deal with this violation have been: (1) to count clusters such as [ʃp, ʃt] as filling a single C slot, and (2) to regard [ʃ, s] as being 'extrametrical' consonants which do not count as part of the syllable template but are appendices. Giegerich (1989: 69–73) discusses these alternatives and rules out the second one since [st] occurs word-internally, e.g. *Meister*, *Hamster*. He would like to accept the first suggestion, which regards [ʃp, ʃt] as complex segments and not sequences. This means that phonetically they are two sounds but phonologically they function as only one unit, occupying one C slot. As is probably now becoming clear, the old question of whether the affricates in German are one phonological unit or two is still very much alive. Giegerich comes to the conclusion that 'Affricates are phonetically complex elements that behave phonologically like single units' (1989: 69). Other recent studies that take this line are Griffen (1985: 123–48), T. A. Hall (1992: 15f.), Ramers and Vater (1992) and Wiese (1988: 60ff.; 1996).

7.3.2 The analysis of vowel length and diphthongs

Another phenomenon which receives attention from syllabic phonology is vowel length or quantity. The parallelism between long vowels and diphthongs

Onset	Rhyme		Onset	Rhyme	
	Nucleus	Coda		Nucleus	Coda
C	V V	C	C	VV	C
b	a u	m	n	a:	m

Figure 7.7   Representation of long vowels and diphthongs

is maintained by symbolizing both of them VV at the CV level, e.g. *Baum* and *nahm* are both CVVC. However, at the phonetic segmental level the long vowel is only realized by one segment as is illustrated in Fig. 7.7.

This is the exact reverse of the treatment of the affricates (T. A. Hall 1992: 18–23). Giegerich (1989: 25) follows a similar course, but uses different symbolism. Wiese (1988: 62–78) has a slightly different scheme, viewing diphthongs as comprising VC, the C being a resonant, at the CV level. He distinguishes between quantity at the syllabic level and length at the phonetic level. All agree, however, that length and tenseness combine at the underlying level to characterize long vowels. The status of length and quantity, one of the classic phonological areas of controversy (see 5.2.1.1), continues to be the subject of debate.

7.4 Syllable boundaries

Where we have disyllabic words it is important for the framing of phonological rules to determine where the boundaries between the syllables lie. The sign to show syllable is [.]: [ta:.gə, tor.tə]. Syllables that end in vowels are called open syllables and those that end in a consonant are closed syllables. Principles have been suggested as to how to divide words into syllables (Benware 1986: 85–7). Firstly, the division of consonant clusters at syllable boundaries must not result in clusters that do not appear in word-initial or word-final position. Thus no syllables will begin with [ŋ] because no words begin with [ŋ]. In [tor.tə] the boundary could not come before [r] ([to.rtə]) since /rt/ is not an admissible initial cluster. Also, the short vowel [ɔ] does not appear in word-final position, where all vowels are long. The boundary, therefore, lies between [r] and [t]: [tor.tə]. Secondly, in setting syllable boundaries, onsets (initial consonant clusters) should be maximized. In the verb [re:gnən], the boundary will be before the [gn], [re:.gnən] since [gn] is an admissible initial cluster. Thirdly, in German, syllable boundaries occur where there are word boundaries. Hence the word-final obstruent devoicing rule specifies devoicing at word and syllable boundaries.

7.5 Changes affecting syllable structure

During the history of German various changes have affected the syllabic structure and phonotactics of German.

7.5.1 Syncope

The syncope of unstressed [ə] in inflectional endings and also in simple disyllabic forms has affected the frequency of postvocalic consonants structures in German. MHG *dienest, market, nacket* have become NHG *Dienst, Markt, nackt*. This change has also happened regularly in verbal inflections: MHG *du nimest, er, sie nimet* have become NHG *du nimmst, er, sie nimmt*. The syncope has not taken place if the verb is regular and its stem ends in /t/ or /d/ (*rettet, redet*), or a combination of /m/ or /n/ preceded by an obstruent (*atmen, atmet; regnen, regnet; zeichnen, zeichnet*). Through syncope NHG has gained nine CC clusters in final position and fifty new CCC clusters. MHG did not have CCCC clusters but NHG has thirty (Meinhold and Stock 1982: 184–6). In colloquial speech syncope has affected the unstressed syllables [-əl], [-əm] and [-ən], changing the nucleus of the syllable from [ə] to a syllabic consonant.

7.5.2 Epenthesis

Epenthesis, the addition of an obstruent, [t], to form a consonant cluster, has also affected NHG, but to a much lesser degree. Epenthetic [t] appears chiefly after -*n*, -*s* and -*ch*, mostly preceded by an unstressed vowel. After [n] and before [l] in NHG there are still examples of alternations between forms with an epenthetic consonant and those without: *eigen, eigentlich; hoffen, hoffentlich*. The main conditioning factor seems to be in the transition of [n] to [l]. The epenthetic [t], being a plosive, makes the transition from alveolar nasal to oral lateral easier. As the speaker goes from one to the other, the point of articulation remains the same, but the manner of articulation changes from nasal to lateral. This change does not normally take place if the -*en* or -*es* is an inflectional ending. Examples after [n]: MHG *ieman, nieman, irgen, allenhalben* – NHG *jemand, niemand, irgend, allenhalben*. It occurs after a stressed vowel in MHG *mâne*, NHG *Mond*. Examples after [s]: MHG *ackes, iez(e), obez, moras, palas, sus* – NHG *Axt, jetzt, Obst, Morast, Palast, sonst*. Examples after [x-ç]: MHG *dornach, habich, predich* – NHG *Dornicht, Habicht, Predigt*. In each the consonant cluster that developed merged with already existing clusters.

7.5.3 Apocope

Apocope, the loss of final unstressed vowels, occurs throughout the German-speaking area and is frequent in colloquial speech: *wart' mal!* (*Warte mal!*) In Upper German (UG) and Low German (LG) most of the final unstressed vowels have been lost but in the Central German (CG) dialects from which, to a large extent, standard NHG has come, most final unstressed vowels have been retained, especially in inflectional endings: *Name, sagte, Tage*. Only in some adverbs, particles and a few nouns has there been apocope: MHG *lihte, abe, mite, herze, vrouwe* – NHG *leicht, ab, mit, Herz, Frau*.

QUESTIONS

1   What is the Sonority Scale?

2   Give an account of CCC clusters in word-initial position.

3   Which of the following initial CC clusters are infrequent: /ʃp sf vr kn fr kv/? Give ONE example of the infrequent clusters.

4   Which of the following CC clusters are not permitted in word-initial position: /tl ŋg pr lʃ rp dl/?

5   Which final consonant clusters are missing from the following groups: /ps pʃ; mp ms mʃ; nt ns; lp lt lk ln/?

6   What is the difference between apocope and syncope?

7   Where is the syllable boundary in: *Gäste, Stärke, Sorte, singen, zeichnen, Wege*?

8   Explain and illustrate consonant epenthesis.

9   Which of the following initial consonant clusters do not occur in German and why: /bm bl br bn bv bs bʃ bf bx/?

10 Which of the following 'nonsense' words would be impermissible in German and why: *Krant, Kort, Rtast, Wost, Tlump, Skopm, Psching, Spwahl, Skuhn, Ksatn*?

8 Foreign sounds

8.0 Introduction

Throughout its history German has been influenced by other languages. This has varied in intensity and in the number of different languages involved at different times. The metaphor that linguists mostly use to describe languages influencing each other is that of borrowing. It is rather a strange metaphor since unlike borrowing in everyday life, when we may return a borrowed book, languages do not return words or sounds they have borrowed. Another way of describing the influences of languages on each other is that of saying that the languages are in contact and that languages transfer words from one language to another. However, the borrowing metaphor is so widely used that we will make use of it in this chapter. Before looking at the exact nature of the influence of foreign languages on the sound system of German, we will review briefly the extent of borrowing throughout the history of German. For general works on borrowing and language contact, see Haugen (1950), Weinreich (1953).

8.1 Borrowing in the history of German

It is at the lexical level that most languages influence each other. Words are borrowed from one language to another with differing results. To illustrate this in general we will use examples of post-1945 English loans in modern German (see 8.2.8). Some words show the same phonetic structure as German (e.g. *Lift*), while others only differ in spelling (*Toast*). Some words, however, introduce potentially new sounds that are not to be found in German (see 8.2.1), e.g. *Thriller*, with an initial interdental fricative [θ], or a new consonant cluster also not to be found in German, as in *Tweed* or *smart* (see 8.2.3).

German has been influenced throughout its development chiefly by Latin, French and English. Other languages have provided fewer loans, e.g. Italian

(*Cembalo, Oper*), Spanish (*Cargo, Vanille*), Slavonic (*Grenze, Peitsche*), Arabic (*Matratze, Sofa*) and Persian (*Joghurt, Tulpe*).

Latin was the language from which German borrowed words during its oldest period. The main areas of vocabulary affected were (1) Christian ritual and ecclesiastical organization and (2) general cultural and economic areas, including horticulture and building. Most of these loans were made in OHG or pre-OHG times.

Many of the central concepts of Christianity were expressed not by loan words, but by loan meanings, using already existing Germanic words and giving them a new or additional Christian meaning: *Geist, Gott, Heiland, Himmel, Hölle*. (We will cite the forms of the loan words in the NHG form to be more accessible.) In many more cases, however, loan words are used, mostly from Latin but a few from Greek: *Altar* (Latin *altâria*), *Engel* (Greek *anggelos*), *Kirche* (Greek *kyriakos*), *Kloster* (Latin *claustrum*), *opfern* (Latin *operârî*), *Priester* (Latin *presbyter*), *segnen* (Latin *signâre*), *Teufel* (Greek *diabolos*).

Words from other more general areas of borrowing, e.g. from military and economic organization are: *Kampf* (Latin *campus*), *Kerker* (Latin *carcer*), *Markt* (Latin *mercâtus*), *Münze* (Latin *monêta*), *Pfeil* (Latin *pîlum*), *Pfund* (Latin *pondus*), *Straße* (Latin (*via*) *strâta*), *Wall* (Latin *vâllum*), *Wein* (Latin *vînum*). But it is in the realm of horticulture that a large number of borrowings from Latin occur: *Kirsche* (Latin *cerasium*), *Kohl* (Latin *caulis*), *Minze* (Latin *menta*), *Pflaume* (Latin *prûnus*), *pfropfen* (Latin *propagâre*), *Senf* (Latin and Greek *sinâpi*). Culinary borrowings are *Küche* and *Pfanne*. Items reflecting Roman building skills with stone and brick are: *Keller* (Latin *cellârium*), *Küche* (Latin *cocina*), *Mauer* (Latin *mûrus*), and *Ziegel* (Latin *têgula*).

In Middle High German times (the Middle Ages) it was from French that borrowings came. This was the Age of Knights and Chivalry and many of the loans reflect this: with chivalric concepts *âventure* (NHG *Abenteur*), *prîs* 'glory' (NHG *Preis*), *turnei* (NHG *Turnier*) and arms and armour *harnas* (NHG *Harnisch*), *lanze* (NHG *Lanze*), *pantzer* (NHG *Panzer*). Some of the borrowings did not survive to NHG: *tjostieren* 'to joust', *schevalier* (NHG *Ritter*) and *garzûn* 'squire'. This over-use of French was parodied by Tannhäuser in about 1250. The French words are in bold.

> Ein **riviere** ich dâ gesach,
> Durch ein **fores** gieng ein bach
> Zetal über ein **plâniure**.

(A river I saw there, through the forest went a stream into a valley through a meadow.)

In the sixteenth century and onwards there was a renewed influx of learned Latin words in the wake of Humanist and Renaissance writing. These affected various specialist areas of language: (1) school and university: *Auditorium, Autor, Bibliothek, Grammatik, Universität, Zensur*; (2) administration: *Akten, Audienz, Faktum, Fiskus, Inventar, Kanzlei, Konferenz*; (3) legal affairs: *Advokat, appellieren, Hypothek, Kaution, Prozess*; and (4) medicine: *Anatomie, Doktor, Medikament, operieren, Patient, Rezept*.

In the seventeenth century French was the main source of borrowing. The terminology for warfare and military matters was largely from French, leavened with some Spanish and Italian. Many of the words were used in the new medium of newspapers as they reported the battles and sieges of the Thirty Years' War (1618–48) and they became familiar to speakers of German: *Armee, Bataillon, Bombe, Garnison, Kaserne, Kommandeur, Pionier, Terrain, Trupp*. Some military words also came from the languages of Eastern Europe: *Haubitze* (Czech *houfnice*), *Horde* (Turkish *ordu* 'army' via Russian), *Husar* (Hungarian *huszar*), *Säbel* (Hungarian *szablya*).

Perhaps even greater than the influence on military vocabulary was that of French on the language of general culture in the seventeenth and eighteenth centuries. All Europe wanted to orientate themselves on the model of the French monarch Louis XIV (1643–1715). Baroque palaces and their grounds gave rise to borrowings such as *Allee, Balkon, Etage, Kaskade, Parterre* and *Terrasse* from French while *Bronze, Fresko, Galerie, Kuppel* (*cupola*) and *Stuck* (*stucco*) came from Italian. Items of clothing and toilette include *Perücke, Parfum, Pomade* and *Weste*. French culinary terms are exemplified by *Bouillon, Dessert, Kotellet, Omelett, Ragout*. Kinship terms such as *Onkel, Tante* and *Cousin, Cousine* and other words such as *Dame* and *Visite* were borrowed at this time.

During the sixteenth and seventeenth centuries there were also a smaller number of borrowings from more exotic languages, particularly with the introduction of items from the New World. In many instances these loans from indigenous languages came through intermediate languages such as Italian, Spanish and Portuguese: *Ananas, Dattel, Kakao, Kokosnuss, Mais, Muskat, Schokolade, Tabak, Vanille, Zitrone*. Arabic has provided *Alakali, Alkohol, Alkove, Kaffee*.

Certain specialist languages were affected by particular languages. For instance, the language of commerce borrowed many words from Italian that still have their Italian form (*Bank, Bankrott, brutto, Konto, netto, Porto*), as did the language of music (*Arie, Ballett, Kapelle, Motette, Oper, Oratorio*), including the instruments: *Bratsche* 'viola', *Fagott* 'bassoon', *Mandoline*.

In the face of a large influx of loan words in the seventeenth century, many in the form of the original language, a reaction against foreign borrowing began. Language societies (*Sprachgesellschaften*) developed, the first in Weimar in 1617. One of their principles, but not the primary one, was to keep German pure from foreign words. This purism expressed itself not only in wanting to keep the language pure but also by suggested translations for loan words, particularly compounds. Some of these suggestions have become an accepted part of the language, often co-existing with foreign words, e.g. *Anschrift* (*Adresse*), *Leidenschaft* (*Passion*), *Tagebuch* (*Journal*), but other suggestions did not catch on and remain historical curiosities: *Jungefernzwinger* (*Nonnenkloster*), *Krautbeschreiber* (*Botaniker*), *Tageleuchter* (*Fenster*). The societies gradually faded in importance but the concept of purism continued, revived by Johann Heinrich Campe (1746–1818) in the eighteenth century and then by the *Allgemeiner Deutscher Sprachverein* in 1885. The tradition of purism has recently had a revival (see 8.3).

In the late seventeenth and throughout the eighteenth century the borrowing of English makes itself felt for the first time. English parliamentary democracy provided loans such as *Bill, Debatte, Parlament* (originally French!), *Juries, Sprecher* or *Speaker*. There are also more general loans such as *Frack, Gentleman, Klub, Pudding*. The nineteenth century saw a flood of English loans enter German from industrial and technical fields: *Bunker, Lokomotive, (Kipp)Lore* 'dump truck' (cf. *lorry*), *shrinken, Tunnel, Viadukt*. Sport was another area of English influence: *Tennis, Fußball* (translation of *football*). Other items include: *fashionable, Rowdy, Snob, Streik*. This influx continued into the twentieth century and reached its height after 1945 (see 8.2.8).

Figure 8.1 shows some of the languages that have influenced German in its historical development and which areas of vocabulary have been affected. For general details about OHG and MHG see 12.1.1 and 12.1.2. General accounts of borrowing in German feature in Schwarz (1967), Schirmer and Mitzka (1969) and Folz (1987).

8.2 Borrowing and the sound system of German

The sound system of German has been influenced by foreign loans in the following ways.

8.2.1 New sounds are introduced

Through the borrowing of an increasing number of words from a language that do not exist in German, new sounds can be introduced into the sound

Period	Areas of vocabulary	Examples	Language(s)
OHG	Christianity, Roman culture	Altar, Bischof; Keller, Ziegel	Latin
MHG	Courtly and knightly culture; Ecclesiastical and theological	Manieren, Palast; Abenteuer, Turnier; Absolution, Zeremonie	French, Latin
16th c.	Humanism, Reformation, Commerce	Mathematik, Zensur; evangelisch, Pastor; Bilanz, Porto	Latin, Italian
17th c.	Military, general, music	Artillerie, Patrouille; Dame, Onkel; Bass, Tenor	French, Italian
18th c.	Politics, literature, general culture	Parlament, Opposition; Charme, Diner	English, French
19th c.	Industry, sport	Lore, Streik; Golf, Tennis	English
20th c.	Politics, business, technology, fashion, food, entertainment	Hearing, Image; Boom; Computer; fair; Make-up; Cocktail; Musical	English

Figure 8.1   Loan words in the history of German

system. Initially speakers may substitute the nearest sound to the foreign one, e.g. the voiceless [ʃ] for the voiced [ʒ] or the sequence of a vowel + velar nasal for a nasal vowel. The length of time and acceptance by native speakers will determine whether a sound becomes accepted with the foreign pronunciation.

8.2.1.1 The voiced post-alveolar [ʒ]

Our first examples concern the voiced post-alveolar fricative [ʒ]. The phoneme /ʒ/ is spelt <g> initially before front vowels (*Giro, Gelee*) or before unstressed [ə] (*Etage, Page, Garage*). Initially before back vowels it is spelt <j> (*Jalousie, Journal*). In NHG it fits well into the phonemic pattern, being the voiced partner of /ʃ/. The near minimal pair: *Giro : schier*, shows them contrasting. The distribution of /ʒ/ is limited. Initially it appears only before vowels: *Genie, Jackett*. Medially it appears only after long vowels (*Rage*) and /n/ (*rangieren* 'to arrange, shunt' and *Orange*). It does not normally show a phonological alternation with voiceless /ʃ/ except possibly in the case of *beige* where for some speakers [beːʃ] would alternate with [ʒ] in *beigenfarbig*. Some linguists disregard /ʒ/ when describing the phonology of NHG (Philipp 1970 and Wurzel (1970). *DAW* includes it in the inventory of standard phonemes (2005: 37). In colloquial speech /ʒ/ is usually devoiced but this is regarded as non-standard by *DAW* (2005: 58).

The phoneme /ʒ/ was borrowed into the standard language through the adoption of French loans. Most of the words containing /ʒ/ are post-MHG borrowings. Paul (2002) gives the following chronology: fifteenth century, *Journal*; sixteenth century, *Courage, Gelatine, Passage, Passagier*; seventeenth century, *engagieren, Gage, Giro* (Italian), *Jalousie, Loge, logieren, Page, rangieren*; eighteenth century, *Etage, Gelee, Genie, genieren, Genre, Jargon, Jongleur, Orange, Regie, Regisseur, Regime*; nineteenth century, *Gendarm, Jackett*; twentieth century, *Garage*. The integration of /ʒ/ into the sound system of German has taken a long time and has occurred gradually. Even today the number of words with /ʒ/ is not frequent but the sequence -*age* is familiar and supports the pronunciation [ʒ].

8.2.1.2 Nasal vowels

French, unlike German, developed nasal vowel phonemes in the course of its history. By the seventeenth century French had developed four nasal vowel phonemes: /ɛ̃/ *fin* 'fine'; /œ̃/ *brun* 'brown'; /ɔ̃/ *bon* 'good'; and /ɑ̃/ *grand* 'big'. In modern French the first two (/ɛ̃/ and /œ̃/) are tending to merge into /ɑ̃/. As we have seen, the seventeenth and eighteenth centuries were a time when there was intense contact between speakers of the two languages. French had enormous prestige among the aristocracy and scholars. Brunt (1983: 1–106) gives an informative account of the influence of French on German. Words containing French nasal vowels have in some cases retained their nasal vowel in German: *Teint* [ɛ̃], *Fonds* [ɔ̃], *Pendant* [ɑ̃]. In other cases the nasal vowel has been replaced by an oral vowel + velar nasal, *Bon* [bɔŋ], *Restaurant* [-raŋ].

Before we deal with the integration of words with nasal vowels into German we will look at their influx over time. Ever since the sixteenth century there has been a steady flow of French words into German. Figure 8.2 shows some examples of French words containing nasal vowels in the history of German. The dates are according to Telling (1988). Munske (1984) made a detailed study of 190 words containing nasal vowels in German, English, Dutch and the Scandinavian languages. Of the 126 words with a nasal vowel as a suffix, only 25 retained the nasal vowel pronunciation as the only pronunciation: [ɔ] *Abandon, Chanson, Jeton, Kotillon*; [a] *nonchalant, Akkompagnement, Agrément, Amendement, Detachement, Enjambement, Räsonnement, Sentiment, Kontenance, Nonchalance, Renaissance, Süffisance, Trance*; [ɛ] *Chagrin, Dessin, Krétin, Mannequin, Marocain, Embonpoint, Point*. In 39 cases the nasal vowel pronunciation was merely a variant with other pronunciations such as oral vowel + velar nasal. In all other cases an

Examples	First recorded	English gloss
Ballon	15th/16th century	'balloon'
Fasson		'style, shape'
Bataillon		'batallion'
Cousin	17th century	'cousin'
Terrain		'terrain'
Appartement		'apartment'
Ressentiment		'resentment'
Balkon		'balcony'
Champignon		'mushroom'
Parfum	18th century	'perfume'
Teint		'complexion'
elegant		'elegant'
Balance		'balance'
Jargon		'jargon'
Salon		'drawing room'
Croissant	19th/20th century	'croissant'
Mannequin		'mannequin'
Elan		'zest, vigour'
Restaurant		'restaurant'
Beton		'concrete'
brisant		'explosive'

Figure 8.2   Loan words with nasal vowels

oral vowel + nasal consonant had been substituted for the original nasal vowel.

8.2.1.3 The case of uvular [R]

As we have seen (4.4.5.2) the articulation of the phoneme /r/ is extremely complex. Apart from the range in the manner of articulation from trill, through fricative and approximant to vowel, the main difference lies in the place of articulation: alveolar or uvular. Both are used in the standard. The alveolar sound is almost certainly Indo-European but it is not clear how old the uvular sound is. An Early NHG phonetician described the /r/ as 'ain hundts buchstab/ wann er zornig die zene blickt und nerret,/ so die zung kraus zittert', which seems to point towards an alveolar or dental trill (Müller 1882: 128). Trautmann (1880: 204–22) maintained that the uvular [R] was introduced by imitation of French pronunciation and is thus the borrowing of a foreign articulation. Most histories of German ignore the question of the origin of uvular [R]. The older British tradition has followed Trautmann's suggestion: Wright (1907: 12), 'This *r* [i.e. alveolar *r*] began to give way to back or uvular *r* in the eighteenth century. In modern times it has spread extensively in towns and North Germany. Its origin in Germany was probably due to the imitation of French pronunciation'; Kirk (1923: 40), 'Its origin [i.e uvular *r*] was probably due to the imitation of its pronunciation in French, where it arose about the middle of the seventeenth century'; and also Chambers and Wilkie (1970: 117), who espouse the French origin for [R]: '*r*, originally a front trill, acquired its back uvular pronunciation in eighteenth century cultured society in imitation of French pronunciation. From there it spread to all social classes and most dialects.' This reflects the authoritative remarks by Bach (1965: 312): 'Unser Gaumen-r dürfte nach französischem Vorbild im 17. Jh. von der gebildeten Schicht auf die deutsche Aussprache übertragen worden sein.' However, several scholars have argued against this importation of uvular [R] and see it rather as an independent development (see Russ 1982: 111–15, with further references). More recent work sees the spread of uvular [R] as having been strengthened by the influence of French (Wells 1985: 273; von Polenz 1994: 90). Voge (1978: 121f.) argues that while the importation of uvular [R] from French seems unlikely, the uvular articulation does gain ground in the eighteenth century. This whole question needs a thorough re-investigation and French influence may well have played a role in supporting one variant, if not in its actual genesis.

8.2.2 'Lost' sounds have been re-introduced

Through sound changes some sounds and combinations of sounds disappeared from German. In later centuries borrowed words containing these sounds or combinations of sounds have been re-introduced in the language.

8.2.2.1 Initial [p] in OHG

Through the second or High German Sound Shift, initial Germanic voiceless plosives were shifted to affricates: English *pound, tide*, German *Pfund, Zeit* [tsait]. Initial Germanic *k* was only shifted in the southernmost varieties of German and then became [x] in Swiss German: *Kind* [xint]. The gap created by shifting *t* to [ts] was filled by the change of Germanic *d* to *t*: *do – tun*. In the case of the gap created by the shifting of Germanic *p* to [pf] this was filled by the introduction of Latin loan words with initial *p*. Some early examples from the eighth century (given in NHG spelling) are: *Palme, Paradies, Pein, Pilgrim* (Seebold 2001: 229–31). The latter <p> was also used irregularly in Upper OHG for initial *b-*. This re-introduction of *p* also affected the Germanic initial consonant clusters *pl-* and *pr-* which were shifted to *pfl-* and *pfr-* (see 8.2.4.1).

8.2.2.2 Unstressed final vowels [-a, -o, -i, -u]

Modern German has four unstressed vowels apart from schwa: [-a] (*prima*), [-o] (*Auto*), [-i] (*Mutti*), and the less frequent [-u] (*Akku, Hindu*) in disyllables. This situation reflects OHG where there were also these four unstressed vowels: *taga, ofto, gibu, nezzi*, and also *-e, hirte*. At the end of the OHG period these vowels all merged in schwa through vowel reduction: MHG *tage, ofte, gibe, netze, hirte*. There are a few relics of *-o* in MHG and in a few adverbs (*jetzo, anhero*) unstressed *-o* was also retained in archaic Chancery language into the eighteenth century. A relic of this in modern German is the correlative *desto*: *desto mehr desto besser* and the compounds *nichtsdestoweniger, nichtsdestotrotz*. There are a few OHG loans with full unstressed vowels that have survived but most of the words with unstressed [-i, -a, -o, -u] in modern German are loans or new derivations that have come gradually into the language. We will deal with the vowels individually.

(i) Words with final *-a*

There are about 460 words, excluding names, that have final [-a] in NHG (Lee 2005: 1–13). They come from two sources: (1) loan words, e.g. *Firma*; (2) word-shortening through clippings or blends, e.g. *Dia*. Further examples of loan words, with approximate date of first recording, are given in Fig. 8.3.

(ii) Words with final *-o*

There are over 380 words, excluding names, that have final [-o] in NHG (Lee 2005: 846–53). They come from three sources: (1) loan words, e.g. *Kino, Solo*; (2) word-shortening through clippings or blends, e.g. *Disko*; (3) derived forms, e.g. *Prol+o*, from the first part of *Proletarier* + the ending *-o*, designating a person. Further examples of clippings are: *Abo < Abonnement, Auto < Automobil, Bio < Biologie, Demo < Demonstration, Euro < Europa, Limo <*

Example	First recorded	Language	English gloss
Drama	16th century	Greek/Latin	'drama'
Schema			'scheme'
Thema			'theme'
Sofa	17th century	Arabic	'sofa'
Villa		Italian	'villa'
Dogma	18th century	Greek	'dogma'
Extra		Latin	'special'
Propaganda		Latin	'propaganda'
Firma	19th century	Italian	'firm'
prima		Latin	'excellent'
Razzia		French/Italian	'police raid'
Pizza	20th century	Italian	'pizza'
Sauna		Finnish	'sauna'

Figure 8.3   Loan words with final -*a*

Example	First recorded	Language	English gloss
Konto	16th century	Italian	'account'
Risiko			'risk'
Ghetto	17th century	Italian	'ghetto'
Piano			'pianoforte'
Porto			'postage'
Embargo	18th century	Italian	'embargo'
Solo			'solo'
Studio			'studio'
Casino	19th century	Italian	'casino'
Cello			'cello'
Foto	20th century	French	'photo'

Figure 8.4   Loan words with final -*o*

Limonade or *Limousine*. Clipping combined with blending has produced *Kripo < Kriminalpolizei*, *Strobo < Stromrechtsboykotteur*. Further examples of derived forms are *Anarcho*, 'anarchist' and *Realo* 'politician (usually from the Greens), with a realistic political outlook'. Further examples of loan words, with approximate date of first recording, are given in Fig. 8.4.

Example	First recorded	Language	English gloss
Juni	16th century	Latin	'June'
Juli			'July'
Costi	17th century	Italian	'there'
Fusti			'certificate of damage'
Gummi	18th century	Latin	'rubber'
Mahagoni		Caribbean	'mahogany'
Potpourri		French	'potpourri'
Makkaroni	19th century	Italian	'maccaroni'
Khaki	20th century	Urdu (via English)	'khaki'

Figure 8.5   Loan words with final -*i*

(iii) Words with final -*i*

There are about 175 words, excluding names, that have final [-i] in NHG (Lee 2005: 486–99). They come from two sources: (1) loan words, e.g. *Gummi*; (2) word-shortening through clippings or blends: *Abi*, *Uni*; *Schiri* < *Schiedsrichter*. Further examples of loan words, with approximate date of first recording, are given in Fig. 8.5.

(iv) Words with final -*u*

There are only about thirty words, excluding names, that have final [-u] in NHG (Lee 2005: 1187–93). They come from two sources: (1) mostly loan words, e.g. *Iglu*; (2) word-shortening through clippings or blends, e.g. *Akku*. Most are quite recent (*Guru, Haiku, Hindu*); the only non-twentieth-century examples are *Kakadu* (eighteenth century) and *Tohuwabohu* (nineteenth century).

8.2.3 New consonant clusters

As well as introducing new sounds, loan words can also introduce new combinations of consonants. Many of these, however, are not frequent and occur mostly in learned and scientific vocabulary.

8.2.3.1 Initial [dʒ-]

The initial cluster [dʒ-], which in colloquial speech often becomes [tʃ], only occurs in a few modern loans. These are mostly from English after 1945 and spelt with *J-*: *Jeans, Jetset, Jingle, Jingoismus, Jive, Job*, and the related forms, *jobben, Jobber, Jodhpur, Jogging, joggen, Joint, Junkie. Jazz*, first recorded in *Duden* in 1929, has alternative pronunciations, [jats] and [dʒes]. *Joker* (*Duden* 1934) also has alternative pronunciations for <J> of [dʒ] and [j]. The nineteenth-century borrowing *Jury* tends to be pronounced in the French way, [ʒyri]. [dʒ-] is spelt <D-> in *Dutyfree*. The spelling has been changed in *Dschungel* and *Dschunke* (Muthmann 1996: 191f.). A recent word, borrowed from Arabic, is *Dschihad* 'Jihad, holy war'.

8.2.3.2 Initial [ps-]

The initial cluster [ps] occurs in a few modern scientific words from Greek: *Psoriasis, Psyche* (seventeenth century), *Psychiatrie, Psychiater, Psychologe, Psychologie* and in the prefix *Pseudo-* (eighteenth and nineteenth century). It also occurs in *Psalm(e), Psalter*, which go back to the eighth century but remained isolated forms.

8.2.3.3 Initial [sk-]

Germanic initial *sk-* has become [ʃ] in NHG, spelt <sch>. Since <ch> in MHG could stand for a stop or a fricative it is not clear when this post-alveolar fricative phoneme /ʃ/ developed. It was probably not until [s] was written <sch> before sonorants in MHG (*snel* > *schnell*) that this change was complete. The word *Skorpion* seems the only survivor with [sk-] from OHG. The cluster [sk-] can also combine with [l] or [r]. The number of words has increased modestly over time as Fig. 8.6 shows.

8.2.3.4 Initial [s] + obstruent or sonorant

With the change of the alveolar [s] to post-alveolar [ʃ] before initial consonants, the clusters [st sp sl sm sn] did not exist. These were re-introduced, particularly in the nineteenth and twentieth centuries. As the loan words became established in German the pronunciation with [s] gave way to that with [ʃ]: *Streik*. As a rule the more recent the loan the higher the chance there is of the [s] pronunciation being used. The clusters /st/ and /sp/ are more frequent than /sl sm sn/. The cluster /sl/ occurs in nineteenth-century loans *Slang, Slogan, Sloop, Slums* from English and *Slibowitz* from Czech. The earliest example of /sn/ is *Snob* (1853) but the latest edition of *DR* (2006) shows *Snack, Sneaker, sniffen, Snowboard*. The cluster /sm/ has *Smaragd* from OHG, *smart, Smoking* 'dinner-jacket' (late ninteenth century),

Example	First recorded	Language	English gloss
Sklave	15th/16th century	Slavonic	'slave'
Skrupel		Latin	'scruple'
Skelett	17th century	Greek	'skeleton'
Skizze		French	'sketch'
skurril			'scurrilous'
Skandal	18th century	French	'scandal'
Skulptur			'sculpture'
Skat	19th century	Italian	'skat'
Skepsis		Greek	'scepticism'
scannen	20th century	English	'to scan'
Skateboard			'skateboard'

Figure 8.6   Loan words with initial [sk]

and post-1945 loans *Smalltalk, Smartcard, Smash, Smoothie* and *Smörgåsbord* (Swedish).

In the case of the clusters /st/ and /sp/ as well as /str/ and /spr spl/ the pronunciation varies between [s] and [ʃ]. Muthmann (1996: 431–43) lists those words where the pronunciation varies between [s] and [ʃ]: *Spaghetti, Spektakel, Sponsor, Spleen, Splitting, Spray, Stadion, Status, Star, Steak, steril, stopp, Stratum, Struktur.* Words with these initial clusters soon became integrated into the German phonotactic system.

8.2.3.5 Some minor clusters

Three minor consonant clusters are [sf-] (*Sphäre*), [sv-] (*Swap*) and [sts-] (*Szene*). The initial clusters [sf-] and [sv-] clusters are not very frequent. The cluster [sf-], spelt <Sph>, features in Greek loans *Sphäre, sphärisch, Sphäroid, Sphinkter, Sphagistik* and *Sphinx.* The cluster [sv-], spelt <Sw>, occurs in some English loan words (*Swap, Sweater, Swimmingpool, Swing, switchen*), and may occur as [sf-] or [sw-] with some speakers.

The tricluster [sts-] only occurs in *Szene* and derived forms, *Szytta, Szintigram* and *Szintillation*, all from Greek roots.

8.2.3.6 The initial cluster [vr-]

If we include Low German as a language that NHG has borrowed from then we have to include the initial cluster [vr-], spelt <wr->. In OHG the pronunciation of <w> was lost, as in English where it is, however, still retained in spelling: *wring, write*. The words that have [vr-] in NHG are mostly agricultural and maritime: *Wrack, Wrasen, wriggen, wringen, Wruke* is the complete list.

8.2.4 The re-introduction of 'lost' consonant clusters

As well as lost sounds, 'lost' consonant clusters that had disappeared from the language have been re-introduced.

8.2.4.1 Initial voiceless labial stop + liquid [pl-], [pr-]

With the shift of Germanic [pl-] to [pfl-] and [pr-] to [pfr-] the gap created is filled with borrowing from Latin. Some examples from the eighth century (given in modern spelling) are: *predigen, Priester, Probst; planen, Platte.*

8.2.4.2 Medial [-mb-]

In MHG medial [-mb-] became assimilated to [mm], then shortened to [m] (*kumbe*r > *Kummer*), thus removing the cluster [-mb-]. This has been re-introduced into German by French loans: *Bombe* (seventeenth century), *Plombe, Hekatomb*e (eighteenth century), *Trombe* and other words, *Gambe, Jambe, Katakombe.*

8.2.4.3 The consonant cluster /tw/

In MHG the word-initial cluster /tw/ occurs in a small number of words, about twenty (Hennig 2001: 343f.). Those that have remained in NHG have either changed the /tw/ to /tsv/ (MHG *twerc*, NHG *Zwerg*; MHG *twingen*, NHG *zwingen*) or /kv/ <qu> (MHG *twalm*, NHG *Qualm*; MHG *twerh*, NHG *quer*). This 'gap' has been filled by loan words. The earliest of these is English *Twist*, 'twist of yarn' (nineteenth century). *Tweed* and *Twill* are recorded in DR (1929) but others such as *Tweeter*, *Twist* (the dance) and *Twinset* are post-1945. *Twen* 'someone in their twenties' is a post-1945 German pseudo-loan formation.

8.2.5 New distribution of already existing sounds and consonant clusters

The distribution of already existing sounds can be changed by the introduction of loan words that contain a sound in a different environment where it did not normally occur, e.g. voiceless alveolar [s] in word-initial position before vowels. In other instances it may also increase the frequency of a sound in a particular environment.

8.2.5.1 Intervocalic voiced labio-dental [-v-]

In MHG there was a contrast between voiceless /f/ and voiced /v/ medially between vowels: *hoffe* 'I hope' and *hove* 'farm'. The voiced /v/ was not very frequent and merged with the voiceless /f/. Where medial [v] does occur, spelt either <v> or <w>, in NHG the words come either from Low German (*Möwe*, *stowen* 'to stew'), from French (*brave, Initiative*), or from other languages: *Lava* (Italian), *Diwan* (Turkish/Persian). The occurrence of intervocalic /v/ in *Löwe* is probably the result of a spelling pronunciation. In this instance a previous intervocalic contrast, lost through merger, has been re-introduced in NHG through foreign loans.

8.2.5.2 Initial voiceless alveolar fricative [s-]

In standard pronunciation in NHG initial <s> is pronounced with some voice. In Austria and South Germany it is devoiced. Whatever the phonetic details, there is no phonemic contrast in initial prevocalic position between a voiced and a voiceless alveolar fricative as there is medially between vowels: *reisen* /z/ vs *reißen* /s/. However, in standard NHG, words with a voiceless initial [s] have been introduced so that contrasts such as *sechs* /z/ vs *Sex* /s/ have arisen. The main sources have been English (*Safe, Set, Single, surfen*) and French (*Saison, Satin, Souffleuse, Souper*). In most cases there is a voiced and a voiceless variant so that the development of this new opposition or new distribution of [s] is possibly rather speculative.

8.2.5.3 Initial alveolar affricate [tʃ-]

In MHG the alveolar affricate [tʃ] occurred in the word *tiutsch* and the incidence of the sound increased in the early modern period. The exception to this was in initial position before vowels. In NHG, however, [tʃ] has gradually increased its frequency and also appears initially before vowels. By the beginning of the twentieth century *Tschako, tschau, tschüss* and *Tschapka* were recorded as well as the names *Tschechen, tschechisch, Tscherkessel-in. DR* (2006) can add *Tschador* and the onomatopoetic *tschilpen* and *tsching* as well as the name *Tschetschnien*. There are also several colloquial Austrian words, such as *Tschepperl* and *Tschick*. Ebner (1998) lists twenty words with initial [tʃ]. Again the extension of this affricate to initial prevocalic position is due to loans.

8.2.6 New morphophonemic alternations

Not only does NHG have new phonemes through borrowing and changes in the distribution of phonemes, but there are also some new morphophonemic alternations. These do not tend to introduce new phonemes but make use of existing phonemes:

/d/ – /z/: *divid+ieren: Divis+ion; kollidieren, Kollision*
/t/ – /s/: *diskutieren, Diskussion; emittieren, Emission*
/ts/ – /k/: *produzieren, Produktion; reduzieren, Reduktion*
/kt/ – /ks/: *annektieren, Annexion; flektieren, Flexion*

8.2.7 New word stress patterns: word-final stress

This mostly concerns the stress that borrowed suffixes bear. Most derivational suffixes in loan words from Latin and French bear the main word stress: + x + ′x (*nerv+ös, Stud+ent*). In native words it is the stem vowel that bears the main stress: ′x + x (*ein+sam, Köch+in*). In loan words the suffix is still stressed, even when it is followed by an unstressed schwa: *Cour′age, Tab′elle*. The following non-native suffixes bear the main word-stress:

Noun and adjective suffixes
-*al*: *horizontal, kontinental*
-*ant*: *Demonstrant, Spekulant; militant, relevant*
-*anz*: *Dominanz, Militanz*
-*ar*: *Kommisar, Velar; modular, zellular*
-*är*: *Funktionär, Revolutionär; legendär, reaktionär*
-(*at*)*ion*: *Konfirmation, Reservation*
-*ei*: *Malerei, Spielerei*
-*ell*: *institutionell, traditionell*
-*ent*: *Korrespondent, Produzent; permanent, turbulent*
-*enz*: *Differenz, Frequenz*
-*esk*: *balladesk, kafkaesk*
-*eur*: *Ingenieur, Masseur*
-*ie*: *Chirurgie, Therapie*
-*ier* [ie:]: *Portier, Saisonier*

-ier [iːr]: *Passagier, Pionier*
-ist: *Alpinist, Chronist*
-(i)tät: *Formalität, Elektrizität*
-iv: *Kollektiv, Missiv, expansiv, subjektiv*
-ös: *infektiös, religiös*
-thek: *Bibliothek, Spielothek*
-ur: *Agentur, Reparatur*
Suffixes with schwa or other vowel after the main stress
-abel: *komfortabel, tolerabel*
-ibel: *divisibel, reduzibel*
-ade: *Blockade, Promenade*
-age: *Kartonage, Reportage*
-elle: *Kriminelle, Salmonelle*
-ieren: *fotografieren, telefonieren*
-ismus: *Kapitalismus, Optimismus*
-itis: *Bronchitis, Cellulitis*
-oge: *Biologe, Geologe*
-ose: *Diagnose, Neurose*

In many French and Latin loan words the stress is on the final vowel, even if it is not a productive suffix. The following are a selection of examples: *Sopr'an, Doktor'and, Konzentr'at, Result'at, Niv'eau, In'sekt, Proj'ekt, Magn'et, Pak'et, Kotol'ett, Tabl'ett, Toil'ette, Vign'ette, rap'id, hybr'id, Men'ü.*

8.2.8 The sounds of English post-1945 loans

In the twentieth century, particularly since 1945, it was English, especially American English, which was the main source of borrowing for German. An investigation by Siegl (1989: 334–87) registered an increase in the number of borrowed words listed in both the Mannheim and Leipzig *Duden Rechtschreibung* volumes from the fourteenth to the eighteenth editions only in the case of English. The number of English loans, or Anglicisms, rose from 868 (2.9 per cent) to 1,404 (3.89 per cent). Surveys of English influence are provided by Carstensen (1965), Stanforth (1968) and Viereck (1984, 1986). A detailed lexicographical work is Carstensen *et al.* (2001). It contains relevant material for our purposes, although the emphasis is on the written language, whereas we are concerned here primarily with the pronunciation of English loans. Fink (1980) investigated the pronunciation of forty-four English words and phrases and found a great variety of pronunciations for each word. Students, academics and pupils were, not surprisingly, the groups whose pronunciation and understanding of English loans was the best. The skill in reproducing English sounds depended to a great extent on the amount of linguistic training of the speaker. Younger speakers were also better than older ones. In this section we shall discuss some ways in which German speakers adapt English loans to their own sound patterns. In many cases information in dictionaries confirms these observations.

8.2.8.1 Pronunciation of English vowels

For the English diphthongs [ei] and [əu] German speakers substitute either [e:] or [ɛ:], e.g. *Trainer*, *Spray*, and [o:], e.g. *Soul*, *Toast*. The long central vowel [ɜ:] (English *girl*, *shirt*) does not exist in German and often [ø:] is substituted for it. Similarly the short unrounded low [ʌ] (*cut*, *cup*) does not exist in German and [a] is used instead by German speakers in words like *Cutter*, and in a few cases even the informal spelling *a* may be found, e.g. *Bags Banny* (*Bugs Bunny*). The vowel in the first component of *Curry-Wurst* is pronounced [œ].

   The low front [æ] in RP (*man*, *sat*) is perceived by German speakers to be closer to [ɛ] than [a] and is consequently pronounced [ɛ]. It is sometimes written *ä* in brand names, e.g. *Das Big-Mäc* (hamburger), or to Germanicize foreign words in informal spellings, e.g. *Cräcker*, *Täcks* 'cream cracker', 'tack'. In other cases words containing English [æ] are pronounced [ɛ] but the vowel is spelt *a* as in English, e.g. the older loan *Tram* (1875) and also modern *trampen* 'to hitch-hike' and *Gag*. This sound substitution reflects an old-fashioned RP value for short <a> in English. The <a> tends nowadays to be pronounced [a], especially in the midlands and north of England (Kerswill 2007: 49).

8.2.8.2 Pronunciation of English consonants

We have already mentioned the English initial cluster [dʒ] that does not exist in German (8.2.3.1). The voiceless affricate [tʃ] is often substituted for it (*Job*, *Jeans*, *Jet*). The German uvular *r* [R] is substituted for the English prevocalic or intervocalic flapped [ɾ] (*Trainer*, *Sherry*). Other differences do not result from the absence of the sound in German but from its different distribution. Intervocalic voiceless [s] occurs in German (*reißen*, *wissen*), but in initial position before vowels a voiced [z] is used in standard German (initial [s] does occur in Austria and south Germany). In general most German speakers use initial [s] without difficulty in English loans (*Safe*, *Set*, *Single*,

Software, Surfing). However, some English loans with <s> do occur with [z], which is an indication of their integration into German. The prefix *Super-* /*super-* which is added to adjectives or nouns (*supermodern, Supershow*) is also pronounced with [z], as is the less common prefix *sub-*. Medial <s> in German is usually pronounced [z], whereas in English it can be pronounced [s]. When German borrows the word *Leasing* into German the medial <s> is pronounced [z].

A general rule of German phonology is that all obstruents in word- or morpheme-final position are voiceless, which is not the case in English, where both voiced and voiceless consonants occur (*cab, cap*). This means that final voiced consonants in English loans become devoiced in German speech: *Job* [tʃɔp], *live* [laif], cf. *Live-Sendung* [laifzɛnduŋ] 'live-broadcast'. The distinction in English between the final consonants in *live* /v/ and *life* /f/ is not maintained in German, where word-final devoicing is applied.

8.2.8.3 Consonant clusters

The English initial consonant cluster *tw-* does not occur in German but with the borrowing of a number of words (*Tweed, Twill, Twinset, twisten*) it has been re-introduced into German (see 8.2.4.3). NHG has no clusters of *s* + consonant in native words due to a sound change of [s] → [ʃ] before initial consonants, leaving only clusters of [ʃ] + consonant: *Spaten, Stück, Schloss, Schrift, schmelzen, schneiden*. English on the other hand has only one cluster of [ʃ] + consonant (*shrimp*); the other clusters are [s] + consonant: *stand, slow, small, snow*. Consequently any words borrowed from English with initial [s] + consonant are either felt to be unassimilated loans and pronounced [sp-, st-] etc. (e.g. *Spike, Star*), or else they become integrated and are pronounced [ʃp-, ʃt-] etc., e.g. *Sport, Stop(p)*. The fluctuation of pronunciation can be seen easily by consulting any monolingual or pronouncing dictionary.

8.3 Attitudes to foreign words

We saw how a tradition of purism developed in German linguistic thought that had a peak in the period after the unification of Germany in the nineteenth century. A wave of nationalistic fervour culminated in the replacement of 760 official postal and transport terms in 1874 by the Postmaster-General Heinrich von Stephan (1831–97) by German equivalents, e.g. *Briefumschlag* for *Couvert*, *Postanweisung* for *Mandat*, *Postkarte* for *Korrespondenzkarte*.

This tradition of purism and translation of foreign words continued into the twentieth century but after 1945 more moderate views prevailed and the *Gesellschaft für deutsche Sprache*, re-founded in 1947, expressly forbade any 'witch-hunt' of foreign words. The Dudenverlag, while still publishing a separate *Fremdwörterbuch*, are happy to accept assimilated loans, especially as technical terms if they are part of a specialist jargon, in the ten-volume *Großes Wörterbuch der deutschen Sprache* (1999). Lay opinions about English loans range from their use being regarded as 'a laziness of thinking', 'besmirching our language' through 'kow-towing to the Americans', 'separating groups in society' to 'endangering national identity' (Stickel 1984: 43–7). In the survey by Stickel and Volz (1999: 19–23) the informants identified English loans as being the main area of language innovation. In addition, 26.5 per cent considered this development to be *besorgniserregend* (giving rise to concern).

An expression of this concern has been the formation and activities of the *Verein Deutsche Sprache*, which was founded in 1997 orginally as *Verein zur Währung der deutschen Sprache* but changed its name in April 2000. It has about 30,000 members and one of its goals is to help German maintain itself from being overwhelmed by English words. It does this by producing an *Anglizismenindex*, with suggestions of German equivalents of English words, awarding 'prizes' for *Sprachpanscher des Jahres* (language adulterator of the year) and writing to institutions and individuals about their linguistic usage. This is all in the tradition of German purism but may be connected with animosity towards foreigners as well and right-wing political views. Pfalzgraf (2003) and (2006) are detailed studies of the situation. In general, critics inveigh against *Denglish* (only recorded in *DR* in 2000 as a pejorative term), a mixture of German and English beloved of advertisers.

In real linguistic terms, however, English words probably amount to no more than 4 per cent of German vocabulary. Siegl (1989) shows how the number of English words in *DR* from 1949 to 1986 only rose from 868 (2.9 per cent) to 1,404 (3.89 per cent). The frequency of English loans varies according to text type. They mostly occur in specialist language vocabulary such as that of computers. Hoberg (2000) and Barbour (2001) play down the alarmist views of those who claim that loans are a danger to German. The speakers in the long history of German have decided which words they want to have in the language. This has also meant that new sounds (8.2.1) or combinations of sounds (8.2.3) have been introduced into German or sounds (8.2.2) or combinations of sounds (8.2.4) that have died out through phonetic change have been re-introduced into German.

QUESTIONS

1 Which new consonants have been introduced into German through loan words?

2 What languages have been the main sources of the borrowing of new sounds into German?

3 How far is [R] a borrowed sound in German?

4 What has been the effect of borrowing on the system of unstressed vowels in German?

5 How has German word stress been affected by borrowing?

6 What consonant clusters have been 're-introduced' into German by borrowing?

7 How has German dealt with nasal vowels in the words it has borrowed from French?

8 In what ways has English provided new sounds and combinations of sounds for German?

9 By examining the form of the following words decide which of them have been borrowed into German: *Orange*, *Pfeife*, *Twen*, *Single*, *Tofu*, *sterben*, *Träne*, *Tschador*, *smart*, *Echo*. How easy was your decision and why?

10 Read and summarize the following extract. How would you as a teacher of German or a German linguist respond to it?

War of words

The use of English terms by German speakers is of increasing concern to linguistic purists in Europe's biggest country, writes Ben Aris (*Guardian*, Tuesday 9 September 2003):

Fed up with the language of Goethe being corrupted with additions such as 'die kiddies' and 'der call centre', Germany's politicians are proposing to ban civil servants from using 'Denglish' – German mixed with English – in the workplace.

Over the last decade Denglish has become widely used by schoolchildren, advertisers and businesses, and traditionalists are starting to fight back.

The trend is being pushed by globalisation, the Germans' love of holidays and the internet, where Germans have adopted the hi-tech jargon wholesale.

Even perfectly good German words such as die Rechenanlage have been abandoned in favour of the more international sounding der computer. At the same time Germans abroad find few speak their language, and the numbers of other nationals studying German continue to fall.

The philological protectionists are hoping to strike a blow for pure German at a cultural conference next month, when 16 states will get together to call on Berlin's 140,000 civil servants to stop using English in the workplace.

The traditionalists meet once a month to pare Anglicisms from the language and include them on a list of banned words. They have also complained to the church for using English in sermons and claim that companies with Denglish names listed on the German stock market are failing faster than those with pure German names.

Abroad, the German language is in trouble, with the number of students choosing to study it falling every year. German education authorities called for a campaign to 'sex up' their language in a desperate effort to encourage more young people to take German at school.

9 Alternations

9.1 Introduction

We have been concerned up to now with the occurrence of sounds in contrast and have established the inventory of vowel and consonant phonemes for German. In this chapter we will deal with the alternation between sounds in different contexts.

Many words do not simply occur in one form. As a basis for our description we will discuss two cases of words that show an alternation of sounds:

(1) a medial voiced obstruent alternates with a word- or morpheme-final voiceless obstruent: *loben – Lob, neiden – Neid, mögen – mag; brave – brav, lesen – las*

(2) a short or long back vowel alternates with a short or long front vowel: *muss – müssen, Tuch – Tücher, Loch – Löcher, Lohn – Löhne, schwach – Schwäche, Waage – wägen*

The first of these alternations is known as word-final devoicing (*Auslautverhärtung*) and is an automatic process conditioned by the phonetic context. The second alternation is known as umlaut, or mutation, and is not automatically conditioned by the phonetic context but by a complex number of conditions, mostly grammatical, e.g. noun plural, Subjunctive II, or by which suffix follows. These conditions will be considered in detail in 9.3.3. We can thus divide sound alternations into automatic alternations and morphophonemic or morphophonological alternations, where the conditioning factors are not automatic nor necessarily phonetic.

9.1.1 Distinctive features

Before we illustrate the wide range of both consonantal and vocalic alternation in German we must first deal with some basic concepts that are used by linguists to describe these.

175

First of all it is necessary to recall our discussion in Chapter 5 about the Prague definition of the phoneme as comprising a bundle of distinctive features shown by a system of oppositions.

Each phonological segment in German can be characterized by a unique set of features that may be present (marked by [+]) or absent (marked by [–]). The most widely used set of distinctive features is derived from those used for English by Chomsky and Halle (1968). Wurzel (1970: 194–208) applied them to German. Benware (1986: Chapter 6) describes several generative rules. They have, however, been subject to some changes over the last few decades. We shall use an eclectic selection of features, informed by the discussion in Kohler (1995), Wiese (1996) and Fox (2005: 64–71).

Most of the features used here are similar to articulatory terms that we have used in Chapters 3 and 4. The major classes are characterized by a [+] or [–] value for certain features. The feature [+consonantal] is used to distinguish the consonants from the vowels. What we have described as manner of articulation is reflected in [+delayed release] for the affricates – used by Fox (2005) and originally from Chomsky and Halle (1968) – and [+continuant] for the fricatives, but the plosives are described as [–delayed release, +obstruent]. The nasals and liquids are [–obstruent]. Benware, Kohler and Wiese do not use a feature to describe the unitary affricates since they analyse them as a cluster of two consonants.

The features for place of articulation also present a few problems. In practice this is a continuum in the oral cavity and the application of a binary [+/–] system to it is rather artificial. It is here that the greatest divergence appears in the descriptions by linguists. One suggestion would be to use features such as [labial], [apical], which show a clear reference to articulation. Another suggestion would be to use less familiar terms such as [anterior], produced in the front of the mouth, i.e. labial and alveolar, and [coronal], produced in the central part of the mouth. We will follow Wiese (1996: 20) and use the features [labial], [dental], [coronal] and [dorsal] to distinguish places of articulation. In addition we will the feature [high], referring to tongue height, to distinguish between /s/ and /ʃ/. Kohler (1995: 161) uses [+/–eng] (narrow), referring to the shape of the groove of the tongue to distinguish between these two sounds. Figure 9.1 sets out the distinctive features of the German consonant system.

Some of the features are the same as, or similar to, traditional articulatory terms for the descriptions of sounds. The feature [nasal] is used in their traditional way for [m n ŋ]. The term [voice] is also used in its traditional meaning. The feature [syllabic] characterizes vowels, and [consonantal], consonants. [+obstruent] refers to plosives and fricatives whereas [–obstruent]

	pf	ts	p	b	t	d	k	g	f	v	s	z	ʃ	ʒ	j	ç	x	m	n	ŋ	l	r	h
syllabic	−	−	−	−	−	−	−	−	−	−	−	−	−	−	−	−	−	−	−	−	−	−	−
consonantal	+	+	+	+	+	+	+	+	+	+	+	+	+	+	+	+	+	+	+	+	+	+	+
delayed release	+	+	−	−	−	−	−	−	−	−	−	−	−	−	−	−	−	−	−	−	−	−	−
continuant	−	−	−	−	−	−	−	−	+	+	+	+	+	+	+	+	+	−	−	−	−	+	+
obstruent	+	+	+	+	+	+	+	+	+	+	+	+	+	+	+	+	+	−	−	−	−	−	+
nasal	−	−	−	−	−	−	−	−	−	−	−	−	−	−	−	−	−	+	+	+	−	−	−
voice	−	−	−	+	−	+	−	+	−	+	−	+	−	+	+	−	−	+	+	+	+	+	−
labial	+	−	+	+	−	−	−	−	+	+	−	−	−	−	−	−	−	+	−	−	−	−	−
anterior	+	+	+	+	+	+	−	−	+	+	+	+	+	−	−	−	−	+	+	−	+	−	−
dental	−	−	−	−	−	−	−	−	+	+	−	−	−	−	−	−	−	−	−	−	−	−	−
coronal	−	+	−	−	+	+	−	−	−	−	−	+	+	+	+	−	−	−	−	−	−	−	−
dorsal	−	−	−	−	−	−	+	+	−	−	−	−	−	−	−	+	+	−	−	+	−	−	−
high	−	−	−	−	−	−	+	+	−	−	−	−	−	+	−	+	+	−	−	+	−	−	−
back	−	−	−	−	−	−	+	+	−	−	−	−	−	−	−	−	−	−	−	+	−	−	−

Figure 9.1   Distinctive features of German consonants

	iː	ɪ	yː	ʏ	uː	ʊ	eː	ɛ	øː	œ	oː	ɔ	ɛː	ɑː	a
syllabic	+	+	+	+	+	+	+	+	+	+	+	+	+	+	+
consonantal	−	−	−	−	−	−	−	−	−	−	−	−	−	−	−
high	+	+	+	+	+	+	−	−	−	−	−	−	−	−	−
low	−	−	−	−	−	−	−	−	−	−	−	−	+	+	+
back	−	−	−	−	+	+	−	−	−	−	+	+	−	+	+
rounded	−	−	+	+	+	+	−	−	+	+	+	+	−	−	−
long	+	−	+	−	+	−	+	−	+	−	+	−	+	+	−

Figure 9.2   Distinctive features of German vowels

describes a group of consonants comprising the nasals and liquids for which the term sonant, or resonant, is also used. The feature [continuant] is used for those sounds whose articulation does not involve any occlusion of the organs of speech in the vocal tract. Other features, such as [high], [back], have typically been used to describe vowels but in generative phonology have been extended to cover both vowels and consonants, [high] being used for palatal, post-alveolar and velar sounds and [back] for velar sounds. The features [anterior] and [coronal] are more unfamiliar, the former designating both labial and alveolar sounds, the latter alveolar or dental sounds.

The vowels of German can be represented by Fig. 9.2 showing their distinctive features.

$$\begin{bmatrix} +\text{obstruent} \\ +\text{voice} \end{bmatrix} \quad -----> [-\text{voice}]/\#$$

Figure 9.3   Rule of word-final obstruent devoicing

The features [rounded] and [long] are used solely to apply to vowels. The other features have occurred in the description of the consonants although no consonants in German are characterized as [low].

9.1.2 Underlying forms and phonological rules

Generative phonology dispenses with the notion of the phoneme altogether and uses phonological distinctive features, as its basic means of distinguishing between words and also for characterizing sounds. It starts with so-called underlying forms, roughly equivalent to base allomorphs to which it also applies phonological rules. Thus the [ra:d-] of *Rades* [ra:dəs] and the [ra:t] of *Rad* are morpheme variants, allomorphs, from which one is chosen as a base, or underlying, form from which the other can be derived by a phonological rule. Through the use of underlying forms and rules this theory aims to be able to make more widely applicable generalizations about the phonology of the language, e.g. instead of saying that intervocalic [b d g v z] become [p t k f s] in word- and syllable-final position a statement can be made that any voiced obstruent becomes voiceless in that position.

In the account of German consonant phonemes we saw how no voiced obstruents occurred word-finally, whereas intervocalically both voiced and voiceless sounds occurred. Thus if [bunt] is the nom. and acc., [bund+əs] the gen., then the underlying form will be either of the two forms. The choice between them will be determined by whether the other one can be derived easily by a phonological rule. A general rule changing voiced obstruents in final position into voiceless obstruents will describe this feature of German consonant distribution. Thus to return to our example, [bund] will be the underlying form and will be changed into [bunt] by a phonological rule which states that 'a voiced obstruent becomes voiceless in word-final position'. This rule consists of three parts: the structural description, i.e. stating what segment it will change, the structural change, describing how the segment has been changed, and lastly the environment of the change. This rule can be formalized as in Fig. 9.3.

The rule has three parts: (1) the structural description: it applies to all voiced obstruents; (2) the structural change: they become voiceless; (3) the context: in word- or syllable-final position.

$$\begin{bmatrix} + \text{continuant} \\ - \text{voice} \\ + \text{back} \end{bmatrix} \quad -\!-\!> \quad [-\text{back}] \quad / \begin{bmatrix} + \text{syllabic} \\ - \text{back} \end{bmatrix}$$

Figure 9.4   Rule fronting [x] to [ç]

The application of such a word-final devoicing rule will derive the nom. and acc. surface form [bunt] from underlying [bund]. The alternation [t]–[d] involves the phonemes /t/ and /d/ and is an automatically, phonetically conditioned alternation. Another alternation that can be described by a phonological rule is that of [x] and [ç], e.g. *Loch* [lɔx], *Löcher* [lœçər]. In this case the underlying form of the plural would be [lœxər] to which a phonological rule would apply, changing it from a velar fricative to a palatal fricative. It might be formulated as in Fig. 9.4.

Here again the rule has three parts: (1) the structural description: it applies to voiceless fricatives that are back ([x] is the only candidate); (2) the structural change: the place of articulation becomes palatal ([ç]); (3) the environment is after a vowel that is front.

The alternation between the underlying voiced [d] and surface [t] was an alternation between units that in a phonemic approach are phonemes. The alternation between [x] and [ç] in a phonemic approach is an alternation between allophones. Generative phonology makes no distinction between these two particular levels of representation, regarding both surface forms as being derived from the application of phonological rules to underlying forms. The underlying forms are sometimes called the deep, or systematic phonemic, level and the derived forms the surface, or systematic phonetic, level. The traditional phonemic level, as used by phonemicists, is referred to as the taxonomic, or autonomous, phonemic level.

9.2 Automatic alternations

These are alternations that are conditioned automatically by the phonetic context. The best-known example is that of word-final devoicing.

9.2.1 Word-final devoicing

This rule devoices any medial voiced obstruent in word- or syllable-final position. The rule is set out in Fig. 9.3. The spelling does not reflect this at all (see 6.2). This rule was introduced into German at the end of the OHG period (see 12.7.2). Examples are: *loben* > *Lob*; *glauben* > *glaubhaft*; *kleiden* > *Kleid*; *Kinder* > *Kindheit*; *schlagen* > *Schlag*; *Tage* > *täglich*; *braver* > *brav*; *lesen* > *las*, *lesbar*. There is one possible example of the devoicing of [ʒ], *beigenfarbig* > *beige*. A detailed investigation into the phonetics and phonology of word and syllable devoicing in German is Brockhaus (1995).

9.2.2 Treatment of schwa

Schwa, which only occurs as an unstressed vowel, is subject to deletion or elision. In informal speech it is invariably deleted in the endings *-em*, *-en*, *-el*. *DAW* (2005: 32–4) sets up complicated rules whereby [ə] is deleted in the ending *-em* only after fricatives, in the ending *-en* it is deleted after plosives and fricatives and in the ending *-el* it is deleted after plosives, fricatives and nasals. These 'rules' are valid for a more careful level of speech than the normal colloquial variety. After the deletion of [ə] the syllabic nasal is assimilated to the point of assimilation of the preceding labial or velar plosive. Thus [leːbn̩] becomes [leːbm̩] and [zaːgn̩] becomes [zaːgŋ̍].

In the third person singular present of regular, or weak, verbs there is an alternation between the ending [-ət] if the stem ends in /t/ or /d/ (*rettet*, *redet*) or a combination of /m/ or /n/ preceded by an obstruent (*atmen*, *atmet*; *regnen*, *regnet*; *zeichnen*, *zeichnet*); and [-t] (no schwa): *glaubt*, *sagt*, *kauft*, *küsst*, *mischt*, *macht*, *stimmt*, *verbannt*. In the case of irregular, or strong, verbs this syncope rule does not apply to verbs with stems in /t/ or /d/, if there is a change of stem vowel in the third person singular present: *findet* (without syncope) but *hält* < *halten*, *tritt* < *treten* and *lädt* < *laden*.

9.2.3 Alternations involving [ɐ]

The vocalization of postvocalic *r* to [ɐ] after long vowels and diphthongs in word- or syllable-final position leads to alternation with a medial [r] in those forms that have inflected forms. The spelling is not affected: *euer* [-ɐ] > *eure*; *ihr* [-ɐ] > *ihre*. In colloquial speech the elision of [ə] in unstressed syllables leads to further vocalization of *r*: *Tür* [-ɐ] > *Türen* [tyːrən] but also [tyːɐn].

9.3 Morphophonological or morphophonemic alternations

Morphophonological, or morphophonemic, alternations are alternations that are not conditioned by the phonetic context but by other factors. These rules affect a differing number of words and are really part of a continuum, but for practical purposes they can be divided into three groups (Haspelmath 2002: 192ff.): relic alternations, common alternations and productive alternations.

9.3.1 Relic alternations

9.3.1.1 Reflexes of the High German Sound Shift

These apply to a small number of words and are not applied to newly created words or borrowings. Native speakers are not normally conscious of their status as alternations. Only by consulting etymological dictionaries and historical grammars do these alternations and connections come to light. In most cases the words in which the alternation occurs belong to different word classes. The alternation between the /ts/ in *sitzen* and the /s/ in *gesessen* is one of the very view examples that occur within a paradigm.

The chief exemplars of these relic alternations are the forms that reflect historically the Second, or High German, Sound Shift. The affricates and voiceless plosives reflect historically geminate consonants (see 12.7.1). The labials are represented by a postvocalic alternation between the affricate /pf/ and the voiceless fricative /f/ (*Tropfen – triefen, rupfen – raufen* 'to pull, to tear (one's hair)', *schöpfen – schaffen*) and also between voiced /b/ and voiceless /p/: *Rabe – Rappe* (Swiss *Rappen* 'a 10-cent coin'), *Knabe – Knappe*. The alveolars are represented by a postvocalic alternation between the affricate /ts/ and the voiceless fricative /s/ (*sitzen – gesessen, stutzen – stoßen, beizen – beißen, netzen – naß*) and also between voiced /d/ and voiceless /t/: *schneiden – geschnitten*. Since in the sound shift Germanic /k/ was not shifted to an affricate the postvocalic alternation among the palato-velars is between a voiceless fricative /x/ and a voiceless plosive /k/: *wachen – wecken, Dach – decken*. But there is also the alternation between /g/ and /k/: *neigen – nicken, Ziege – Zicke, Hage – Hecke*.

9.3.1.2 Some Germanic consonant alternations

A related group of alternations that appear to overlap with these relics of the Second Sound Shift are those that are labelled 'grammatical change'. They occur chiefly among the strong verbs. Sometimes they are also said to be accounted for by Verner's Law, a sub-set of the First, or Germanic, Sound Shift. These can be exemplified by an alternation between voiced and voiceless alveolar plosives: *leiden – gelitten, schneiden – geschnitten, sieden – gesotten*. The alternation between *ziehen* and *gezogen* normally fits in here, although the medial <h> is no longer pronounced. Many of the older alternations were levelled out in favour of one consonant: MHG *ih was – wir wâren* > NHG *ich war, wir waren*. The /s/ – /r/ still survives in *gewesen – war(en)*.

The suffix *-t* was used in the past to form nouns from verbs (*fahren – Fahrt*), but it is no longer productive in NHG. In the case of those verbs whose stem ended in an obstruent this became a voiceless fricative before the *-t*. In many cases the meaning of the noun is different from that of the verb: *geben – Gift* 'poison'. Examples of this relic alternation with labials: *graben – Gruft* (with the ablaut of stem vowel); palato-velars: *schlagen – Schlacht, tragen – Tracht, mögen* (originally 'to be able to') *– Macht*.

9.3.2 Common alternations

These apply to a larger number of items but tend not to apply to new words. Native speakers can probably recognize these alternations.

9.3.2.1 Vowel gradation

The irregular or strong verbs in German are characterized by a change of stem vowel to indicate differences in tense: present *singen* – past/preterite *sang* – past participle *gesungen*. These changes of stem vowel are known as vowel gradation or ablaut. They are not random but are patterned. In some verbs the infinitive has the same stem vowel as the past participle (*treten – getreten*), in others the stem vowel of the past is the same as that of the past participle (*ritt – geritten*). Historically in OHG and MHG there were six main patterns, called *Ablautreihen* (ablaut series), but due to vowel change and morphological levelling these classes have splintered into relic groups. In addition, the number of strong verbs has been reduced drastically through loss or the verb becoming regular (for details, see Russ 1978a: 114–19, 137f. and 154–9; Augst 1977). *DG* (1984: para. 208) lists thirty-nine vowel patterns that exist in NHG for 173 verbs, excluding prefixed and compound verbs, but sixteen of these are represented by only one verb each. The forms of the strong verbs will be taken from *DG* (1984: para. 220).

The patterns with the most verbs can be seen in Fig. 9.5.

Even within these patterns a phonological regularity occurs. The distribution of vowel length in the preterite of *reiten* and *bleiben* is conditioned by the final consonant of the stem. In verbs whose stem ends in a voiceless obstruent (*reiten, greifen, beißen, streichen*), the vowel in the preterite and past participle is short (*ritten, geritten; griffen, gegriffen; bissen, gebissen, strichen, gestrichen*), whereas in verbs whose stem ends in a voiced obstruent, or no consonant, the vowel in the preterite and past participle is long (*blieben, geblieben; mieden,*

Vowel pattern	present	preterite	Past participle	Number
ei – i – i	reiten	ritt(en)	geritten	23
i – a – u	binden	band(en)	gebunden	19
ei – i: – i:	bleiben	blieb(en)	geblieben	16
i: – o – o	fließen	floss(en)	geflossen	11
i: – o: – o:	biegen	bog(en)	gebogen	11
e – a – o	bergen	Barg(en)	geborgen	9

Figure 9.5   Vowel gradation patterns

gemieden; stiegen, gestiegen; priesen, gepriesen; liehen, geliehen). If we put these two groups together we have thirty-nine verbs showing the same pattern. There is a similar regulation of vowel length in the vowel in the preterite and past participle of *fließen*, with a short vowel before a voiceless obstruent (*flossen, geflossen*) and *biegen*, with a long vowel before a voiced obstruent or /r/, or if the stem ends in a vowel (*schoben, geschoben; fror, gefroren; floh, geflohen*). If we merge these two groups we have twenty-two verbs showing the same pattern. There is one exception in the vowel length regulation in the *fließen, biegen* groups: the verb *bieten*, whose stem ends in a voiceless plosive, nevertheless has a long vowel in the preterite and past participle: *boten, geboten*.

Another more subtle regulation of vowel quality occurs with verbs of the patterns, *i – a – u* and *e – a – o*. All the verbs with this pattern have a stem that ends in CC, of which the second consonant is an obstruent but the preceding consonant is always a nasal (*binden, finden, schwinden, sinken, trinken, winden*) or a liquid (/r/ or /l/) (*bergen, gelten, helfen, melken, schelten, sterben, werbe, werden* – preterite *ward* is old-fashioned, *werfen* and *bersten*, which has two consonants after /r/). DG has also counted verbs such as *singen, sang, gesungen* into the *i – a – u* pattern. Historically the velar nasal /ŋ/ has developed from a cluster of nasal + voiced palato-velar plosive. Thus these verbs fit into the pattern of verbs whose stem ends in a nasal + obstruent: [ziŋgən]. Originally these vowels had a stem in [e] that was raised to [i] before a nasal + obstruent (cf. Latin *ventus*, NHG *Wind*).

These tantalizing glimpses of earlier regularity have always challenged linguists to try and systematize the vowel gradations. The infinitive was not suitable to describe the pattern since it contained a variety of different vowels, so linguists turned their attention to the other parts of the verbs. Halle (1953) used as his starting point the stem vowels of the preterite, of which there are only four, which occurred both short and long: [u(:)], *trug, wusch, fuhr, schund*; [o(:)], *bot, zog, fror, goss*; [i(:)], *lief, hieß, kniff, fing*; [a(:)], *gab, traf, nahm, rann, half.* Using rules to derive other parts of the verbs he sets up seven classes, ranging from a membership of thirty-six down to one, representing 117 verbs. Generative linguists have described the strong verbs along similar lines. Ross (1967) sets up seven classes according to the varying stem forms of the verbs, like Wurzel (1970: 63–79). However, the rules proposed are not purely phonological but make use of more abstract features such as 'the present stem vowel = vowel in the past participle' (*geben – gegeben*) and 'preterite stem vowel = vowel in the past participle' (*boten – geboten*). These features are then given +/− values.

Apart from the distribution of vowel length and occurrence of [i u] before nasals the vowel alternations are independent of phonetic environment. Although there is only a very small group of simplex verbs (173), these do occur very frequently. Also some of these verbs form prefixed and compound verbs that retained the strong verb vowel gradations; for example, *nehmen* has sixty prefixed and compound forms while *kommen* has ninety-two prefixed and compound forms. They do seem to enjoy a certain amount of productivity. There is also some evidence that native speakers recognize these features. Although there is a mass of evidence from colloquial and dialect speech to show that strong verbs are becoming weak, there is also the evidence of jocular forms, such as *gewunken*, and colloquial forms, such as *frägt – frug – gefragen* for *fragt – fragte – gefragt*, that the intuition of native speakers does recognize some of the vowel gradation patterns.

9.3.2.2 Alternations in loan words

(i) Alternations between obstruents

The borrowing of a large number of loan words from Latin and Greek has led to the gradual adoption of borrowed consonantal alternations. The following alternations exist: (1) /t/ in a verb alternating with /s/ in a noun: *diskutieren, Diskussion; kompromittieren, Kompromiss;* /t/ in an adjective alternating with /s/ in a noun: *chaotisch, Chaos; caritativ, Caritas;* (2) /d/ in a verb and /z/ in a noun: *elidieren, Elision; suspendieren, Suspension;* (3) voiced obstruent in a verb alternating with a voiceless obstruent before the suffixes *-t, -tion, -tur: transkribieren, Transkription, Transkript; fungieren, Funktion; reagieren, Reaktion; korrigieren, Korrektur.*

(ii) Alternations involving the affricate /ts/

The letters <t> and <c> before front vowels in loan words are pronounced [ts] and often spelt <z> in established loans, e.g. *Zigarette, Elektrizität.* This alveolar affricate /ts/ frequently alternates with /k/: (1) /ts/ in a verb alternates with /k/ in a noun and/or adjective: *provozieren, Provokation, Provokateur, provokatorisch; musizieren, Musik, musikalisch*; (2) the same alternation also occurs before the suffixes *-tion, -t*: *produzieren, Produkt, Produktion; obduzieren, Obduktion*; (3) /ts/ in a noun alternates with /t/ in an adjective: *Evidenz, evident; Äquivalenz, äquivalent; Prominenz, prominent*.

9.3.3 Productive alternations: umlaut

Productive alternations apply to a large number of words and are often applied to newly formed words. Most native speakers will recognize that this alternation exists.

The prime example of a productive morphophonological alternation is umlaut. Historically it is a fronting, or palatalization, of a back vowel, including the fronting of the low vowel [a] to [e], under the influence of a following high front vowel or semi-vowel, e.g. [i iː j]. During the course of the history of German, specifically in MHG when unstressed vowels became reduced to schwa, the umlaut rule was no longer phonetically conditioned. Instead in NHG it has become an alternation between front rounded and back rounded vowels and between the front unrounded [e] and the low unrounded [a] in certain grammatical categories: (1) Noun plurals (9.3.3.1): *Gast – Gäste; Loch – Löcher*; (2) Comparison of adjectives (9.3.3.2): *lang – länger; groß – größer*; (3) 2nd and 3rd person sg. pres. of strong verbs (9.3.3.3): *schlafen – schläfst – schläft*; (4) in the Subjunctive II form; (5) after certain word formation suffixes (9.3.3.5).

Umlaut has been treated in several different ways according to different linguistic schools of thought:

(1) In traditional descriptions, occurrence of umlaut has been examined separately in each grammatical category (*DG* 1984).
(2) In a structural approach (Koekkoek 1965) umlaut has been seen more as an accompaniment to the main segmental morphemes.
(3) In a generative approach two directions have been discernible:
    (a) a purely phonological approach with abstract underlying forms. Bach and King (1970) illustrate this with the schema in Fig. 9.6: the umlaut rule is made to function phonetically by setting up abstract forms with unstressed [i]. A vowel reduction rule, not motivated by NHG forms, then produced the relevant surface forms;
    (b) a morphological approach (Wurzel 1970) that differentiates between: (i) suffixes marked [+umlaut], [+umlaut causing]

underlying forms	bu:xir	gasti	armu
umlaut rule	by:xir	gesti	n/a
vowel reduction	by:xər	gestə	armə

Figure 9.6   Umlaut and underlying forms

(+*umlauterzwingend*, +*umlautbewirkend*); (ii) stems marked [+pl. umlaut], [+comparative umlaut], [+derivational umlaut]. Umlaut is also triggered by clusters of morphological features, e.g. [+verb, +strong, +sg., −1st pers.].
Russ (1977) and Bergmeier and Fries (1979) are a critique of these theories. A theoretical discussion is Wiese (1996: 181–94).

In our present account we will be accept that umlaut is conditioned by different factors and see how in some areas it is productive and in others not so. However, rather than complicate matters everything connected with umlaut will be dealt with in this section.

9.3.3.1 Umlaut in noun plurals

Umlaut occurs in nouns of all three genders in NHG and together with the endings -*er*, -*e* or absence of ending. The ending -*er* is always accompanied by umlauting the stem vowel of the singular where possible with neuter nouns (*Buch* – *Bücher*, *Loch* – *Löcher*) and a few masculine nouns (*Mann* – *Männer*, *Wald* – *Wälder*). In the case of the absence of ending, this only occurs with nouns ending in -*el*, -*en* and -*er*: *Mäntel*, *Gärten*, *Väter*. These nouns are usually regarded as allomorphs of the nouns ending in -*e*, such as *Tage*.
Augst (1975) is a detailed examination of the plural system, giving statistics for the occurrence of endings and umlaut. The ending -*e* accompanied by umlauting of the stem vowel occurs in the majority of cases among feminine nouns whose stem vowel is susceptible to umlaut: *Hand* – *Hände*, *Wurst* – *Würste* (forty-seven out of fifty-one examples according to Augst 1975: 43–6). Among the neuter nouns there is a much smaller number of nouns with umlaut and -*e* in the plural: *Flöße* 'rafts', *Klöster* (7 out of 101 examples according to Augst 1975: 46–8). However, in the formation of the plural in masculine monosyllabic nouns that add -*e* it is more difficult to say whether presence or absence of umlaut is the rule or the exception. It is not possible to predict the occurrence of umlaut from the phonetic ending of the stem. Of the pair *Aal* and *Saal*, both end in [l] and both add -*e* in the plural but it is only *Saal* that undergoes umlaut: *Säle*. Augst (1975: 39–43) reports that of 696 masculine

nouns with a stem vowel susceptible to umlaut, 297 showed umlaut and 409 did not.

However, those masculine nouns that take umlaut are very often frequently used monosyllabic forms. German grammars for second language learners very often stress the frequency of the use of umlaut and Korte (1986: 22) wants to set up as a rule that masculine nouns regularly take umlaut in the plural and Leys (1986: 303) wants to set up as a prototypical rule that masculine nouns show umlaut in the plural. Historically it is certainly true that the umlaut plural has increased its incidence among masculine nouns, being applied to loan words: *Pass, Plan, Rang, Tanz, Trumpf* (Paul 1920, 2: para. 10). Regional usage also differs slightly. In South Germany and Austria there are more words that have a plural umlaut, e.g. *Krägen* (Eichhoff 1977–2000: 4, map 79) and especially for Austria (Tatzreiter 1988: 82f.). Russ (1989: especially 63–5) was an attempt, using nonsense words with a group of twenty-five informants, to try and determine which of the two plural formations, with or without umlaut, was more regular for masculine nouns. The result was not clear. Globally, more words used umlaut in the plural: 172 (26.5 per cent) of the words were recorded with an umlaut plural plus -*e* by the informants, whereas 160 (24.6 per cent) of the words were recorded with only an -*e* ending and no umlaut. Among the individual words, there were thirteen words where the informants predominantly chose umlaut and nine words where the predominant choice was no umlaut. For three words the presence or absence of umlaut was equal. To sum up: the question of a productivity of umlaut in plural formation of masculine nouns was unclear, but there seemed a tendency for umlauted forms to predominate.

9.3.3.2 Umlaut in the comparison of adjectives

Another grammatical area where umlaut is used is in the formation of comparative and superlative forms for adjectives: *alt – älter – ältest*. Historically the forms with umlaut are the older but they represent a small, though frequently occurring, group. Augst (1971) maintains that the forms without umlaut are the regular ones. Out of his corpus of 141 monosyllabic adjectives only 25 occurred always with umlaut. These are mostly monosyllabic forms with the stem vowel *a, o* or *u*: *alt, arg, arm, hart, kalt, krank, lang, nah, scharf, schwach, schwarz, stark, warm; grob, groß, hoch; dumm, jung, klug, kurz*. Some words fluctuate (*bang, blass, fromm, glatt, karg, krumm, nass, rot, schmal*), although *DG* (1984: 518) recommends that the forms without umlaut are to be preferred in the standard language.

9.3.3.3 Umlaut in the present tense of strong verbs

As well as changing their stem vowel to form the past tense (*singen – sang*), strong verbs with stem vowels that are susceptible to umlaut (short and long *u*, *o* and *a*, as well as the diphthong *au*) umlaut the vowel in the second and third person singular present: *stoßen – stößt, fallen – fällt, tragen – trägt, laufen – läuft*. The only exceptions to this are: *kommen – kommt, rufen – ruft, saugen – saugt* and *schaffen* 'to create' *– schafft*.

9.3.3.4 Umlaut in Subjunctive II

Subjunctive II (SII) is formed from the past stem of strong and irregular verbs. The most frequent forms are *wär-* + endings and *hätt-* + endings. All the modal auxiliary verbs except *wollen* and *sollen*, plus *wissen*, form their SII forms by umlauting their past indicative forms: *durfte – dürfte, konnte – könnte, mochte – möchte, musste – müsste, wusste – wüsste*. The verb *brauchen*, which has come to be used as a modal auxiliary, has developed an analogical SII form with umlaut (*bräuchte*), although *Duden Grammatik* does not yet regard it as standard. In many instances the periphrastic construction of *würde* + infinitive has taken over from the synthetic subjunctive forms of strong verbs such as *fände*. Jäger (1971: 256–61), in his investigation of the subjunctive in written German, lists seventy-one verbs that occur with a synthetic SII form, excluding *sein* and *haben*, of which fifty-three, including prefixed and compound forms, have a stem vowel that is susceptible to umlaut. The most frequent of these are: *käme* (*kommen*), *gäbe* (*geben*), *wüsste* (*wissen*) and *stünde* (*stehen*).

9.3.3.5 Umlaut in derivational morphology

Wurzel (1970: 118–24), in his treatment of umlaut in derivational morphology, distinguishes between suffixes that always cause umlaut ([+*umlauterzwing-end*]) and those that only cause umlaut sometimes ([+*umlautbewirkend*]), and even then only in connection with certain stems. Benware (1986: 140) expands this ability to cause umlaut to 'always', 'few exceptions', 'sporadically' and 'frequently'. However, the detailed text-based study by Wellmann (1975: 38f.) shows that it is rather more a case of a continuum of umlaut with different noun suffixes. This can be seen in Fig. 9.7.

A similar picture emerges for adjectival suffixes, based on Kühnhold *et al.* (1978: 50ff.), although there are fewer of them as Fig. 9.8 shows.

Umlaut also occurs in the derivation of verbs. There are no clear suffixes that determine umlaut but there is a difference between the formation of

Suffix	%	+umlaut	−umlaut
-lein	95	Stündlein	Muttilein
-chen	90	Fässchen	Frauchen
-el	90	Bündel	Achtel
-e (abstract)	90	Länge	Starre
-in	90	Wölfin	Gattin
Ge … (-e)	90	Gelände	Gelaufe
-nis (neuter)	80	Verlöbnis	Erfordernis
-ling	80	Häftling	Rundling
-ner	70	Söldner	Afrikaner
-ler	70	Ausflügler	Sportler

Figure 9.7   Occurrence of umlaut with noun suffixes

Suffix	%	+umlaut	−umlaut
-lich	70	männlich	fraulich
-ig	40	bärtig	grasig
-isch	15	höhnisch	schulisch

Figure 9.8   Occurrence of umlaut with adjective suffixes

intransitive and transitive verbs. In the case of the former forms without umlaut predominate, whereas in the formation of transitive verbs umlaut predominates. Even in this instance there is a further distinction among transitive verbs formed from nouns where both umlauted and non-umlauted forms occur: *schroten < Schrot, salben < Salbe; häufen < Haufen, krönen < Krone*. Among transitive verbs formed from adjectives (*kränken < krank, lähmen < lahm*) about 80 per cent show umlaut (Kühnhold and Wellmann 1973: 24f.).

QUESTIONS

1   Illustrate the following distinctive features: [delayed release], [coronal], [high], [rounded].

2   Which of the following 'rules' are automatic alternations: word-final devoicing, umlaut, syncope in verbs, vowel gradation?

3   How far is vowel length predictable in the past tense of irregular verbs?

4   Give examples of two relic alternations.

5   How far do morphophonemic alternations apply to loan words?

6   Describe the phonetic process of umlaut.

7   In which grammatical categories in German is umlaut productive?

8   Which German noun suffixes have the greatest productivity with regard to
    umlaut?

9   Invent a list of ten nonsense words (see Russ 1989) with vowels that can take
    umlaut. Disguise them by also choosing ten words with vowels that cannot
    take umlaut. Then ask a group of foreign learners of German to put all the
    words into the plural. How many words actually occur with an umlauted
    vowel?

10 How far can the vowel gradation patterns of strong verbs be simplified to help
    foreign learners of German learn them?

10 Suprasegmental features and syllables

10.0 Introduction

The previous chapters have dealt with the segmental sounds of German, i.e those sounds that can be arrived at by the segmentation of the speech chain into C and V units. In this chapter we will deal with other phenomena that cover more than a single C and V place. These are called suprasegmental elements. The chief among them are word stress and intonation. We will not treat other features such as tempo and rhythm. Among the works that deal with these topics are MacCarthy (1975: 8–16); Kohler (1995: 186–200); C. Hall (2003: 109–37); Fox (2005: 88–100).

10.1 Word stress

It is a feature of languages like German that among the vowels in disyllabic words, one of the vowels is more prominent than the other, e.g. *Friéde*, *Aúto*, *Spónti*, *Pízza*. This prominence may express itself in more force of articulation, loudness, higher pitch and length. Such syllables are stressed, or accented. This stress is known as word stress and can best be shown by the pronunciation of words in isolation. Not all words, however, are stressed even in isolation. Definite and indefinite articles, monosyllabic prepositions and many other functional words never bear the stress. Some unstressed function words also undergo phonetic reduction but this is a function of sentence stress.

10.2 The placement of stress

The role of word stress in German is a complex one, but in general it is predictable and rules for its occurrence can be given.

In simple disyllabic words containing schwa, the stress falls on the other syllable: *bítte*, *beréit*. We can thus have both pattern 'stressed + unstressed' and 'unstressed + stressed'. We will mark a main stress with the accent mark ´ on the vowel. In making statements of stress placement rules a certain amount of morphological information is needed and also one needs to know whether we are describing native or foreign words.

Most monomorphemic disyllabic words, i.e. those that cannot be analysed into morphemes, have the ´x x stress pattern even if the unstressed vowel is not schwa: *Héring*, *Árbeit*, *Gúmmi*, *Théma*, *Kíno*, *Híndu*. In trisyllabic words with a final unstressed syllable the stress will always occur on the penultimate syllable. This is the case with *Forélle*, *Holúnder*, *Hornísse*, *lebéndig* and *Wachólder*, which are generally regarded as exceptions to stress rules. This regularity, which we can call the Penultimate Syllable Stress Rule, has the advantage that it can not only describe the stress placement but also account for the stress shift in such forms as *Proféssor* to *Professóren*, and *Jápan* to *Japáner*. The conditioning factor seems to be the suffix. To describe the regularities of stress it is best to distinguish between stems, or underived forms, and affixes. The unstressed suffixes of German can be divided into two groups: one which keeps the stress placement of the original form (*Kőnig – Kőnigin*), and a second group which makes the stress conform to the Penultimate Syllable Stress Rule, which involves a stress shift: *Jápan > Japáner*. Most native suffixes belong to the first group, e.g. *-chen* (*Wagen > Wägelchen*), *-heit* (*dunkel > Dunkelheit*), *-igkeit* (*müde > Müdigkeit*), *-ig* (*Kugel > kugelig*), *-lich* (*lesen > leserlich*), *-nis* (*hindern > Hindernis*), *-tum* (*Beamte > Beamtentum*), *-ung* (*verwirklichen > Verwirklichung*). In most cases there could be no shift anyway since the unstressed vowel *e* occurs before the suffix. The suffixes *-isch* and *-(i)aner* belong to the second group (*Amérika > Amerikáner*), as do the plural *-en/-e*: *Charákter*, *Charaktére*. Even those nouns that are of foreign origin and have final syllable stress follow the Penultimate Syllable Stress Rule before the suffixes of the second group: *Energíe > enérgisch*.

10.2.1 Suffixes

Suffixes fall into two main groups in German: (1) those that are always unstressed, and (2) those that are always stressed.

Group 1 comprises mostly native suffixes: (nouns) *-chen* (*Häuschen*), *-el* (*Deckel*), *-er* (*Bäcker*) (with variants *-ler – Sportler –* and *-ner*: *Pförtner*), *-heit/- keit* (*Freiheit*), *-ie* [-iə] (*Studie*) (new singular from loan word *Studien*), *-in* (*Lehrerin*), *-lein* (*Fräulein*), *-ling* (*Sträfling*), *-nis* (*Erkenntnis*), *-schaft* (*Landschaft*), *-tum* (*Eigentum*), *-ung* (*Werbung*); (adjectives) *-bar* (*denkbar*), *-ern* (*hölzern*), -*haft* (*wohnhaft*), -*ig* (*milchig*), -*isch* (*kindisch*), -*lich* (*glaublich*), -*los* (*hilflos*), -*mäßig* (*rechtsmäßig*), -*sam* (*langsam*).

Group 2 comprises mostly foreign suffixes: (nouns) -*ant*/-*ent* (*Lieferant, Student*), -*anz*/-*enz* (*Toleranz, Prominenz*), -*ar* (*Missionar*), -*är* (*Millionär*), -*erei* (*Bäckerei*), -*ie* (*Philosophie*), -*ier* (*Bankier*), -(*at*)*ion* (*Kontamination, Definition*), -*ismus* (*Kapitalismus*), -*ität* (*Qualität*), -*ist* (*Kapitalist*), -*ör* (*Frisör*); (adjectives) -*abel*/-*ibel* (*akzeptabel, sensibel*), -*al*/-*ell* (*ideal, aktuell*), -*ar*/-*är* (*atomar, humanitär*), -*iv* (*dekorativ*), -*os*/-*ös* (*kurios, nervös*).

The suffix -*ik* is an anomaly in that is stressed in some words, e.g. *Republík*, but not in others, e.g. *Grammátik*. According to Muthmann (1988: 477–83) there are seventeen words where the suffix -*ik* is stressed (*Musík, Physík*), but by far the greater number (eighty) where the stress is on the preceding syllable: *Lógik, Pánik, Phonétik*.

10.2.2 Prefixes

Prefixes occur with nouns, adjectives and verbs. These instances occur in verb morphology. Simple verb forms in German consist of a stressed followed by an unstressed syllable, *kómmen, káufen*. Derived verb forms in German are of basically two types: (1) verbs with an unstressed prefix occurring before the verbal stem: *ent+kommen, ver+kaufen*; (2) stressed prefixes before the verbal stem: *abfahren, mitkommen*.

The unstressed prefixes in Type 1 verbs are never separated from the verb stem: *Ich verkaufe das Buch, Ich verkaufte das Buch, Ich habe das Buch verkauft*. They are known as inseparable verbs. The inseparable prefixes are: *be-* (*bezahlen*), *ent-* (*entkommen*), *er-* (*erzählen*), *ge-* (*gehören*), *ver-* (*verkaufen*), *zer-* (*zerstören*).

The stressed prefixes of Type 2 verbs can be separated from the verb stem: *Ich fahre heute ab, Ich fuhr gestern ab, Ich bin gestern abgefahren*. They are known as separable prefixes and are always stressed. These separable prefixes are: *ab-* (*abgeben*), *an-* (*anfangen*), *auf-* (*aufstehen*), *aus-* (*aussteigen*), *bei-* (*beitragen*), *ein-* (*einsteigen*), *empor-* (*emporkommen*), *fort-* (*fortfahren*), *los-* (*loslassen*), *nach-* (*nachtragen*), *nieder-* (*niederschlagen*), *weg-* (*weggehen*).

In other instances, however, the placement of stress, i.e. on the prefix or verb stem, is distinctive. This is the case with the verbal prefixes *durch, über, um* and *unter*. When they are stressed they are separable and when they are unstressed they are inseparable. This stress contrast correlates with a semantic contrast. Fig. 10.1 gives examples of this.

There is a larger list of contrasting words in Rausch and Rausch (1991: 161f.). Kühnhold and Wellmann (1973) gives some statistics from the corpus

prefix	verb	meaning (stressed)	meaning (unstressed)
durch	brechen	'to break (in two)'	'to break (through)'
durch	laufen	'to wear out'	'to run through'
durch	schneiden	'to cut through'	'to pierce' (fig.)
durch	setzen	'to carry through'	'to infiltrate'
über	fahren	'to cross over'	'to knock down'
über	gehen	'to turn into sth.'	'to pass over'
über	setzen	'to take across'	'to translate'
über	treten	'to go over, to flood'	'to cross, infringe'
um	bauen	'to renovate'	'to enclose'
um	fahren	'to run down'	'to bypass'
um	reißen	'to tear down'	'to outline'
um	ziehen	'to move house'	'to surround'
unter	schieben	'to push underneath'	'to insinuate'
unter	stehen	'to take shelter'	'to be subject to'
unter	stellen	'to store'	'to make subordinate to, to suppose'
unter	ziehen	'to put on underneath'	'to undergo sth.'

Figure 10.1   Semantic contrasts in the use of verbal prefixes *durch-*, *über-*, *um-* and *unter-*

about the frequency of separable and inseparable verbs with *durch-*, *über-*, *um-* and *unter-*. There are 343 verbs with separable *durch-* as against 265 with inseparable *durch-*. In the case of *über-* the relationship is reversed: only 105 separable verbs as against 278 inseparable ones. With *um-* the situation is more even, with 232 separable verbs and 213 inseparable ones. The prefix *unter-* occurs with 60 separable verbs and 77 inseparable verbs.

The description of stress placement is further complicated by the fact that there are also verbs with two prefixes. Again Kühnhold and Wellmann (1973) give some facts about the occurrence of these prefixes. In the corpus there were only 220 verbs with a double prefix, a modest 2.2 per cent of all verbs. There were four patterns: (1) a stressed prefix followed by an unstressed one: *auf+er+stehen*, *an+ver+trauen* (154 verbs); (2) an unstressed prefix followed by a stressed one: *be+ab+sichtigen*, *ver+an+lassen* (45 verbs); (3) two unstressed prefixes: *be+miss+trauen*, *ver+ge+waltigen* (12 verbs); and (4) two stressed prefixes: *wieder+auf+bauen*, *wieder+ein+setzen* (9 verbs, all with the prefix *wieder-*). This last pattern no longer exists orthographically as a unified verb since the new spelling reform always splits *wieder* from compounds with separable prefixes of their own such as *aufbauen*.

10.2.3 Adjectival prefixes

The prefix *un-* is a very productive adjectival prefix that occurs both stressed and unstressed. The morphological structure of words that use it varies from simple words to derived forms with prefixes and suffixes, including past participles. The *un-* is stressed in the majority of forms: (1) before a simple stem: *un+fair, un+schön;* (2) before a derived stem: *un+ehrlich;* (3) before a past participle: *ungelernt, ungesüßt;* (4) before a prefix that is itself normally stressed: *un+ab+hängig, un+an+nehmbar, un+auf+fällig, un+aus+führbar, un+ent+schlossen, un+er+kannt, un+ver+dient, un+voll+ständig, un+vor+sichtig, un+zu+frieden.*

In a large group of words, especially adjectives ending in the suffixes *-lich, -ig, -sam, -bar* and *–haft,* the stress alternates between the *un-* and the stem vowel: *ún+berechenbar* and *un+beréchenbar.* In some instances there is a semantic distinction between the two forms. Benware (1986: 104) illustrates this: *Sein Bericht klang únglaublich* ('His report was not to be believed') and *Das ist eine ungláubliche Summe* ('That is an enormous sum').

A small number of words with *un-* only have the stress on the stem syllable: *un+dénklich, un+éndlich, un+fásslich, un+ságbar, un+ságlich, un+zählbar, un+zählig.* They show a semantic development away from their literal meaning as negatives to taking on an augmentative meaning as in the use of *Un-* in such nouns as *Un+summe* 'an immense sum', *Unmenge* 'an immense amount'.

10.2.4 Compounds

10.2.4.1 Compound nouns

Compounding is the combination of two stems to form another word, e.g. *Schlaf+Sack = Schlafsack.* This process can occur with nouns, adjectives, adverbs and verbs but it is most productive in the case of nouns (Fleischer and Barz 1992: 87–145). Most compounds consist of a basic component or head (*Grundwort* or *Determinatum*), which gives noun compounds their grammatical gender, and a determining first component or modifier (*Bestimmungswort* or *Determinans*), e.g. *Haustür,* where *Haus* is the modifer and *-tür* the head. This type can be called a subordinating compound (*Determinativkompositum*). The modifier restricts the meaning of the head in the compound. The simple word *Tür* can cover an opening/closing means of access to many things, whereas a compound restricts its meaning to one item, to one type of opening or a certain type of door: *Autotür, Garagentür, Kellertür, Toilettentür;*

Doppeltür, Drehtür, Klapptür, Pendeltür; Außentür, Innentür, Seitentür, Vordertür; Gittertür, Glastür, Stahltür.

Compound nouns normally follow a 'Left Stress Rule' whereby the leftmost, or first, component is stressed: *Háustür, Áutotür*. This holds true even for longer compounds, e.g. *Kíndheitserinnerungen, Héringsschwarm*. All the major parts of speech occur as leftmost modifiers and retain the leftmost stress: *Autoschlüssel* (noun + noun), *Großstadt* (adj. + noun), *Dreirad* (numeral + noun), *Innenkurve* (adverb + noun), *Ichform* (pronoun + noun) and *Bratpfanne* (verb + noun). Most noun compounds in German are subordinating compounds.

The type of nominal compound represented by words like *Taugenichts*, where the head of the compound lies outside its components also follows the Left Stress Rule. Morphologically these compounds refer to a person by paraphrasing what the person does or is. The components of the compound are different parts of speech from the compound itself. Thus *Tauge-* is a verbal stem and *nichts* a negative pronoun. This is known as an exocentric compound. Other examples are: *Störenfried, Nimmersatt, Dreikäsehoch*.

There are also co-ordinating (or appositional) compounds, where the two components are of equal weight: A *Stadtstaat* 'city-state' is both a *Stadt* and a *Staat*. They comprise: (1) designations for clothing: *Strumpfhose, Schürzenkleid*; (2) people: *Fürstbischof, Dichterkomponist, Waisenkind*; (3) expressions for ideologies: *Marxismus-Leninismus*; (4) geographical names: *Schleswig-Holstein, Baden-Württemberg*. These types of compounds are exceptions to the normal 'Left Stress Rule' and have two main stresses, one on the main vowel of each component, or even a greater stress on the right component.

Other exceptions to the 'Left Stress Rule' are compounds with contrastive stress: *Ostermóntag*, as against *Ostersónntag*, as well as several similar expressions, such as *Karfréitag, Pfingstsónntag*. The trio *Jahrhúndert* 'century', *Jahrtáusend*, 'millennium', *Jahrzéhnt* 'decade' shows stress always on the last component. Other exceptions are the points of the compass (*Nordóst, Nordwést, Südóst, Südwést*) and some geographical names (*Südáfrika, Ostásien, Südgeórgien*). The alphabetisms, words formed from and pronounced as letters of the alphabet, such as *CD, PC* also have the stress on the second component. Longer forms such as *LKW* and *PKW* similarly stress the last component but also have variants with the stress on the first component.

A noun compound can have three components A, B, C. We can have either the stress pattern *Rótweinpunsch* or *Stadtbáuamt*. The difference in stress pattern can reflect the morphological structure of the compound. *Rótweinpunsch* is [A B] C with a non-branching head. *Stadtbáuaumt*, on the other hand, is A [B C] with a branching (or compound) head.

10.2.4.2 Compound adjectives

Compound adjectives can also be formed in German. The head is an adjective and the modifier usually a noun (*lebensnah*) or another adjective (*hellblau*). Exceptionally a verb stem occurs: *röstfrisch, tropfnass*. As with nouns, subordinating compounds are the main type and have the main stress on the leftmost component. Co-ordinating adjective compounds also occur, e.g. *taubstumm*. They are less frequent than the subordinating type among the adjectives but more frequent than the nominal co-ordinating compounds. Other examples are *nasskalt, süßsauer, feuchtwarm* and the national colours such as *blauweiß, schwarzrotgold*. Derived adjectives are often divided by a hyphen: *deutsch-französisch, wissenschaftlich-technisch*. As is the case with co-ordinating noun compounds they have two equal main stresses, one on the main vowel in each component. In some instances there are contrasting stress patterns linked with contrasting meaning: *blút+arm* 'anaemic', 'colourless' and *blút+árm* 'very poor'; *stéin+reich* 'stony' and *stéin+réich* 'very rich'. The stress pattern, x ´x, also goes for co-ordinative compound adjectives: *rotgrún* (coalition between SPD and the Greens), *blauwéiß* (the Bavarian colours). The stress in these compounds contrasts with *dúnkelrot* 'dark red' and *bláuweiß* 'a bluey white'.

10.2.4.3 Compound verbs

Compounds among verbs are even more restricted. The use of verbal stems, nouns and adjectives as modifiers, e.g. *trennschleifen* (from *trennen+schleifen*) 'to cut off', *kupferkaschieren* 'to copper-bond' and *buntweben* 'to colour weave', are typical of technical language. There are, however, some genuine verbal compounds with a noun or adjective modifier: as a direct object of a verb (*achtgeben, danksagen, stattfinden, teilnehmen*); representing a state (*stillsitzen, übrigbleiben*); functioning as an adverb (*blindschreiben, falschspielen, schieflaufen*). Their stress pattern is still regular, stressing the leftmost element. The most productive process of forming compound verbs, however, is with the separable verbal prefixes *ab-, an-, auf-, aus-, bei-, durch-, hinter-, los-, nach-, über, um-, unter-, vor-, wider-, zu-*, which all occur as free morphemes. Their status as compounds is controversial and we have treated them as prefixes. Some linguists refer to them as pre-verbs (Donalies 2002).

10.2.4.4 Compound particles

Many uninflected words occur that are of the pattern x ´x: *infolge, obwohl*. These are represented by prepositions, conjunctions and adverbs. Most of the words originate in Early NHG by the incorporation of two words into one (*Univerbierung*). The first is a preposition, the second an article or a noun. Their origin can be found in Paul (2002). Thus there are the conjunctions: *damit, indem, nachdem, obwohl, sofern, soweit, wenngleich, wiewohl, zumal.* Prepositions with this pattern are: *anstatt, aufgrund, gegenüber, infolge, zufolge, zugunsten.* Forms like *entlang, entsprechend* are regular in that they contain an initial unstressed prefix.

Adverbs are rather more complex. There are a number that contain prefixes that are usually stressed: *abseits, anlässlich, ausschließlich, außerhalb, eingangs, einschließlich, nachher, oberhalb, unfern, unweit, zuzüglich.* The directional adverbs always show the pattern x ´x (*einher, hinaus, hinein, heraus, herein*) since they are combining with separable verbal prefixes, e.g. *aus, ein.*

The particle *da-* (*davon*), with its variant *dar-* before vowels (*darauf*), forms prepositional adverbs. These normally have the stress pattern x ´x (*dadúrch*), but when they are used in deictic function the stress pattern is reversed (*dádurch*). This dual patterning goes for all the prepositional adverbs: *dabei, dadurch, dahinten, dahinter.* The interrogative and relative particle *wo-/wor-* (*wovon, worauf*) can also pattern in this way.

There are also a number of adverbs that comprise a noun followed by a preposition: *bergauf, bergab.* These also show the stress pattern x ´x.

10.3 Sentence stress and weak forms

We have established that many words, particularly those belonging to the main word-classes (noun, adjective and verb), have a stress pattern that characterizes them. In addition to this there is sentence stress when in a sentence a speaker may emphasize one or more particular words according to their semantic importance (emphasized word in bold): *Ich habe sie* **gestern** *gesehen.* **Dieses** *Buch empfehle ich Ihnen.* **Warum** *bist du nicht gekommen?*

In many cases the other words, which are unstressed, are reduced in phonetic form. For example, the conjunction [unt] can be reduced to [un] with loss of [t], to [ən] with centralization and loss of lip-rounding and to a syllabic nasal [n̩], often taking its place of articulation from neighbouring sounds, [m̩] near labials and [ŋ̩] near velars. These reduced forms of [unt] are called 'weak forms'. This concept has been well established in English through Daniel Jones but MacCarthy (1975: 13–15) first applied it to German and Kohler (1995: 211–20), who lectured for a time in the Department of Phonetics in Edinburgh, extended its application in more detail. Benware (1986: 125–36) and C. Hall (2003: 148–55) also take it into account. An independent treatment of the same phenomenon was developed by Meinhold (1973), but is more accessible in Meinhold and Stock (1982: 95–8), who deal with the whole range of what they call phonostylistic reductions, for example the elision of unstressed vowels in the endings [-əl], [-əm] and [-ən].

Most of the material presented here is based on Kohler (1995: 211–16). Among all the different cases some general processes can be discerned. These are: the loss of alveolar plosives in final position, e.g. [nɪç] *nicht*; shortening of long vowels, e.g. [du] *du*, [ʃɔn] schon; and vocalization of postvocalic *r*, e.g. [ɛɐ] *er*. The following illustrate some examples from several different word classes:

(1) personal pronouns: *du*, [duː] > [du] > [de], *er* [eːr] > [eɐ] > [ɛɐ] > [ɐ], *ihnen* [iːnen] > [inn̩] > [in] > [in, im, iŋ] (all the other pronouns show weak forms);

(2) the definite and indefinite articles: *der* [deːr] > [deɐ] > [dɛɐ] > [dɐ], *den* [deːn] > [den] > [dən] > [dn̩] > [n, m, ŋ], *das* [das] > [s], *ein(en)* [ainən] > [ainn̩] > [ən] > [n, m, ŋ], *eine* [ainə] > [nə] (all the other article forms and *dessen, deren, denen* show weak forms);

(3) some irregular verb forms: *ist* [ist] > [is] > [s] (final [t] is deleted in *bist* and *sind*), haben [haːbən] > [(h)am] > [m], *werden* [veːrdən] > [veɐn] > [vɛɐn] – the *d* is also elided and the *r* vocalized in *wurden, würden, geworden*; *hast* and *hat* lose their initial [h]: [ast], [at];

(4) some frequently used prepositions: *über* [yːbɐ] > [ʏbɐ] > [ʏβɐ], *für* [fyːr] > [fʏɐ] > [fɐ], *von* [fɔn] > [fn̩] (*vor, nach* and *in* are also affected);

(5) a small number of conjunctions: *und* [unt] > [un] > [n̩], *aber* [aːbɐ] > [aβɐ], *oder* [oːdɐr] > [odɐ] > [ədɐ] (the vowels in *wie* and *da* become shortened);

(6) some adverbs: *jetzt* [jɛtst] > [jets] > [jəts], *mal* [maːl] > [mal] > [ma], *nun* [nuːn] > [nun] > [nʊn].

10.4 Intonation

For many years the study of German intonation was sadly neglected. Schindler and Thürmann (1971) contains a much smaller number of items on suprasegmentals than segmental sounds. An early work in English is Barker (1925). The area was taken up in Germany by von Essen (1964). Meier (1984) is a general bibliography but contains a number of items on German. Other accessible studies are Fox (1984 and 2005: 94–101); MacCarthy (1975: 17–28); Kohler (1995: 195–200); C. Hall (2003: 116–37).

Utterances are not spoken all on one pitch level but rise and fall to give the impression of tunes. Unlike music there are no fixed scales of notes but considerable variety of pitch. The symbolization of intonation is difficult and different schemes are in use. All of them, however, show the rise, fall or level pitch of the voice. We will follow von Essen (1964: 16) and Fox (1984: 7) who use [–] for stressed syllables and [.] for unstressed syllables.

The changes in pitch are usually located in the syllable that has the most stress in the utterance. This syllable forms the nucleus of the tone, or intonation, group. The minimum group is a simple sentence: *Heute ist Dienstag.* Complex sentences may contain more than one tone group (‖ marks the boundary of a tone group): *Wir sollten nach Freiburg fahren,* ‖ *aber wir hatten keine Lust.* Within each tone group there is a nucleus, the stressed syllable, which shows the most pitch changes and sometimes one or more stress groups, comprising a stressed syllable and unstressed syllables. In our examples the nuclei would be *Diens-, Frei-* and *Lust.* The syllables between the nucleus and the first stressed syllable of the tone group are known collectively as the head, and any unstressed syllables before the head are known as the pre-head. The only obligatory part of the tone group is the nucleus. Likewise any syllables after the nucleus are known as the tail. Our examples can thus be divided as follows:

| (1) | | Heute ist | Diens- | tag | −.−. |
| (no pre-head) | | ǀ head | ǀ nucleus | ǀ tail | |

| (2) | Wir | ǀ wollten nach ǀ | Frei- | burg fahren | .−..−.−. |
| | pre-head | ǀ head | ǀ nucleus | ǀ tail | |

| (3) | | aber wir hatten keine Lust | | | ..−¯.−.− |
| (no pre-head) | | ǀ head | ǀ nucleus | ǀ (no tail) | |

The crucial changes in pitch affect the nucleus. Following C. Hall (2003) we can classify the intonation patterns of German, based around the nucleus, into five types. The patterns are also typical of certain types of sentence. Since there is an overlap in the sentence types that occur with the falling pattern and the rising-falling pattern it seems best to deal with them together. For the same reasons the rising and falling-rising patterns will be grouped together.

Type 1 has a tone group with a falling pattern:

(1) *Er hat jetzt genug geschlafen.*   .. −. −. _.
(2) *Schreiben Sie bitte bald!*   −.. −. _
(3) *Wann fährst du nach Hause?*   . −.. −.

Type 1a has a tone group with a rising-falling pattern:

(4) *Er hat gewonnen!*   ... −.
(5) *Trink doch deine Milch!*   −. −. −

(6) *Wie alt bist du?*　　　　. — —.

(7) *Wunderbar!*　　　　　　—..

Both these patterns are used typically for statements (1,4), commands (2,5) and questions containing *w*-words such as *wann, was, wer, wie, wo* (3,6). Type 1a is also used for exclamations (7).

Type 2 has a tone group with a rising pattern:

(1) *Spielst du mit?*　　　　_. —

(2) *Was schreibst du jetzt?*　　_—. —

Type 2a has a tone group with a falling-rising pattern:

(3) *Bist du jetzt müde?*　　　　　　　　　.. —_

(4) *Übrigens, ‖ (wir wollen euch nächste Woche besuchen).*　_. —.

(5) *Achtung!*　　　　　　　　　　　　　—.

Both these patterns are used typically for questions which can be answered by *yes* or *no* (1,3), and for questions containing *w*-words such as *wann, was, wer, wie, wo* to make them more polite and friendly or to confirm their content (2). Type 2a is also used for non-final, or dependent, tone groups (4) and friendly warnings (5).

Type 3 has a tone group with a level pattern:

(1) *Wenn wir Zeit hätten, (würden wir jetzt verreisen).*　—._—.

(2) *Möchtest du Bier oder Wein?*　　　　　—.. ——. —

(3) *Ich möchte Äpfel, Birnen, Bananen und Pflaumen.*　.—. —. —.. —. —.

(4) *(guten) Abend; Danke.*　　　　　　—. —. ; —.

This pattern is used typically for non-final, or dependent, tone groups (1), the first part of so-called alternative questions (2), for lists, except for the last item (3) and for ritual greetings and non-committal expressions (4).

There is no agreement on the number of distinct intonation patterns in German. Kohler distinguishes six tones (1995: 198f.) whereas MacCarthy (1975: 18–23) has two basic tunes, one of which is sub-divided into a tune that ends on a high level pitch while the other rises to a high pitch. Writing about intonation can only give some pointers to listen to. The real exploration of this topic, as with phonology in general, comes from the spoken word itself.

QUESTIONS

1   Illustrate the 'Penultimate Syllable Stress Rule' in German.

2   Give four examples of suffixes that are stressed.

3 In which of the following words is the suffix *-ik* stressed: *Mathematik*, *Rhythmik*, *Rubrik*, *Germanistik*, *Plastik*, *Fabrik*?

4 Which of the following prefixes are always unstressed: *auf-*, *durch-*, *ent-*, *er-*, *um-*, *ver-*?

5 Illustrate the 'Left Stress Rule' in German noun compounds.

6 What exceptions are there to the 'Left Stress Rule' in noun compounds?

7 What aspects of word stress in German are particularly difficult for the foreign learner? What handy rules-of-thumb could you provide?

8 Illustrate the weak forms of the personal pronouns.

9 Illustrate TWO patterns in German intonation.

10 Get two native speakers to speak the following short dialogue and transcribe the intonation patterns:

   A. Hallo, Manfred! Entschuldige. Meine Uhr ist stehen geblieben. Kannst du mir mal sagen, wie spät es ist?
   B. Ja, selbstverständlich! Genau zehn vor acht.
   A. Vielen Dank auch! Mach's gut! Tschüss und schönes Wochende!
   B. Gleichfalls und grüß' bitte Heidrun!

11 Pluricentric and regional variation

11.0 Introduction

One of the main parameters of variation in German is that of region. The German of Hamburg or Berlin is different from that of Munich or Stuttgart.

The phonological features of each area are dependent on the phonological structure of the local dialects (see Fig. 11.1).

11.1 German dialects

The structure and status of dialect in German-speaking countries is a well-researched subject (see Russ 1989). In this chapter we merely want to give a few pointers to some of the interesting and relevant characteristics of the phonetic structure of German dialects. We shall concentrate on a selection of dialects. Figure 11.1 is a rather simplified map of the main dialect areas of German. Some of the dialect features mentioned here we will have encountered in the descriptions of the individual vowels and consonants in Chapters 3 and 4.

The main division is into Low German and High German dialects. The Low German dialects have a consonant system that has not undergone the Second, or High German, Sound Shift, similar to English or Dutch (see 12.7.1). It also has the following other phonetic features:

a) Retention of voiceless stops as in English with no High German sound shift: *Peerd* (*Pferd*), *slapen* (*schlafen*), *Kopp* (*Kopf*), *Tied* (*Zeit*), *Water* (*Wasser*), *heet* (*hieß*), *maken* (*machen*), *sik* (*sich*). Also *d* instead of HG *t*: *Disch* (*Tisch*), *Dag* (*Tag*).

b) Intervocalic and word-final HG *b*, *g* are usually voiced fricatives, voiceless at the end of words (although sometimes written <b, g>) – *gewen*

Figure 11.1   Main dialect areas in the German-speaking countries

(*geben*), *af* (*ab*); *kreegen* (*kriegen*), *Dag* [dax] (*Tag*) – and sometimes intervocalic *d* or *t* has become *r*: *harrn* (*hatten*).

c) Initial *st*, *sp* are often pronounced [st, sp].

d) Retention of long high monophthongs: *Tied* (*Zeit*), *Lüüd* (*Leute*), *Huus* (*Haus*).

e) Monophthongs for HG *ei*, *au* (from MHG *ei*, *ou*): *weet* (*weiß*) 'I know', *ok* (*auch*).

f) Apocope of final unstressed *-e*: *Lüüd* (*Leute*).

LG also has the following morphological features:

a) No *ge-* in past participles.
b) No difference between acc. and dat. sg. in personal pronouns: *mi* (= HG *mir, mich*).
c) Frequent use of *-s* plural: *Bekers* (*Becher*), *Buddels* ('bottles'), *Deerns* ('girls'), *Dokters* (*Doktoren*).
d) The form *he* for masc. 3rd pers. sing. pronoun, HG *er*.
e) In the present plural of the verb there is only one form for all three persons: *wi, ji, se snakt Platt* 'we, you, they speak Low German'. The form *snakt* is characteristic of West LG whereas *snacken* is characteristic of East LG.

The High German dialects, which have formed the basis of NHG, can be divided into Central German and Upper German. The main criterion has been the extent to which the Second Sound Shift has been carried through (see Fig. 12.6). The Upper German dialects have carried it through to the same extent as the standard language and in southern Alemannic and Austro-Bavarian even further in shifting initial [k] to [x] or even the affricate [kx].

Alemannic, or West UG, mainly represented by the Swiss German, or High Alemannic, dialects, has the following phonetic characteristics (Low Alemannic in Alsace is very similar):

a) Retention of MHG long, high closed vowels as monophthongs: *Zyt* (NHG *Zeit*), *Stüür* (NHG *Steuer*), *us* (NHG *aus*).
b) Retention of MHG diphthongs as diphthongs: *Liebe* (NHG *Liebe*), *füere* (NHG *führen*), *Buech* (NHG *Buch*).
c) Voiceless velar fricative [x] for NHG initial [k]: *Chind*.
d) Vowels in open syllables short (*sagen*), and not lengthened as in NHG.
e) Apocope in many cases: *Reis* (NHG *Reise*).

Swabian is a special sub-dialect of Alemannic which shows diphthongs, like NHG, for the Alemannic monophthongal high front vowel. Swabian has the following additional phonetic characteristics:

a) Loss of final and pre-consonantal *-n*: *Rege* (*Regen*), *Sonnenschei* (*Sonnenschein*), *Maa* (*Mann*), *ois* (*uns*), *feif* (*fünf*).
b) Loss of final *-e*: *Sach* (*Sache*), *bleed* (*blöde*), *i lach* (*ich lache*).
c) Derounding of front rounded vowels (*Entrundung*): *scheene* (*schöne*), *Fresch* (*Frösche*); *Schissl* (*Schüssel*); *heid* (*heute*), *Fraend* (*Freund*).
d) Representation of NHG /ai/ and /au/ by two diphthongs according to their MHG origin. NHG /ai/ represents a merger of MHG *î* and *ei*, e.g. NHG

drei, sei represent MHG *drî, sî*, while NHG *zwei, eine* represent MHG *zwei, eine*. In Swabian MHG *î* and *ei* have separate reflexes: MHG *drî, sî*, Swabian [drəi, səi]: MHG *zwei, eine*, Swabian *zwoi, oine*. A similar situation exists for NHG /au/ which is a merger of MHG *û* and *ou*: *Sau, draußen; auch, laufen* (MHG *sû, drûzen; ouch, loufen*). Swabian has [əu] for MHG *û*: [səu, drəusə, əu, ləuf].

e) Merger of voiced and voiceless consonants (*Konsonantenschwächung*): *iiber* (*über*), *ibich* (*üppig*); *leide* (*läuten, leiten*); *frooge* (*fragen*), *bage* (*backen*); *beese* (*böse*), *beise* (*beißen*).

f) Development of *s* to *sch* before medial and final stops: *isch* (*ist*), *fescht* (*fest*), *zerscht* (*zuerst*), *Obscht* (*Obst*).

g) The retention of diphthongs for MHG *ie, üe*, and *uo*: *Zwieble* (*Zwiebel*), *grieß* (*grüß*, MHG *grüez*), *guet*.

East of the river Lech, Bavarian, East UG, or more correctly, Austro-Bavarian, begins. It is a very large dialect area taking in most of Bavaria and Austria apart from the western state of Vorarlberg. It has the following phonetic characteristics:

a) Rounding of [a] to [o]: *Salåd* (*Salat*), *Tåg* (*Tag*).

b) NHG *ei* (from MHG *ei*, not MHG *î*) becomes [oa]: *oans* (*eins*), *zwoa* (*zwei*), *hoaß* (*heiß*).

c) Derounding of front rounded vowels: *bäs* (*böse*), *Kia* (*Kühe*), *Fiass* (*Füße*, MHG *vüeze*).

d) Central Bavarian shows vocalization of postvocalic *r* and *l*: *Woat* (*Wort*), *Soiz* (*Salz*).

e) New front rounded vowels produced by vocalization of *l* in some cases: *vui* (*viel*), *Ködn* (*Kälte*).

f) Central Bavarian has consonant lenition: *Blååz* (*Platz*), *Babba* (*Papa*), *danzn* (*tanzen*), *bäddn* (*beten*), *Glawia* (*Klavier*), *Gnocha* (*Knochen*), *lägga* (*lecken*), *schmegga* (*schmecken*).

g) Regulation of vowel quantity. A long vowel is followed by a short lenis consonant and a short vowel by a long fortis consonant.

h) Apocope of final unstressed vowels: *I nimm* (*ich nehme*), *zwoa Dåg* (*zwei Tage*).

In South and Central Germany the front rounded vowels, short and long *ü, ö* [ʏ, yː, œ, øː], are derounded and merge with the unrounded front vowels *i, e* [ɪ, iː, ɛ, ɛː, eː]. Thus *Biene, Bühne* come to have the same stressed vowel [iː] and the stressed vowels *vermissen, müssen* merge in [ɪ] and those of *Söhne, Sehne* in [eː]. Speakers again fluctuate in the use of unrounded and rounded vowels. This reflects the situation in the local dialects where all the front rounded vowels have been derounded. Not all regional differences find their way into colloquial and near-standard varieties. In this chapter, we will deal principally with the differences between the codified varieties in Germany, Austria and Switzerland, but some widely used dialectally influenced forms will also surface.

11.2 The ambiguity of the term 'German'

A complication is that the term 'German' is ambiguous. On the one hand there is the national political reference to the German Federal Republic and on the other hand there is the linguistic reference to the language used in the German Federal Republic, Austria and the largest part of Switzerland. The German language used in the three countries differs in pronunciation, grammar and vocabulary, but not to the extent that we would want to speak of three languages. Historically the relationship between these three national varieties has changed over the years. Since Germany is the most populous country, with a successful economy, and a founder member of the European Union, it has often been seen as the main guardian of standard German. Other varieties were often seen as deviations from a *Duden*-driven norm.

11.3 Pluricentric variation

However, since the 1990s there has been a movement among linguists to redress this asymmetric relationship. German has begun to be regarded as a pluricentric language with several different national centres and varieties. We shall be looking at three centres: Germany, Austria and Switzerland. Up to the re-unification of Germany there was a fourth national variety, that of the German Democratic Republic (*Deutsche Demokratische Republik*). Ebner (1998) and Meyer (1989) give details of the standard in Austria and Switzerland, called Austrian Standard German (ASG) and Swiss Standard German (SSG) respectively (Clyne 1995: 20–65). Ammon (1995) is a pioneering and detailed work, summarizing research and providing copious examples. A problem remained in that it was unclear what to call the national standard language in the German Federal Republic. Clyne (1995: 23f.) suggests German Standard German (GSG). Older scholars had used designations such as *Binnendeutsch* (Internal German). Ammon uses the terms *das österreichische Standarddeutsch, das schweizerische Standarddeutsch, das deutsche Standarddeutsch*.

The pronunciations, grammatical constructions and words typical of these national varieties are: Austrianisms (*Austriazismen*) for Austria, Helveticisms (*Helvetizismen* or *Helvetismen*) for Switzerland. However, what were the forms typical of GSG to be called? Again Ammon rides to the rescue with the term Teutonisms (*Teutonismen*) (1995; 1998). However, these terms have not found their way into the most ambitious project for the description of the national varieties of German, the *Variantenwörterbuch des Deutschen* (Ammon *et al.* 2004: xviii–xx), where a raft of geographical labels is used instead, e.g. *A-ost* (eastern Austria), *A-west* (western Austria); *CH-zentral* (central Switzerland); *D-nord* (north Germany), *D-süd* (south Germany). The main reason is that many words that are labelled as Austrian (for example) only appear in parts of the country. This is perhaps most typical when applied to Germany. As is well known there are many words that are typically north German or typically south German. Our main concern here will be with pronunciation and that does not show so much internal variation in each state, apart from Germany itself. Ammon *et al.* (2004: li–lxi) deal with pluricentric differences in pronunciation in general. Eichhoff (1977–2000) presents a few maps that deal with phonetic variation and because of the coverage of the whole German-speaking area these are extremely instructive. Examples from Eichhoff (1978, vol. 2) are: the pronunciation of the initial consonant in *Chemie* as [ç] in North and Central Germany and [k] in South Germany (Map 112); the development of a pre-palatal [ʃ] in *der letzte* and *der erste* characterizes the south-west including Switzerland and Tyrol (Maps 113, 114); the initial plosive spelt <g> of the past participle prefix *ge-* (*gehabt*) appears as the fricative [j] in the Lower Rhineland and in Saxony and around Berlin (Map 115); the stress in words such as *Tabak*, *Kaffee* and *Tunnel* also varies regionally (Maps 109–111), the stress occurring on the first syllable more often in the north of Germany.

11.3.1 Pronunciation in Switzerland

Switzerland is different from the other German-speaking countries in that SSG is chiefly a written language. In everyday conversation a Swiss German dialect is used. This situation is known as diglossia, with a Swiss German dialect as the so-called 'Low' Variety and SSG as the so-called 'High' Variety. SSG is not simply restricted to the written language but is used in the Federal Parliament, formal speeches, teaching most subjects at school and university. It is also used in national radio and television news and finally in conversation with those who do not understand a Swiss German dialect (see Russ 1987, Haas 1988 and Rasch 1998). Boesch (1957) was an attempt to provide some guidelines for the pronunciation of SSG that would follow a middle way between the two extremes of clinging slavishly to *Siebs* and using a heavily dialectally influenced pronunciation. This has been partially successful and some of the suggestions were incorporated into the nineteenth edition of *Siebs*. *DAW*, on the other hand, has maintained that the standard should be supraregional and has not recorded any Swiss pronunciations in any of its editions. There are, however, differences in SSG from ASG and GSG that range from the pronunciation of individual vowels and consonants to the positioning of stress. Meyer (1989: 25–36) and Ammon (1995: 255–8) list a number of examples.

11.3.1.1 Vocalic differences

Most differences affect the distribution of phonetic features in individual words. These mainly affect the incidence of short and long vowels, the pronunciation of <y> as [i:], the use of diphthongs occurring in Swiss German dialects and the omission of unstressed [-ə] in some foreign words.

(1) In SSG the vowels in the following words (in bold) are long but short in GSG: *Amboss, Andacht, brachte, Gedächtnis, Lorbeer, Nachbar, Rache, rächen, Viertel, Vorteil*. This results in a difference in pronunciation between *Rost* 'rust' (with short vowel) and *Rost* 'grill' (with a long vowel). We also find the opposite with words where the vowel is short in SSG but long in GSG: *Barsch, Erde, düster, Geburt, hapern, Harz, hätscheln, Jagd, Krebs, Nische, Obst, pusten, Städte, Wuchs*. This is especially the case in words containing *-it* (*Appetit, Liter, Profit*), *-atik* (*Thematik*), *-atisch* (*dramatisch*), *-iz* (*Miliz*), and before *-tsch-* (*hätscheln, watscheln*).

(2) In some foreign loans the vowel spelt <y> is pronounced [i:] in SSG and not [y:]: *Asyl, Gymnasium, Libyen, Physik, Pyramide, System, Zylinder*.

(3) Swiss German dialects have a row of diphthongs, [iə, yə, uə], that do not occur in GSG, although we assume that they were present in MHG. They occur in place names (*Spiez, Brienz, Flüelen, Üetliberg, Buochs, Muolen*), surnames (*Dieth, Lienert, Ruoff, Büeler*) and first names (*Rüedi, Ueli*). Boesch (1957: 35–9) has an extensive list of place-names.

(4) In the pronunciation of French loan words a final <e> is often not pronounced: *Chance, Chauffeuse, Coiffeuse, Drainage, Garage, Nuance*. Exceptions are *Clique, Crème* and *Enquête*, which retain a final [-ə].

11.3.1.2 Consonantal differences

There is a remarkable range of pronunciation differences in the consonant system. These range from the devoicing of lenis obstruents, through the use of a plosive in *-ig*, the sole use of the velar fricative [x] for postvocalic <ch>, the treatment of nasal vowels in the suffix *-ment*, the retention of the [r] in

-*er*, the omission of the glottal stop to the pronunciation of long intervocalic consonants.

(5) A general feature of the pronunciation of the lenis obstruents in SSG is that they are devoiced. This is reflected in SSG where loan words with orthographic <v> are pronounced [f]: *Advent, Advocat, Evangelium, Kadaver, Klavier, nervös, November, Provinz, Revier, Vikar, violett, Vizepräsident.*

(6) One striking difference is that the suffix <-*ig*> is, contrary to *Siebs* and *DAW*, to be pronounced with a final plosive [-ik] and not a fricative.

(7) The digraph <ch> is pronounced as a voiceless velar fricative in informal SSG whereas in more formal speech [x] and [ç] are prescribed.

(8) The suffix -*ment, Departement*, is pronounced as [mɛnt] and not [mɑŋ] or [mɑ̃].

(9) In the final syllable -*er* the articulation of the [r] as a fricative or trill is retained.

(10) The glottal stop is largely absent, especially in such words as *Ver+ein, sich er+innern.*

(11) There is also the tendency for orthographically doubled consonants (*pp, tt, ff, ss, mm* etc.) to be pronounced long (*hoffen* [hɔfːə]), which reflects Swiss German dialect.

11.3.1.3 Differences in stress

The stress on many French loans is on the first syllable in SSG instead of the second as in GSG: x′x → ′x x (*Asphalt, Billet, Budget, Buffet, Filet*). This accent shift also goes for three-letter acronyms: ′*AHV* (*Alters- und Hinterlassenenversicherung*), ′*SBB* (*Schweizerische Bundesbahnen*), whereas in ASG and GSG the last letter is stressed: *AK′H* (*Allgemeines Krankenhaus*), *AB′M* (*Arbeitsbeschaffungsmaßnahmen*).

11.3.2 Pronunciation in Austria

The spoken language of educated Austrians shows a number of deviations from the *Siebs* and *DAW*, some of which are also current in southern Germany. There is a widespread use of dialect and colloquial language in Austria in spoken communication. The distribution of the different forms has been examined by Wiesinger (1988: 9–30) and Moosmüller (1991). Lipold (1988) and Ammon (1995: 150–4) will be used for most of the following examples. Ebner (1998) brings some examples in the entries in his dictionary, but not in the introduction. Specifically geared for usage in Austria is the *Österreichisches Wörterbuch*, which has appeared regularly in new editions. However, it only sporadically shows pronunciation.

11.3.2.1 Vocalic differences

ASG shares with SSG several differences of pronunciation from GSG. These affect the length of vowels, the quality of vowels and diphthongs and the frequent omission of the final [-ə] in foreign loans.

(1) As with SSG there are also differences in the quantity between the GSG and Austrian usage. The following stressed vowels (in bold) are short in GSG but long in ASG: *Geschoß*, *ob*, *Rebhuhn*, *Walnuss*, *Politik*, *Profit*, *Notiz*, *absolut*. In contrast, the following stressed vowels (in bold) are long in GSG but short in ASG: *Geburt*, *artig*, *zart*, *Nische*, *Liter*, *Obst*, *Probst*, *Nüster*; and in unstressed syllables: *Amboß*, *spielbar*, *Altertum*, *Balkan*, *Schlendrian*.

(2) The diphthong spelt <ei> is pronounced with a half-open first component, [ɛi].

(3) The short vowel spelt <a> has became a back rounded [ɔ] or back [ɒ] in Austrian dialect in original native words, old loans and some names. However, more recent loans, e.g. *Kassa*, *Taxi*, *Klasse*, and names, e.g. *Dagmar*, *Sandra*, show a front vowel, [a]. This front [a] is very widespread in spoken ASG for names. Thus the border town of *Passau*, other geographical names such as *Prag*, *Amerika*, and Christian names such as *Anna*, *Alexander*, are pronounced with [ɒ] in Bavaria and [a] in Austria (Wiesinger 1990: 452f.).

(4) Another vocalic feature ASG shares with SSG is that the final -*e* of loan words such as *Nuance*, *Chance* is not pronounced; exceptionally, as in SSG, in *Clique* ASG retains the pronunciation of the final [-ə].

11.3.2.2 Consonantal differences

ASG shares with SSG several features of the consonant system.

(5) Unlike GSG but like SSG the lenis obstruents of ASG are devoiced.

(6) Another feature ASG shares with SSG is that the suffix -*ig* is pronounced with a final plosive, e.g. [-ik] in ASG.

(7) Those words spelt with initial *Ch-* before a front vowel, e.g. *China*, *Chirurg*, *Chemie*, are also pronounced with a plosive [k] instead of a palatal fricative [ç]. This type of pronunciation, however, also occurs in southern Germany.

11.3.2.3 Differences in stress

There is also a tendency to stress loans on the initial syllable, as also occurs in SSG, e.g. *'Attentat, 'Kopie, 'Marzipan, 'Uniform, 'Vatikan*. Other ASG differences in stress placement are *Mathe'matik, Roko'ko, Ta'bak* as against GSG *Mathema'tik, 'Rokoko, 'Tabak*. Lipold (1988: 47–54) has a detailed list of ASG words with a different pronunciation from GSG. Stress in place-names is described in Hornung (1988). In the east of Austria some place-names are pronounced with stress on the final syllable, e.g. *Land'eck* instead of *'Landeck*. Those names that end in *-au* are subject to variation, e.g. *Wa'chau*, with final stress, but *'Ramsau*, with initial stress.

11.3.3 Features of pronunciation typical of Germany

These are termed Teutonisms (*Aussprache-Teutonismen*) by Ammon (1995: 334), who uses the *reine und gemäßigte Hochlautung* of *Siebs* and the *Standardlautung* of both *DAW* and *GWDA*.

Germany comprises a much larger area than Austria and Switzerland and has more inhabitants. This difference is reflected in the range of dialects used in the three countries. Swiss German dialects all belong to the Alemannic dialect group. Austrian dialects, on the other hand, belong to the Bavarian dialect group, apart from the states of Vorarlberg and Tyrol, whose dialects are Alemannic. The Alemannic and Bavarian dialect groups do, however, together form the largest part of the UG dialect group. In Germany we have not only UG dialects (see Fig. 11.1), but also CG dialects and LG dialects, the latter not participating in the Second Sound Shift (see Chapter 12). Even within these major groupings of LG, CG and UG there are numerous sub-divisions (for details see König 1994: 230 and 239ff.; Barbour and Stevenson 1990: 146ff.). The consequences are that many of the pronunciation features that occur in Germany are regionally restricted. They have to be labelled North German (*Norddeutsch*) or South German (*Süddeutsch*) and even these are rather simplified distinctions. In fact most of the features that are viewed in Austria and Switzerland as typically German are North German.

There has always been an interest in trying to ascertain the regional distribution of pronunciation features. Once the strait jacket of *Siebs* was sloughed off and more attention paid to what the actual pronunciation of speakers was, then investigations could begin. One of the most detailed is König (1989). He investigated the pronunciation of forty-four speakers, all with *Abitur*, who had each grown up in one place. He examined their speech in reading word lists, minimal pairs and individual words. On the basis of the recorded responses

König and his team produced maps. But since the research was done before re-unification in 1990 they were only of the old Federal Republic. Nevertheless they remain an interesting record of regional variation among educated speakers and we will use the findings to illustrate our examples. Some of the challenges and changes that German pronunciation is undergoing can be found in Eichinger and Kallmeyer (2005).

11.3.3.1 Vocalic differences

These comprise a wide variety of features, but not dialectal features such as derounding or lowering.

(1) The use of a short vowel in monosyllabic words such as *Bad, Glas, Grab, grob* is found in North German speech. South German as well as ASG and SSG have a long vowel in these forms. König (1989: 2, 152, Map QU. 16) has short vowels in *Bad, Glas, Gras* and *Rad* in the north.

(2) The large-scale use of long half-close [e:] for <ä> is a feature of North German speech: *Bär, Käse, spät.* König (1989: 2, 122, Map E.16) has [e:] in *Schnäbel* and *Mähne* in the north and north-east.

(3) The final <-e> of French loan words is pronounced in Germany (*Bandage, Chance, Garage*) but not in ASG and SSG.

(4) Differences of length exist between GSG and ASG and SSG. In the following words the vowel is long in GSG but short in ASG and SSG: (before *t*) *Appetit, dramatisch, Fabrik, Kritik, Liter, Notiz, Profit, thematisch*; in individual words, *Afrika, Jagd, Nische, Nüstern, Obst.* To a lesser extent a number of words have a short vowel in GSG and a long vowel in ASG and SSG: *Chef, Geschoß, Rebhuhn, Walnuss, Walross.*

11.3.3.2 Consonantal differences

There is a broad spectrum of consonantal differences.

(5) Vocalization of <r> after long vowels occurs in the whole of Germany and also in colloquial speech in Austria. However, after a short vowel it is typical of North German speech (*Stern, Wort*), but also occurs in Bavaria. König (1989: 2, 201, Map R.26) shows the distribution of vocalization for *gern* and *Korb.*

(6) The syllable [-ər] is vocalized to [ɐ]. This occurs throughout Germany and in colloquial speech in Austria as well but not in SSG. König (1989: 2, 323, Map NS.8) has [ɐ] for -*er* in *Fenster* in the north, [ɐ, ə] in the centre and [ə] in the south.

(7) The word-final velar nasal [ŋ] appears as [ŋk] in the north-west and central west (König 1989: 2, 152, Map N.1 *Ding, Täuschung*).

(8) The word-initial affricate [pf] is replaced by the fricative [f] in the north and centre (König 1989: 2, 259, Map P.8 *Pferd, Pflanze*).

(9) Initial <s> before vowels is fully voiced in the north and centre as far south as Hesse (König 1989: 2, 319, Map S.1 *Sichel, Sohn, Seil*).

(10) In the suffix *-ig* the final consonant is a fricative according to *Siebs*, *DAW* and *GWDA* but this is mainly in the north and northern centre, as far south as north Hesse (König 1989: 2, 152, Map NS.4a *Pfennig, winzig*). Normally not regarded as part of the standard, but in North Germany most words spelt with word- or stem-final *-g* (e.g. *Tag, Berg, sagt, Talg*) are pronounced with a fricative, [x] after a back vowel and [ç] after *r, l* and front vowels: [tax, bɛrç, zaxt, talç]. König (1989: 2, 303, Map G.2 *Tag*) shows fricative values in the north. Individual speakers fluctuate between [k] and [x, ç] in many words. This reflects the local dialects where all standard word- and stem-final *g*'s are pronounced as fricatives.

QUESTIONS

1 Explain the notion of 'pluricentric' with reference to German.

2 What are the pluricentric varieties of German?

3 How are words designated that are chiefly used in (a) Austria and (b) Switzerland?

4 Illustrate regional variation with reference to consonants.

5 How does the suffix *-ig* show variation in German?

6 Give examples of some features of North German pronunciation.

7 Illustrate variation in word stress among the different varieties of German.

8 How can we account for the range of regional variation in German?

9 Turn this Low German version of the Christmas story from Luke 2 into High German. What are the major systematic consonantal differences that you find between the two versions?

   1 In düsse Tied käm vun den Kaiser Augustus en Order rut, dat jedereen sick in de Stüerlisten inschriewen schull. 2 Düt wär ganz wat Nies – dat wörr to'n ersten Mal dörchföhrt – un domols wär Kyrenius Stattholer öwer Syrien. 3 Na, jedereen mak sick denn ock up de Reis' na sin Heimatstadt und leet sick inschriewen. 4 So güng ock

Josef vun Galiläa ut de Stadt Nazareth na Judäa, na David sin Heimatstadt – de heet Bethlehem – denn he hör to David sin Sipp un Familie 5 un wull sick inschriewen laten mit Maria, de em antruut wär. Un de schull Moder warn. 6 As se dor wärn, käm de Tied dat se to liggn kamen schull. 7 Un se bröch ehren ersten Söhn to Welt un wickel em in Windeln un lä em in en Kriff; denn se harrn sünst keen Platz in de Harbarg. 8 Un nu wärn in desülwige Gegend Schäpers buten up dat Feld. De heeln nachts bi das Veehwark de Wach. 9 Un wat passeer? Mit een Mal stünn den Herrn sin Engel vör ehr, un unsen Herrgodd sin Herrlikeit lücht öwer ehr up. Do verfehrn se sick banni. 10 Un de Engel sä to ehr: 'Man jo keen Angst! Nä, en grote Freud heff ick ju to vertelln – un all' de Lüd schüllt dat to weten kriegen – 11 denn för ju is hüt de Heiland born. De herr Christus is dat, in David sin Stadt. 12 Un dat schall för ju dat Teeken wesn; ji ward finn'n dat Kind inwickelt in Windeln, un liggn deit dat in ein Krüff.' 13 Un knapp harr he't seggt, do swew üm den Engel en grote Swarm vun unsen Herrgod sin Hofstaat. De löwden Godd un sungen: 14 'Low un Ehr dor baben för unsen Herrgodd un Freden hier nerrn up de Eer för Minschen, de dat hartli meent un den goden Willn hebt!'

(From *Dat Ole un dat Nie Testament in unse Moderspraak*, translated by J. Jessen, Göttingen: Vandenhoeck & Ruprecht, 1962, p. 111.)

10 Identify the dialect of one of the following three passages and give detailed reasons for your choice.

(i) Nach Bethlehem unterwegs

> Drauss tuats schneebebberln
> koid (= kalt) blost der Wind.
> Jetz gschiecht, was gescheng muaß,
> fürs himmlische Kind.
>
> Drauss tuats schneebebberln
> der Weg ist weit.
> D'Mari moant schüchtern:
> ''s is höchste Zeit!'
>
> Drauss tuats schneebebberln
> hell is de Nacht,
> Schleun di nur, Sepperl,
> und gib fein Acht!
>
> Drauss tuats schneebebberln
> halts nur fest zamm;
> 's muaß ja as Kind bald
> a Hoametl ham.

(ii) A home help gives her morning timetable

> Am Morgeds ha i derfa aischt aufschtau om secksa, ond ha missa na die Klaine en d'Schual richta, die send en d'Oberschuul ganga uf Kircha na, Kirchhaim also na, ond na ha i missa abschtauba ond blocka (= bohnern) ond mobba (= moppen), was m'r ja bei eis dahoit et so g'nau tut, ond au et Zeit håt. Ond nå

em – wenn e fetig gewea be om-a naine rom, na han i derfa zom Aikaufa mit-em Täschle laufa, ond natiirlich au a ôgwohnte Sach, on nå hå(t) m'r Zeit gheet von, von halbolfa oder om olfa bis om halbois, då send die Klaine komma von d'r Schuul, då håt missa nå d's Ässa fe'tig sai. Mai Scheffe, d'Frau Dokt(e)r, dui isch zairschta scho ällamål mit en d'Kuche, aber na mo se gmerkt håt, daß d'Elis a bißle jetzt sich auskennt, nå isch-e wägblieba ond i ha a sälber nå a Fraid dra kriegt, wem-m'r håt derfa so sälbschtendig au mål kocha, on des Sach macha, was m'r ja dahoim sosch et so däf, ond au no et ka, wem-m'r von d'r Schul awäg, on mai Schef, d'r Härr Dokt(e)r, där isch erscht von d't Sprächschtond komma mittagets om zwoi, nå ha m'r då missa nomål d's Ässa a bißle gwärma ond auftraga, on na ha m'r vielleicht gschpiilt on d'Kuche fe(r)tich gmacht bis om drui.

(iii) The Christmas story, Luke 2:1–16, in Bärndütsch:

1 I dere Zyt het der Cheiser Augustus befole, me söll i sym Rych e Stüür-Schatzig düefüere. 2 Das isch denn ds erschte Mal passiert, wo der Quirinius isch Landvogt vo Syrie gsi. 3 Da sy alli uf d Reis, für sech ga la yschetze, jede a sy Heimatort. 4 O der Josef isch vo Galiläa, us der Stadt Nazaret, nach Judäa gwanderet, i d Davidsstadt, wo Betlehem heisst. Er het drum zu de Nachfahre vom David ghört. 5 Dert het er sech welle la yschetze zäme mit der Maria, syr Brut. Die het es Chind erwartet. 6 Wo si dert sy aacho, isch d Geburt nache gsi, 7 und si het iren erschte Suhn übercho. Sie het ne gwicklet und i ne Chrüpfe gleit. Es het drum für se süsch kei Platz gha i der Herbärg. 8 I der glyche Gäget sy Hirte uf em Fäld gsi, wo d Nacht düre bi irne Tier Wach ghalte hei. 9 Da chunt en Ängel vo Gott, em Herr, zue ne, und e hälle Schyn von Gott lüuchtet um sen ume. Si sy natürlech starch erchlüpft. 10 Aber der Ängel seit zue ne: 'Heit nid Angscht, lueget, i bringe nech e guete Bricht, e grossi Fröid, wo ds ganze Volk aageit. 11 Hütt isch nämlech i der Davids-Stadt öie Retter uf de Wält cho. Es isch Chrischtus, der Herr. 12 Und a däm chöit der's merke: Dihr findet das Chindli gwicklet und in nere Chrüpfe'. 13 Uf einisch sy umen Ängel ume grossi Schare vom Himelsheer gsi, die hei Gott globet und gseit: 14 'Ehr für Gott i der Höchi, und uf der Ärde Fride für d Mönsche, won är lieb hat'. 15 D Ängel sy wider im Himel verschwunde, und d Hirte hei zunenand geseit: 'Mir wei doch uf Betlehem yne di Sach ga luege, wo da passiert isch, und won nis der Herr het z wüsse ta'. 16 Si hei pressiert und hei d Maria und der Josef gfunde und ds Chindli i der Chrüpfe.

12 Sound changes

12.0 Preliminaries

Having dealt with the synchronic description of German, including regional variation in the standard languages in Germany, Austria and Switzerland, this chapter will show how this system developed out of German in the past. Much of this is, of course, reconstruction, but has been the subject of intense and detailed research for over 150 years. We will not describe the sound systems of past stages of German in detail but will use examples chosen from handbooks and secondary literature. After sketching some necessary information on the history of German and outlining some ways in which sounds change over time we will illustrate the changes.

12.1 History of German

Before describing the changes involved in the development of the German sound system it is necessary to explain some background to our description. As mentioned in 1.1.3 we can divide the historical development of German into four periods: Old High German (OHG), Middle High German (MHG), Early New High German (ENHG), and New High German (NHG). We will expand on the characteristics of each period in a separate section. There is a number of introductory works to the history of German: Schmidt (1996) is being continuously revised, Schildt (1991) is a condensed survey, while Wells (1985) is a more detailed work. Brundin (2004) and Ernst (2005) are more recent accessible works. König (1994) has a number of maps and diagrams that bring this subject to life.

12.1.1 Old High German

The oldest stage of the language is called Old High German and is taken to run from 750 to 1050. The first OHG texts appear from the late eighth century.

Figure 12.1   Map of OHG scriptoria and dialect areas

German was used in glossaries to help clerics understand Latin, then in inter-linear translations to emerge finally in finished translations, such as that of Tatian's Gospel Harmony. The oldest book in German is considered to be a Latin–German glossary called *Abrogans* (*c.*770 in Freising) after the first Latin word. Old High German (770–1050) is primarily the product of the clerical culture which existed in scriptoria such as the monasteries of Fulda in central Germany, Reichenau in southern Germany and St Gallen in Switzerland. It is more realistic to speak of several kinds of OHG than of one particular kind, since all the literary monuments from OHG times show quite a marked difference in spelling and form according to where they come from. It is normally assumed that the differences in writing reflected dialectal differences in pronunciation, each dialect region having one or more centres which produced literary works (see Fig. 12.1). For example, St Gallen and Reichenau were the centres of the Alemannic dialect. Notker Labeo (950–1022) translated the works of Boethius, Aristotle and the Psalms (*c.*1000) and is an important writer of late OHG. Among the centres of the

Bavarian dialect were Mondsee and Freising. The centre of the East Franconian dialect in OHG was the famous monastery at Fulda founded by Boniface and the most famous work written in East Franconian is the anonymous translation from the Latin version of the Gospel Harmony by Tatian (*c.*830). The so-called *Isidor* (*c.*790–800), which is a translation of the *Tractatus de fide catholica contra Judaeos* by Bishop Isidore of Seville, is also an important work. It probably came from the South Franconian region, possibly Lorraine, but its exact provenance and author are uncertain. Otfrid, who was a monk at Weissenburg (now Wissembourg in Alsace), wrote his *Evangelienbuch* (*c.*863–71) in South Rhine Franconian but we know little about his life. Some of our examples will be taken from *Notker, Tatian, Isidor* and *Otfrid*.

The phonology of OHG has a detailed treatment in Penzl (1971). An introductory text is Penzl (1986), while Sonderegger (1987) is an excellent work for more advanced students. Reiffenstein (2004) is the fullest up-to-date account that also includes inflectional forms.

12.1.1.1 Some OHG texts

The following extracts give a brief glimpse into what OHG looked like. They are from different areas and dates. They are given with an English translation but without a detailed commentary on the forms.

(i) Isidor

unbiuuizzsende sindun huueo in dheru dhrinissu sii ein got, fater endi sunu endi heilac gheist: nalles sie dhrîe godâ, oh ist in dhesêm dhrim heidem ein namo dhes unchideilden meghines.

'They are ignorant (about) how there is one God in the Trinity, Father, Son and Holy Ghost: these all are not three gods but one name of the undivided power in three persons.'

(ii) Tatian

Uuarun thô hirta in thero lantskeffi uuahhante inti bihaltante nahtuuahta ubar ero euuit. Quam thara gotes engil inti gistuont nâh in, inti gotes berahtnessi bischein sie; giforhtun sie im thô in mihhilero forhtu.

'There were shepherds watching in the country and keeping nightwatch over their sheep. There came the angel of the Lord and stood near them and God's glory shone around them and they were afraid with a great fear.'

(iii) Otfrid

> Tho truhtin Krist gebóran uuard (thes méra ih sagên nu ni thárf)
> Thaz blidi wórolt uuurti theru sáligun gibúrti
> Thaz ouh gidán uuurti, si in éuuon ni firuuúrti
> (Iz wás iru anan hénti, tho dét es druhtin énti)
> Tho quamun óstana in thaz lant thie erkantun súnnun fart,
> Stérrono girústi; thaz uuuárun iro listi.

'When Christ the Lord was born (I don't need to say more of this story) so that the world would be happy from this blessed birth, it would not be eternally lost. (It was at the time when the Lord put an end to it.) There came (wise men) from the east into the land, they knew the path of the sun, the formation of the stars, that was their skill.'

(iv) Notker

Part of Psalm 23

Truhten selbo rihtet mih, unde nîehtes ne brístet mir. In déro stéte dar uuéida ist, hábet er mih kesezzet. Er hábet mih kezógen bi démo uuazere dero labo. Hábet mîna sêla fóne úbele ze gûote bechêret. Léita mih after dîen stîgon des rehtes, umbe sînen námen.

'The Lord rules me and nothing is lacking to me. He has put me in the place where there is pasture. He has drawn me near the water of refreshment. He has converted my soul from evil to good. He leads me on the paths of righteousness for his name's sake.'

12.1.2 Middle High German

Middle High German is usually regarded as extending from 1050 to 1350 and was widely used for works of literature. Within MHG there is a period (1170–1250) that is known as 'classical MHG'. This is the period when the great literary courtly epics such Hartmann von Aue's *Erec*, Gottfried von Strasbourg's *Tristan* and Wolfram von Eschenbach's *Parzifal* as well as the poetry of Walter von der Vogelweide were written. The normalized forms of MHG grammars and texts, illustrated by the poem of Walther von der Vogelweide (12.1.2.1), are the work of nineteenth century philologists. The exact nature of the MHG literary language, often referred to as 'classical' Middle High German, has been hotly debated. Many of the writers of MHG avoided forms and rhymes that were felt to belong too obviously to one particular region. This nod in the development of a supraregional language variety came to an end with the demise of knightly and courtly literature. However, there were two important developments in MHG times that laid the basis for the genesis of the modern standard language.

One important difference between OHG and MHG is that in MHG times the German-speaking area increased in size. Previously it had extended in the east as far as the rivers Elbe and Saale, but in the Middle Ages colonists pushed into Slavic territories and founded villages and towns which soon grew into areas of German settlement; some groups even travelled as far as present-day Hungary and Romania. All the German territory east of the Elbe was colonized in the thirteenth century. These were larger dialect areas where the dialects of the settlers from different regions were mixed together to produce new dialects (see Fig. 1.1).

The second important development was the explosion in the use of written German by those not skilled in Latin. The upsurge and growth of independent towns meant that German was used for local laws and business dealings. The written documents of the time show a distinct regional variation in usage since there was no political centre to standardize usage. Also, many preachers, especially mystics such as Meister Eckhart and Berthold von Regensburg, used German in their sermons. The new technical sciences, such as mining, used German in their instructional manuals.

An elementary introduction to MHG is Walshe (1974), whereas Penzl (1989) is more advanced.

12.1.2.1 MHG texts

Walther von der Vogelweide

The vowels with a circumflex, e.g. *ûf*, are long; and *iu* is probably phonetically [y:].

> **ich saz ûf eime steine**
> ich saz ûf eime steine
> und dahte bein mit beine
> dar ûf satzt ich den ellenbogen
> ich hete in mîne hant gesmogen
> daz kinne und ein mîn wange
> dô dâhte ich mir vil ange
> wie man zer werlte solte leben

deheinen rât kunde ich gegeben
wie man driu dinc erwurbe
der keines niht verdurbe
diu zwei sint êre und varnde guot
daz dicke ein ander schaden tuot
daz dritte ist gotes hulde
der zweier übergulde
die wolte ich gerne in einen schrîn
jâ leider desn mac niht gesîn
daz guot und weltlich êre
und gotes hulde mêre
zesamene in ein herze komen
stîg unde wege sint in benomen
untriuwe ist in der sâze
gewalt vert ûf der strâze
fride unde reht sint sêre wunt
diu driu enhabent geleites niht
diu zwei enwerden ê gesunt

12.1.3 Early New High German and the development of the NHG standard

Standard languages, particularly those in western Europe, have evolved in a
number of similar ways (Besch 1988; Schmitt 1988). The prerequisite is literal-
ization, that is the writing down of texts in the language, which now functions
as a written as well as a spoken medium. According to Einar Haugen (1966)
there are four stages in the development of standard and national languages: (a)
Selection of Norms or 'What is the best language?', (b) Elaboration of Function
or 'Can the language be used in all situations?', (c) Codification or 'Where can
you find the right usage?', (d) Acceptance or 'Standard Language for all'.

Since the area where German was spoken had no political centre the selection of a norm was very complicated. The two most influential events for the
selection of a norm in the early modern period were the invention of printing
and the Reformation. Printing, using moveable type, was perfected in Germany
in Mainz by Johannes Gutenberg (c.1400–68), who produced his famous Latin
Bible in 1455. Printing soon spread to many other towns such as Cologne, Strasbourg, Nuremberg, Augsburg and Basel. Regional printers' language varieties
arose during the sixteenth century with centres in the Upper Rhine area (Strasbourg, Basle), Swabia (Augsburg), Bavaria and Austria (Munich, Vienna), the
West Central German area (Mainz, Frankfurt), East Franconia (Nuremberg,
Bamberg) and the East Central German (ECG) region (Leipzig, Wittenberg).

Through printing texts could be distributed throughout a wide area and reach a very large audience.

The other decisive event to occur in the sixteenth century was the Reformation. Martin Luther (1483–1546) was instrumental in focussing attention on the written language of the East Central German area, in particular Wittenberg, where Low and High German met. His translation of the Bible and his extensive publications sounded the death knell for Low German and also Upper German (UG) as the varieties that would shape the incipient standard. His German output alone in 1519–20 amounted to about half of all works published in German (Tschirch 1969: 100). Josten (1976) discovered that among the personal authorities cited as models of linguistic usage, Martin Luther's language was the most frequently considered to be the best. It was based on East Central German usage.

This ECG written language was intelligible to both north and south Germans. It may have differed in a number of ways from other regional written languages such as *das gemeine Deutsch* (lit. 'common German', i.e. understood by everyone), which was used in Upper Germany, or the standard form of Middle Low German, which was current in North Germany and was used as a lingua franca among the towns of the Hanseatic league. The following phonological and grammatical features are usually cited as being the most important in distinguishing this East Central German type, used by Luther, from Upper German and Low German:

> diphthongs in the words *Zeit, Haus* (MHG *zît, hûs*) as against monophthongs in LG and Alemannic;
>
> monophthongs in words like *lieb* [li:p], *Bruder* (MHG *liep, bruoder*) as against diphthongs in UG;
>
> the retention of the unstressed final -*e* as against its loss (apocope) in some endings, e.g. dat. *zu Hause*, and the loss of the unstressed vowel (syncope) in some prefixes, e.g. in the past participle *gestellt*, or in the prefix *be-* (*bestellt*);
>
> the pronunciation [k] for *ch* before *s* in *sechs, Ochsen* as against assimilation to *ss* in LG and some small areas in UG;
>
> a long [e:] in the words *gehen, stehen* as against the use of a long [a:] in Alemannic;
>
> -*chen* as the main diminutive ending (*Stückchen*) as against forms with -*l*, e.g. -*li*, -*le*, -*erl* in UG;
>
> attributive adjectives with a pronominal ending in the nom. sg. neuter, e.g. *mein lieb+es Kind*, as against no inflection of the adjective in some LG and UG dialects;

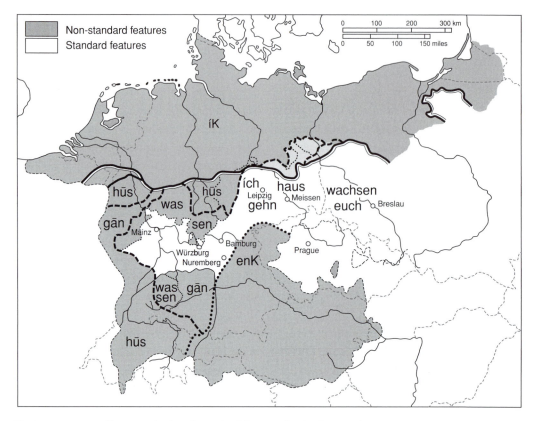

Figure 12.2   Non-standard and standard features in the German language area

personal pronoun forms for the first and second person sg. with the accusative ending in -*ch* (*mich*, *dich*) and the dative in -*r* (*mir*, *dir*), as against one single form for the acc. and dat. in LG (Bach 1965: 249).

Figure 12.2 (from Frings 1957: Map 42) shows the distribution of these features in German dialects.

We have seen how in OHG German was restricted in its use but during the Early NHG period it became extended to all types of texts. In OHG there were first glossaries, then interlinear translations, full translations and then finally independent works, most of these being religious works written by clerics. In MHG times the range broadened to include epic and lyric poetry as a reflection of courtly and knightly society. The use of German gained added ground in administrative functions as independent medieval towns grew and became important. The importance of the bourgeoisie was instrumental in leading the way. The use of the vernacular in Reformation broadsheets and pamphlets and the translation of the Bible were also important factors in the elaboration of function for German. In the seventeenth century, German began to be used as the medium of instruction in the new Protestant universities such as Halle and Göttingen. However, it wasn't until the eighteenth century that German finally gained the victory over its competitor Latin in academic and all other works.

The codification of German occupied scholars from the late fifteenth century onwards. But what can be codified? Spelling, grammar, vocabulary, pronunciation have all been subject to this process with varying degrees of success. Making of grammars and dictionaries of German is linked with the names of Schottel (1663), Gottsched (1748) and Adelung (1794). There was never a German academy as there was in France but German language societies (*Sprachgesellschaften*) developed which in the seventeenth century strove to uphold linguistic standards and the purity of the language in the face of competition from French and Latin loans (see Chapter 8). By the middle of the eighteenth century the variety that we know as the NHG standard written language was firmly established. The spelling was fully codified by 1900 but as we have seen in Chapter 1 attempts at standardizing pronunciation, begun in 1898, have not been so successful.

The East Central German variety that Martin Luther used for his works, including his translation of the Bible, quickly spread to most Protestant areas of German-speaking Europe. By the beginning of the seventeenth century it had ousted Low German as a written language and by the latter half of the seventeenth century it was the main basis of the written language used in Switzerland. Its progress was not so quick in the Roman Catholic southeast but by the middle of the eighteenth century it had found acceptance even there. This ECG written variety of German underwent changes in orthography, grammar and vocabulary in the seventeenth century. Luther, however, had laid the foundations for the acceptance of one variety of written German as a standard. What was important was that the East Central German area had become the focus of attention. This variety, closely connected with Martin Luther, and also containing Upper German elements, comes in the eighteenth century to be spread to other regions. Diffusion occurred chiefly through imitation of literary works in the eighteenth century and universal education in the nineteenth and twentieth centuries. The prime factor was seen as the need to communicate throughout the whole country and in every situation.

Wegera (1986) is an accessible collection of the most important articles on the theories surrounding the origin of standard NHG. Van der Elst (1987) is a survey of the problems of the emergence of NHG, using illustrative text material. Hartweg and Wegera (1989: 36–48) is a useful guide through the maze of theories and deals with phonological developments.

12.2 Sound change

As we have seen, sounds vary according to different contexts. There are a number of ways in which sounds change and there is a short catalogue of them in 12.4. In many cases these variations are either unnoticed by speakers or sometimes they can have a sociolinguistic value, either being considered prestigious and worthy of being imitated or else being stigmatized. We can really speak of sound change proper when these variants of sounds that have arisen change the pattern of the language. Usually this comes about by phonemic mergers or splits (12.5).

Some linguists deal with these variants and changes as the addition of rules to a speaker's grammar. As language is acquired by following generations these rules can be restructured in form and this is when linguistic change takes place. The arising of variants and the subsequent change in the phonemes of a language these linguists regard as belonging to dealing with surface phonetic phenomena. However, in some ways these two descriptions of changes are not contradictory. Basically sound change is described by starting with correspondences between two historical stages of a language: MHG *î, iu, û* 'corresponds' to NHG [ai, oi, au]. We then turn the correspondence into a process and say that MHG *î, iu, û* 'have become' NHG [ai, oi, au]. We have an initial state and a final state. This could equally well be framed in a rule. In every case we also have to discover what the initial state is. In other words we have to fill the letters of texts in the past with phonetic detail (12.3).

Sound change is usually regarded as regular; every instance of a particular sound will have changed into another sound: all the MHG *î* sounds will have become [ai]. Any exceptions are due to other factors such as analogy or dialect borrowing. In the case of the diphthongization of MHG *î, iu, û* to NHG [ai, oi, au], there is no diphthongization of *î* in MHG *vrîthof* 'cemetery' since *vrît-*, 'hedged garden', came to be identified with *Friede* 'peace'. The words *Luke, Düne* are Low German loans and *Uhr* comes from French. These were borrowed later and did not undergo diphthongization. There are also irregular sound changes that only affect a limited number of words: MHG *â* has become [o:] in NHG in a small number of words (12.6.6), e.g. MHG *âne*, NHG *ohne*.

Sounds very often develop in tandem. The change of MHG *î, iu, û* to NHG [ai, oi, au] is a good example of a series (*Reihe*) where all the sounds change in parallel. This change is often referred to as *Reihenschritt* (series change).

The causation of sound change is complicated and often speculative (Russ 1978b). Some guides to sound change with reference to German are to be found in Moulton (1961), Penzl (1975: 19–26), Wells (1985: 68–94) and Szulc (1987: 6–20).

12.3 Sound change and spelling

In reconstructed sound changes before written records are available (for instance the shift of the Germanic voiceless stops to affricates and fricatives) there is no problem with spelling. There are only the initial stages of the change, usually in another language, and the end stages. For changes that occur when written records are available, then, the problem is deducing from the orthography the phonetic and phonemic value of the letters representing the sounds. This is the case for most of the changes between OHG and NHG. In these instances there are several methods that can be used to fill the dead letters with some phonetic flesh. More detail can be found in Penzl (1975: 22–6) and Russ (1986).

12.3.1 Statements on pronunciation by contemporary phoneticians and grammarians

Normally these are only available in modern times. Sometimes they are not very specific as in the statement by Valentin Ickelsamer in his *Teutsche Grammatica* of 1535: 'Das /b/ und /p/ sein auch gleich/ allain das /p/ ist herter dann das /b/. Also auch das /t/ dann das /d/' (The b and p are also the same, except that the p is harder than the b. Thus t is harder than d) (reprinted in Müller 1882: 130). This simply tells us that sounds are different but not how. However, Ickelsamer is much more explicit about the articulation of *f*: 'Das /f/ wurdt geblasen durch die zene/ auf die unteren lebtzen gelegt/ und stymmet wie nass oder grün holtz am feüre seüt' (The *f* is blown through the teeth, placed on the lower lips and sounds like wet or green wood crackling on a fire) (Müller 1882: 128). Here we see that <f> is clearly labio-dental as we know from NHG.

12.3.2 Loan words

Words either loaned into other languages or borrowed from them often help to show us how a sound may have been pronounced. This presupposes that the original borrowed sound has not changed. When German *Stollen* 'gallery (in a mine), also Christmas cake with layers' was borrowed by Czech *stola*, the *s* was already pronounced [ʃ].

12.3.3 Phonological development in the language itself

In normalized MHG all the long vowels were marked ˆ but in the original manuscripts the ˆ is often lacking. However, the different development of the vowels reveals the distinction between long and short vowels. MHG *wibe* 'woman', *libe* 'life' (dat. sg.) have become diphthongs in NHG whereas *siben* 'seven', *riben* 'rubbed' have become long vowels: NHG *Weibe, Leibe* [ai] vs *sieben, rieben* [iː]. We can assume that the vowels in the two sets of words were pronounced differently since they are pronounced differently in NHG.

12.3.4 Spelling conventions and variants

In many texts, particularly in Early NHG, the spelling seems to be in a great state of flux. Many words are spelt differently even in the same sentence. For example, the NHG word *Zeit* is written in one text *zeit, zeyt, zit, zyt*, and the NHG word *Bein* 'leg' is written *bein, beyn, bain*. There is an overlapping of the signs *ei, ey* in the spelling of these two words. In some words they alternate with *i, y* and in other words with *ai*. If, instead of looking at the individual signs, we look at groups of signs, then the fluctuation seems less random and more capable of regular description. In the example of *Zeit* and *Bein* we have two groups of variable spellings, one comprising <i, y, ei, ey> and another comprising <ei, ey, ai>. Since there are two sets of signs, even though *ei* and *ey* occur in both of them, it is assumed that we are dealing with two different sounds that are in opposition. In fact group 1 represents MHG *î* and group 2 represents MHG *ei* (Philipp 1968: 4f. and 93ff.).

There are also inverse (or wrong) spellings, e.g. MHG *daz* being written *das* and MHG *alles* being written *allez*. This shows that the opposition in MHG between /z/ (from Germanic *t*) and /s/ is merging or has merged.

12.3.5 Rhymes and puns

One of the pieces of evidence that there were two short *e*-sounds in MHG is provided by the study of rhymes. MHG /e/, from Germanic short *a* by *i*-mutation (*bezzer* 'better'; cf. Gothic *batiza*), does not normally rhyme with MHG /ɛ/ (also written *ä*, or *ë*), from Germanic short *e* (*ezzen* 'to eat').

12.3.6 Related languages and dialects

In some cases sounds or oppositions between phonemes that were probably used in the past but no longer exist in the present standard are still in existence in dialects or related languages. Most Swiss German dialects still distinguish the reflexes of MHG /e/ and /ë/. However, there are no dialects that distinguish between MHG /z/ < Germanic *t* (*daz*) and /s/ (*des*). The digraphs *th, dh* are used in OHG for the Germanic interdental fricative [θ] that still exists in English and Icelandic.

12.4 Types of phonetic change

Phonetic change occurs when the articulation of a sound is modified. In many cases the change results in a phonemic change through merger or split (12.5). In this section we list a catalogue of phonetic changes, giving an example from the history of German (more details in Dieth 1968: 281–333). Further details of the changes – whether they are regular, what phonemic pattern they represent – will feature in 12.6 and 12.7.

12.4.1 Vowels

Vowel changes can affect the height of the tongue. The tongue can be lowered (MHG *sumer* > NHG *Sommer*). This mostly affects short vowels. The tongue height can be raised (MHG *swære* > NHG *schwer*). This mostly affects long vowels. Other changes affect the position of the tongue in the mouth. The umlaut vowels come about by fronting (OHG *hôren* > MHG *hœren*). In backing, the tongue is retracted (MHG *âne* > NHG *ohne*). Changes can also affect the position of the lips. In MHG *zwelf* > NHG *zwölf*, we have a case of rounding, whereas in MHG *küssen* > NHG *Kissen*, we have derounding. Changes affecting the quantity of vowels are the lengthening of short vowels in open syllables (see 12.6.3.1), e.g. MHG *siben* > NHG *sieben*, or the shortening of long vowels before consonant clusters: MHG *dâhte* > NHG *dachte*. Long vowels are always susceptible to becoming diphthongs: MHG *mîn niuwez hûs* > NHG *mein neues Haus*. Diphthongs themselves are also prone to becoming monophthongs: MHG *liebe* > *grüene*, *buoch* > NHG *Liebe*, *grün*, *Buch*.

12.4.2 Consonants

Changes to consonants affect their manner of articulation, place of articulation and their voicing. Plosives can become affricates or fricatives: English *pound*, NHG *Pfund*; English *sleeping*, NHG *schlafend*. The opposite change is not so frequent, but fricatives can change into plosives, mostly before other obstruents: MHG *vuohs* (*h* = fricative), NHG *Fuchs*. Shift in the place of articulation is not so common, except for neighbouring places: MHG *s* becomes [ʃ] before initial obstruents (MHG *snel*, NHG *schnell*). The values of voice can change. Medially between vowels, obstruents (particularly fricatives) become voiced: OHG *lesan*, NHG *lesen*. Devoicing occurs very often in certain phonetic contexts, e.g. in word-final position: MHG *wîb*, MHG *wîp*. Nasal consonants when occurring in clusters with plosives can 'spread' their nasality and assimilate a following plosive: MHG *kumber*, NHG *Kummer*. Liquids, since they have vowel-like qualities, often become vocalized; this has affected postvocalic /r/ in NHG *Uhr* [u:ɐ] and /l/, but only in Central Bavarian: [soits], *Salz*.

12.5 Phonemic change

Historical phonology not only deals with the changes in the realization of the phonemes but also with changes in the phonemic patterns of the language. This includes not only the number of phonemes and their oppositions but also the distribution of the phonemes.

There are three chief types of phonemic change: merger, split and shift (see Penzl 1971: 22–7; Russ 1978a: 24–8).

12.5.1 Merger

Through phonemic merger a phonemic opposition is lost and two phonemes merge into one, either in all positions (unconditioned merger) or only in certain positions (conditioned merger). The resulting phoneme may be one of the original members of the opposition or it may be a phoneme with a different realization. Merger can be illustrated by the pattern: /A/ : /B/ > /C/. An example of this is seen in German when through the NHG diphthongization the 'new' diphthongs merge with the 'old' MHG diphthongs: MHG *mîn, iuch, bûch* : *bein, vröude, ouch* > NHG *mein, euch, Bauch; Bein, Freude, auch*.

Conditioned merger, sometimes called 'split with merger', involves not the number of phonemes but their distribution. In MHG after /l/ and /r/ the phonemes /w/ and /b/ contrasted: MHG *swalwe* : *selbe*; *varwe* : *gestorben*. In NHG they have merged in /b/ in this position: *Schwalbe, selbe; Farbe, gestorben*.

12.5.2 Split

In phonemic split, sometimes called primary split, new phonemes are introduced. Where there was an allophonic variation there is now a phonemic contrast. Usually phonemic split comes about through another change that removes the allophonic conditioning factors. A classic case of this is umlaut or *i*-mutation. In OHG back rounded vowels developed front rounded allophones before an unstressed *i, i:* or *j*: OHG *skôni* [skø:ni] and *skôno* [sko:no]. In MHG the unstressed -*i* and -*o* vowels merged in schwa and the allophonic difference became a phonemic one that was also distinguished in spelling: MHG *schœne, schône*, NHG *schön, schon*.

12.5.3 Shift

In the case of phonemic shift it is the distinctive features of the phonemes that change. The early OHG contrast /th/ : /d/ (*thû : duon*), between a fricative and plosive became /d/ : /t/ in later OHG and MHG, a contrast between a voiced plosive and a voiceless plosive: *du : tuon* (NHG *du, tun*).

12.6 Vowel changes

12.6.1 Diphthongization and monophthongization

NHG has three diphthongs (/ai/, /au/ and /oi/) and three long high vowels (/iː/, /yː/ and /uː/). In the development of German these vowels have been involved in different changes. NHG also has the long mid vowels /eː/, /øː/ and /oː/ that in the standard have only been affected marginally by the changes in the diphthongs and long high vowels. For the history of the long half-open /ɛː/ see 12.6.5.1.

12.6.1.1 The development of OHG *ai* and *au*

There were also the diphthongs /ai/ and /au/ in OHG, spelt <ei> and <ou> (*stein, ouga*, NHG *Stein, Auge*) that represented Germanic *ai* and *au*. However, Germanic *ai* and *au* were also represented in OHG by the long monophthongs <ê> and <ô>. The long <ê> occurred before /r/, the Germanic medial velar fricative (spelt <h>), and /w/, and finally: *mêre, zêh* (preterite of *zîhan* 'to accuse'), *snêwes, wê* (NHG *mehr, verzieh* (new analogical form), *Schnees* (with loss of intervocalic *w*), *Weh*). The diphthong /ei/ appears elsewhere (*stein, heil*) and contrasts with the monophthong in final position: *skrei : wê*. The monophthong *ô* appears before the Germanic medial velar fricative (spelt <h>) and the alveolars *t, d, s, z* (fricative from Germanic *t*), *n, r* and *l*: *hôh, rôt, tôd, lôs, gôz, lôn, ôra, kôl* (Latin *caulis*) (NHG *hoch, rot, tot, los(e)*, *goss* (shortened in NHG before a voiceless fricative), *Lohn, Ohr, Kohl*). Elsewhere /au/ appears: *loub, loufan, ouga*. The diphthong and monophthong contrast before <h>: *hôh : ouh* 'also'. This final sound represents the Germanic voiceless velar fricative [x] and the voiceless velar fricative that arose in the Second Sound Shift (see 12.7.1) in postvocalic position from the Germanic plosive *k*.

This monophthong is an example of a phonemic split that came about by allophonic change. Allophones arose under certain conditions, subsequently becoming phonemes by a change in the phonetic conditions. At one time

Germanic *ai* must have had two main allophones, a half-open monophthong [ɛ:] before Germanic *h*, *r* and the semi-vowels *w* and *j*, and a diphthongal allophone, [ei] or [ɛi], elsewhere. Similarly, Germanic *au* must have had a half-open monophthongal allophone [ɔ:] before Germanic *h* and the alveolars *t*, *d*, *s*, *z*, *n*, *r* and *l*, and a diphthong, [ou] or [ɔu], elsewhere. In both cases the allophones were conditioned by the following consonant, or lack of consonant. A change in the quality of the following consonants brought about the change of status of the monophthongal allophones to phonemes. The semi-vowel *j* disappeared in final position and created a phonemic opposition between the monophthong /ê/ and the diphthong /ei/. OHG *wê*: *ei* represents Gothic *wái* and pre-OHG *aij*. Then through the merger of the reflexes of Germanic *h* and *k* in final position the monophthong /ô/ came to contrast with the diphthong /au/: *zêh*: *eih* 'oak'; *hôh*: *ouh*.

12.6.1.2 Diphthongization in OHG

These new monophthongs from Germanic *ai* and *au* appear to have 'forced' Germanic *ô* and *ê²* into becoming diphthongs in OHG in order to avoid merging with them. These diphthongs, mostly spelt <uo> and <ie> but <ua> and <ia> in Otfrid (*buoch*, *bruodar*, NHG *Buch*, *Bruder*; *hiar*, *kriacho*, NHG *hier*, *Grieche*), were not conditioned in any way and constitute a phonemic shift. These spellings and the diphthongal pronunciation were continued into MHG: *buoch*, *bruoder*; *hier*, *Krieche*. These diphthongs represent Germanic *ô* and the so-called Germanic *ê²* (of uncertain origin, see Russ 1978a: 42f.). Gothic examples show the monophthongal forms: *bôka*, *brôthar*, *hêr*, *krêks*. In MHG a third diphthong, *üe*, the umlaut of MHG *uo* (*güete*), joined this series of vowels. In addition there is a merger of some of the reflexes of Germanic *eu*, which became *io* in OHG (*biotan*, MHG *bieten*, with OHG/MHG *ie*). The development of Germanic *eu* is complicated by two factors: (1) before *a*, *e*, *o* Germanic *eu* became *io* (*dionôn*, *lioht*) and (2) before *i*, *j*, *u*, *eu* became *iu* (*diutisk*, *hiutu*). This was the regular development in the Franconian dialects. In Upper German *eu* became *iu* before labials and velars even if there was *a*, *e*, *o* in the following syllable. Thus we have Franconian *thiob*, *liogan* 'to tell lies'; UG *thiuba*, *liugan*; NHG *Dieb*, *lügen* (an analogical form in NHG modelled on the noun *Lüge*); Early NHG *liegen*. There was thus a phonemic split of Germanic *eu* into *io* and *iu* in OHG. In MHG *io* merged with *ie* (*dienen*, from *io*, and *Spiegel* from *ie*), while *iu* became the monophthong [y:] and merged with the umlaut of *û* (*liute*, *hiuser*) and was consequently diphthongized.

12.6.1.3 Monophthongization in NHG

The 'new' MHG diphthongs /ie, üe, uo/ are represented in NHG by the long high monophthongs: *Liebe, Güte, Buch*. The spelling has not changed in the case of MHG *ie,* but the *e* has become a length sign. Phonetically this change implies a weakening of the second element, its disappearance, and the consequent lengthening of the first element. Phonemically these long high monophthongs merged with the MHG short vowels *i, ü, u* when they were lengthened: MHG *siben : lieben; über : trüebe; stube : buobe;* NHG *sieben, lieben; über, trübe; Stube, Bube.*

12.6.1.4 Diphthongization in NHG

The MHG long close vowels *î, iu, û* are represented in NHG by the falling diphthongs /ai/ (spelt <ei>), /oi/ (spelt <eu> and <äu>), and /au/ (spelt <au>). A handy mnemonic is *mîn niuwez hûs,* NHG *mein neues Haus,* containing all the relevant sounds. The MHG diphthongs *ei, öu, ou* are also represented in NHG by the same falling diphthongs /ai, oi, au/ respectively. Whereas in MHG there was a contrast between *pîn* and *bein, vriunt* and *vröude, bûch* and *auch,* there is no contrast in NHG. The vowels in the pairs of words are spelt the same and also pronounced the same: *Pein, Bein; Freund, Freude; Bauch, auch.* The MHG phonemic distinction between the series /î, iu, û/ and /ei, öu, ou/ no longer exists; the two sets of phonemes have merged in NHG. The long vowels probably became overlong [ii, yy, uu], the two components became differentiated in tongue height, [ei, øy, ou]. Later [ei] and [ou] were lowered to [ai] and [au], merging with the old diphthongs /ei, ou/. The diphthong [øy] became [oi] by derounding and backness adjustment. All the CG and UG dialects show diphthongs for MHG /î, iu, û/, except High Alemannic (mostly Swiss German), and the dialect of the west part of Thuringia (see Fig. 12.3). The phonetic detail of the diphthongs in the dialects often differs from the standard. The merger of the new and old diphthongs is not found in the dialects. The occurrence of the merger in the standard language is probably due to the fact that when digraphs were first used in ECG for MHG /î, iu, û/ they were the same signs as were used for MHG /ei, öu, ou/. Since both these sets of phonemes were written with the same signs they eventually became pronounced in the same way. A structural cause of the diphthongization may have been the lengthening of MHG short /i, ü, u/ in open syllables that 'pushed' the MHG long high vowels into becoming diphthongs and thus avoided merging with them (Penzl 1975: 117f.).

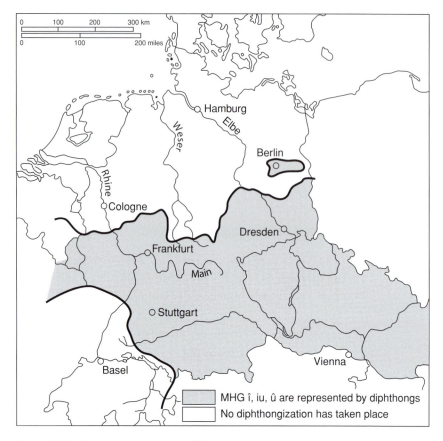

Figure 12.3   Map of NHG diphthongs in German dialects

The map legend reads:

MHG î, iu, û are represented by diphthongs

No diphthongization has taken place

12.6.2 Development of umlaut vowels

One of the typological characteristics of modern German is that it contains both short and long front rounded vowels (*füllen, Bücher, Löcher, hören*) that in some cases also alternate with short and long *u* and *o*. There is also an alternation between the diphthongs *au* and *eu*; in addition, short and long *a* alternate with *e*. These vowels are known as umlaut vowels. They have not always existed in German. They started out as allophones and then through the weakening of unstressed vowels to [-ə] they became phonemes.

The OHG reflex of Germanic short *a* when followed by *i*, *î* or *j*, except before the consonant clusters *ht*, *hs*, was a close *e*. This pronunciation whereby a back vowel is fronted before a high front vowel is known as umlaut or *i*-mutation. The resultant sound, written <e> in OHG, is considered to be phonetically more close than Germanic short *e*, which is also written <e>. Germanic *a* was not only fronted by *i*-mutation but also raised. However, umlaut did not only affect *a* but all short and long back vowels and the OHG diphthongs *uo* (from Germanic *ô*) and *ou*. All these vowels developed palatal or fronted allophones under the influence of *i, î* or *j* that followed. In OHG, however, only the umlaut of short *a* received orthographic recognition. This is known as primary umlaut (*Primärumlaut*). The other mutated or fronted vowel allophones were not written with special signs until MHG, and even then only sporadically. The mutation of the other vowels and diphthongs is known as secondary umlaut (*Sekundärumlaut*). The umlaut sign, the 'two dots' (¨), was originally a small *e* written over the vowel. In MHG there are other signs used for umlaut vowels: <iu> for [y:], <æ> for long [ɛ:] and <œ> for long [ø:].

It would be wrong to think that there were two separate umlaut processes. There are rather two stages of one process. Primary and secondary umlaut represent two different stages of the phonemicization of the umlaut allophones. Examples of primary umlaut are: OHG *ih faru, du feris, er ferit*; *gast* (sg.), *gesti* (pl.); *kraft, kreftig*. Examples of secondary umlaut are: MHG *wahsen, wähset*, OHG *wahsit*; MHG *loh, löcher*, OHG *lohhir*; MHG *künne* 'family, kin', OHG *kunni*; MHG *nâmen, næme*, OHG *nâmî*; MHG *rôt, rœte*, OHG *rôti*; MHG *hûs, hiuser*, OHG *hûsir*; MHG *guot, güete*, OHG *guotî*; MHG *loufen, löufet*, OHG *loufit*. The secondary umlaut of short *a* resulted from the umlaut allophone [æ] not being raised to [e] before the consonant clusters *ht, hs* (OHG *mahtîg, wahsit*). As in other examples of phonemic split, the allophones in complementary distribution became phonemes when the conditioning factors changed or disappeared. In this case the conditioning factors were the *i, î* or *j* of the following syllable. By MHG all the OHG unstressed vowels (except in some derivational suffixes, e.g. *-lîch, -lîn, -inne*, where the vowel may have retained its quality by some subsidiary stress) were reduced to [-ə].

12.6.3 Changes in vowel quantity

12.6.3.1 Lengthening

Disyllabic words in MHG containing a stressed vowel followed by an unstressed vowel had different syllable types from NHG. There were in fact three types (the initial and final consonants will be disregarded):

(1) VCCv: *hazzen, messe, brücke, knappe, ritter, schaffen* (V = any short vowel, CC = a long consonant and v = [ə]);
(2) VCv: *haben, reden, sagen, lesen, beten*;
(3) VVCv: *âbent, slâfen, brâdem* 'vapour', *vrâgen, râten* (VV = any long vowel or diphthong).

There are two stages in the development from MHG to NHG. Firstly, short vowels before single voiced consonants were lengthened: MHG *siben, stube, eben, haben, oben* > NHG *sieben, Stube, eben, haben, oben.* Syllable type 2 (VCv, MHG *haben*) merged with syllable type 3 (VVCv, MHG *âbent*); this is referred to traditionally as lengthening in open syllables (*Tonsilbendehnung*). Secondly, long consonants were shortened. In NHG there are no long consonants except at the boundaries of words and morphemes (*nicht tun, Süddeutschland, Schiff-fahrt*). In NHG length of vowel alone is sufficient to show the difference between the two types of syllable, [ʃafən] : [ʃlaːfən]; no difference of length of consonants is necessary. In NHG orthography the double consonant in *schaffen* merely signifies that the preceding vowel is short (see 6.1.2).

The lengthening resulted in just two syllable types, which differed from each other in both vowel and consonant length: (1) VCCv *schaffen,* and (2) VVCv *schlafen.* In other Germanic languages, e.g. Swedish, we have the same situation where vowel and consonant length are predictable: a short vowel before a long consonant (*tack* 'thanks'), and a long vowel before a short consonant (*tak* 'roof'). Furthermore, in German, the long consonants tended to be voiceless and the short consonants voiced. However, this adjustment, making vowel and consonant length interdependent, did not happen in the development of German.

Firstly, in MHG there was a contrast between single /t/ and double /tt/ in medial position (MHG *bëten* 'to pray', *betten* 'beds'), so a voiceless consonant occurred in both syllable types. In NHG there were both short and long vowels before MHG /t/: MHG *schate, site, beten, bote* > NHG *Schatten, Sitte, beten, Bote.* If we assume a merger of MHG medial /t/ and /tt/ in /tt/ [tt] then the regular development of short vowels before /tt/ would be to remain short, e.g. *Schatten, Sitte.* In other words the sequence VCv would have merged with VCCv if the C = [t]. In those case where the vowel was lengthened it is due to either analogy with other forms or to the fact that the words became spelt with a single <t> and a vowel before a medial consonant would be pronounced long. The main words where we have a lengthened vowel before NHG /t/ are: *beten, Bote, geboten, jäten, Kater, kneten, Knoten, Kröte, Spaten, treten, Vater, waten.* Some of these are verbs and probably have long vowels by analogy with other verbs in the same vowel gradation class. For details see Russ (1969) and (1982: 131–4).

Secondly, there were gaps in the distribution of individual consonants, for instance VVp, VVk, Vbb, Vdd, Vgg did not occur or only very infrequently in MHG. This did not remain the case and from the fifteenth century, through borrowing, words with these structures entered German: (1) from LG, *Laken, Luke* 'hatch', *Pökel* 'brine, pickle', *rekeln* 'to loll around', *Takel, hapern* 'to be short of', *Kaper*, *Stapel*, and (2) from French, *Lupe*, *Tüte*. The sequence VC, with C being a voiced plosive and spelt <bb>, <dd>, <gg>, existed in LG. From the sixteenth century onwards words with that structure were borrowed into NHG: *Ebbe*, *Robbe*; *buddeln*, *Kladde*; *Flagge*, *schmuggeln*. This development is reflected in the infrequent occurrence of short vowels before medial voiced plosives and of long vowels before voiceless plosives, except for /t/, in NHG (see 5.3.1).

Phonemically the lengthening of short vowels in open syllables is an example of shift with merger. MHG short /i, ü, u/ did not merge with MHG /î, iu, û/ since the latter had become diphthongs, but with the long close monophthongs that resulted from the monophthongization of MHG /ie, üe, uo/: MHG *siben* : *lieben* > NHG *sieben, lieben*; MHG *übel* : *rüebe* > NHG *Übel, Rübe*; MHG *stube* : *buobe* > NHG *Stube, Bube*. MHG short /a/ merged with MHG long /â/: MHG *sagen* : *vrâgen* > NHG *sagen, fragen*. MHG short /o/ merged with MHG long /ô/: MHG *boden* : *tôdes* > NHG *Boden, Todes*. MHG short /ö/ merged with MHG long /œ/: MHG *knödel* : *bloede* > NHG *Knödel, blöde*. MHG short /e/, /ë/ and /ä/, when they were lengthened, merged with MHG long /æ/ and /ê/ in a long half-close /e:/, or half-open /ɛ:/, if the resultant phoneme was spelt <ä > (see 12.6.5.1): MHG *zeln, denen, gëben, vrävel(e)* : *lære, sêle* > NHG *zählen, dehnen, geben, Frevel, Leere, Seele*.

12.6.3.2 Shortening

The corollary to the lengthening of short vowels is the shortening of long vowels before consonant clusters. It occurs most frequently before MHG *ch* or *h + t* (MHG *brâchte, dâchte* > NHG *brachte, dachte*), or before *ch* (MHG *schâch, râche* > NHG *Schach, Rache*). In some instances the vowel that was shortened was a diphthong (MHG *viehte, lieht* > NHG *Fichte, Licht*). MHG medial <ng > became <nc > in final position. This is a pointer to the digraph representing a consonant cluster [ŋk] before which any long vowels were shortened (MHG *vienc, gienc, hienc* > NHG *fing, ging, hing*, with <ng > representing the new velar nasal phoneme /ŋ/; see 12.7.5). Shortening, again sometimes of a diphthong, also took place before voiceless obstruents: MHG *gôz, vlôz, müezen, muoter* > NHG *goss, floss, müssen, Mutter*.

12.6.4 Changes in vowel quality

These changes affect the tongue height and lip position of the short and long vowels. None of the changes is regular; rather, each affects a limited number of words, very often in certain phonetic environments.

12.6.4.1 Lowering

In our description of the vowels of NHG we noted how the short vowels were open and the long vowels close. MHG short *ü* and *u* have been lowered in NHG to *ö* and *o*. In some words they have even been lengthened: *König, Söhne*. This lowering has mostly occurred in a few words before /n/ (MHG *nunne, günnen, sunder, sunne, künnen, münech* > NHG *Nonne, gönnen* 'to grant', *sondern, Sonne, können, Mönch*) and before /m/ (MHG *sumer, vrum* > NHG *Sommer, fromm* 'pious'). There is an isolated example before /g/: MHG *mügen* > NHG *mögen*.

Raising of vowels does not occur in the standard but in some CG dialects.

12.6.4.2 Rounding and derounding

The vowels produced by the process of umlaut were chiefly front rounded vowels. In many dialects, e.g. Bavarian, Low Alemannic and Central German dialects, these have lost their lip-rounding and merged with the corresponding unrounded vowels. This has also happened in English, cf. NHG *Brücke*, English *bridge*. In NHG there is a small group of words with /i/ for MHG /ü/ (MHG *fündling, sprütze, bümez, gümpel, küssen, bülez* > NHG *Findling* 'foundling', *Spritze, Bimsstein* 'pumice', *Gimpel* 'bullfinch', *Kissen, Pilz*) and one word with MHG *ö* and NHG *e*: *nörz* > *Nerz* 'mink'.

In other cases in NHG there is a front rounded vowel, either *ü* or *ö*, where in MHG there was an unrounded vowel, *i* or *e*. Examples of /e/ to /ö/: MHG *derren, ergetzen, helle, leffel, leschen, lewe, pekeln, schepfen, stenen, swern, welben, zwelf* > NHG *dörren, ergötzen, Hölle, Löffel, löschen, Löwe, pökeln, schöpfen, stöhnen, schwören, wölben, zwölf*. In many cases the presence of a labial consonant may have encouraged the rounding. Examples of the change /i/ to /ü/ are less frequent: MHG *flistern, wirde, wirz* > NHG *flüstern, Würde, Gewürz*. These words also reflect the situation in most of the Alemannic dialects and East Franconian where this rounding has regularly taken place before certain consonants.

12.6.5 The *e*-sounds

In classical MHG there were five *e*-sounds, three short and two long. Two of the short vowels and one of the long vowels arose from umlaut (see 12.6.2).

12.6.5.1 Origin of /ɛ:/

In MHG there was a contrast between a long half-close /ê/ [e:], *mêre*, and a half-open /æ/ [ɛ:], *mære* 'news' (cf. NHG *Märchen*). In standard NHG there is also a similar distinction between *Beeren* and *Bären*. However, in the north and east of Germany many speakers substitute [e:] for [ɛ:], showing a merger of the two sounds. In fact, NHG /ɛ:/ is not really the exact continuation of MHG /æ/ since it comes from five separate MHG sources: (1) MHG /æ/ in *fähig*, *Käse*; (2) MHG /ä/ when lengthened in an open syllable in *Ähre* 'ear of corn', *Träne*; (3) MHG /ë/ when lengthened in an open syllable in *Käfig, erwägen*; (4) MHG /e/ when lengthened in an open syllable in *ähnlich, nähren, zählen*; and (5) by analogy it occurs in *Fäden, Hähne, Läden*. All these words are connected by their spelling with the letter <ä>. NHG /ɛ:/ is in most cases a spelling pronunciation of words where <ä> represents a long vowel (Moulton 1961: 34f.).

12.6.5.2 The short *e*-sounds

In MHG there were three short MHG *e*-phonemes: /ä/ (from *a* by secondary umlaut), /ë/ and /e/ (from *a* by primary umlaut). These have all merged in NHG in one phoneme, the half-open /ɛ/: MHG *mähtec, ëzzen, besser* > NHG *mächtig, essen, besser*. The phoneme /ɛ/ is spelt <e> but <ä> if there is a morphologically related word with a stem vowel <a>: *Gäste* because of *Gast*, *schwächer* because of *schwach*, *rächen* because of *Rache*.

12.6.6 The retraction of long /a:/

In NHG long open /a:/ is a back vowel but the lips are neutral in its articulation. In many varieties of German this sound has been not only pronounced as far back in the oral cavity as possible but also raised in the direction of /o:/ and taken on lip-rounding. This change is often referred to as *Verdumpfung* (darkening). In standard NHG there are a number of words in which /o:/ corresponds to MHG /a:/: NHG *Monat, Mond, ohne, Schlot, Woge* < MHG *mânôt, mâne, âne, slât, wâc*.

12.7 Consonantal changes
12.7.1 Second, or High German, Sound Shift

The affricates /pf/ and /ts/ that set off NHG from the other Germanic languages arose through the Second, or High German, Sound Shift. Germanic had a series of voiceless plosives *p, t, k* and in pre-OHG these were geminated or doubled medially when they were followed by *i, j* or in some cases *r* and *l*. This gemination only happened in OHG, Old Saxon, Old English and Old

	p	pp	t	tt	k	kk
Initially	pf		z [ts]			
Medially	f, ff	pf	z, zz [s]	z, zz, tz [ts]	ch, hh [xx]	ck, cch [kk, kx]
Finally	f		z [s]		h [x]	

Figure 12.4   The development of Germanic voiceless plosives in OHG

Frisian and is often called the West Germanic consonant gemination. Since they changed further in OHG some Old Saxon examples are clearer. We can contrast the forms with simple consonants in Gothic: Gothic *ga-skapjan*, Old Saxon *skeppian*; Gothic *satjan*, Old Saxon *settian*; Gothic *uf-rakjan*, Old Saxon *rekkian*. Voiced consonants and fricatives were also affected by the gemination: Gothic *sibja, bidjan, hugjan, hafjan, hlahjan*; Old Saxon *sibbia, biddian, huggian, hebbian*, Old English *hliehhan*.

The Germanic voiceless plosives underwent a radical change in OHG and are represented either by affricates or by long voiceless fricatives. Some of the changes did not take place in every dialect of OHG and in fact the dialects of NHG are classified according to how Germanic *p, t, k* developed.

Figure 12.4 shows the development in OHG of the Germanic voiceless plosives and the long voiceless geminates produced by the West German consonant gemination.

Germanic *p* is either represented in OHG by an affricate [pf], written <pf> or <ph> (or even <f> in Notker), or by a voiceless geminate labio-dental fricative [ff], written <f> or <ff>. Medial geminate *pp* is represented by the affricate *pf*. Examples are: initially, English *path, plough* – OHG *pfad, pfluog*; medially, corresponding to a geminate, Old Saxon *skeppian* – OHG *scephen*; medially, corresponding to a simple plosive, English *open* – OHG *offan*, Gothic *slêpan* – OHG *slâfan*; finally, after vowels, English *ship* – OHG *skif*; after liquids and nasals, Old English *healpan, weorpan*, English *stump* – OHG *helphan, werpfan, stumpf*. After liquids the affricate was replaced by a fricative in the ninth century (*helfan*). Some affricates remained in this position until MHG (*scharpf*), but in NHG this has been reduced to a fricative (*scharf*). In NHG the only example of [pf] after a liquid is *Karpfen*.

Germanic *t* is represented in OHG by an affricate [ts], written *z, zz* or *tz*, or else by a voiceless fricative written *z* or *zz*. There is an orthographic overlap in the signs since both <z> and <zz> are used medially for the affricate and the fricative. The different texts represent different systems. Tatian and Otfrid make no distinction, at least after short vowels: *sizzen* (affricate) and *wazzar* (fricative). After long vowels and diphthongs the fricative is often written *z*: *grôze*. The affricate occurred infrequently after long vowels and diphthongs. Isidor, however, makes a clear distinction between the affricate and fricative after short vowels, long vowels and diphthongs: *ezssant, fuozssi* (fricative), and *sitzit* (affricate). Notker also makes a distinction between affricate and fricative by writing the latter *z* after short vowels and the former *zz*: *wazer* (fricative), *sizzen* (affricate). In NHG the affricate is written <tz> medially after short vowels (*Hitze*) and <z> after long vowels and diphthongs (*Brezel, heizen*), while the fricative is written <ss> and <ß>: *essen, Füße*. Examples of affricates are: initially, English *tide*, Dutch *twee*, Gothic *tiuhan* – OHG *zît, zwei, ziohan*; medially corresponding to a geminate, Old Saxon *settian* – OHG *sitzan*. Examples of the fricatives are: medially corresponding to a plosive, English *water*, Gothic *itan lêtan* – OHG *wazzar, ezzan, lâzan*, NHG *lassen*; finally after vowels, English *that, what, foot* – OHG *daz, waz, fuoz*; finally after liquids and nasals, Dutch *zwart*, English *holt, unto* – OHG *swarz, holz, unz*.

The exact phonetic nature of the fricative is uncertain, but it was probably voiceless. It was either dental or alveolar, and also probably pre-dorsal, that is the part of the tongue used to approach the dental or alveolar region to produce the friction was the front part of the dorsum, or back, of the tongue.

Initially before vowels Germanic *k* is always written <k> by Otfrid (*kind, kan, kuning*), whereas Tatian only writes <k> before *i* and *e* (*kind, kennen*); elsewhere it is written <c>: *calb, corn, cuning*. Before liquids and nasals Otfrid writes <k>, while Tatian has <k> before *n* (*kneht*), but <c> before *l* and *r* (*clophôn, crippea*). Isidor and Notker write initial Germanic *k* as <ch>: *chomen*. Medially Germanic *k* is written <ch> by Notker (*rîche*), and Otfrid (*rîchi*), but <hh> by Isidor and Tatian (*rihhi*). The interpretation of the digraph <ch> as affricate, fricative or aspirated plosive is not clear. The dialect reflexes gives us some pointers. Germanic *k* has only been shifted initially and medially when geminate in Upper German. The expected affricate [kx] only occurs in the southernmost parts of Alemannic and Bavarian in the south of Switzerland and Austria. In Alemannic the affricate has been 'smoothed' to a fricative [x] which is current in Swiss German and as far north as Freiburg.

Examples of the reflexes of Germanic *k* initially are: probably a plosive as in NHG, English *corn, kin* – OHG *chorn, kunni*; medially, corresponding to a geminate, Old Saxon *wekkian* – OHG *wecken* (the spelling *cch* in some UG sources may reflect an affricate or fricative pronunciation); medially, a fricative corresponding to a simple plosive, Gothic *brikan, sôkjan, táikns* – OHG *brehhan, suohhen, zeihhan*; finally after vowels, also a fricative, Gothic *sik, mik*, Swedish *tak* 'roof' – OHG *sih, mih, dah*.

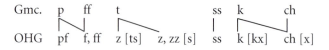

The phonemic pattern of the Sound Shift is largely split with merger, except that the affricates and the fricative /z, zz/ are new phonemes, as is shown in Fig. 12.5.

12.7.1.1 The geographical distribution of the Second Sound Shift

The extent of the shifting of Germanic *p, t, k* varies from south to north. In the far south, in the High Alemannic and South Bavarian dialects, all the Germanic voiceless stops have been shifted initially, medially and finally, whereas in Low German, English and Dutch none of them has been shifted. The material to chart this spread was gathered in the nineteenth century when Georg Wenker (1852–1911) and Ferdinand Wrede (1863–1934) sent out a list of forty sentences to be translated into the dialect of each village. They were sent to every primary school (*Volksschule*) of the German Empire at that time. The question asked was: 'Wie heißt in der Mundart Ihres Dorfes?' (What is this in the dialect of your village?) and one example sentence was: 'Der gute alte Mann ist mit dem Pferd durchs Eis gebrochen und in das kalte Wasser gefallen' (The good old man has fallen through the ice with the horse and into the cold water). This sentence shows three forms whose development reflects the sound shift: *Pferd* (LG *Peerd*, *gebrochen* (LG *braken*), *Wasser* (LG *Water*). On the basis of the answers, maps were drawn showing the extent of the sounds that had undergone the sound shift. The geographical distribution of other sounds was also dealt with. These dialect geographical maps were part of the *Deutscher Sprachatlas* (DSA). Figure 12.6 shows the extent of the shifting.

The isoglosses of the second sound shift spread out from the south to the north in the shape of a fan. The shift of medial Germanic *k* and initial and medial Germanic *t* (isogloss 1) defines the whole of the High German speech area against Low German and Dutch. The shift of initial *k* (isogloss 5) is much more limited and serves to mark off High Alemannic from Low Alemannic and Swabian. The shift of initial and medial geminate Germanic *pp* (isogloss 4) divides UG from CG. The latter can be divided into West CG, where initial *p* remains unshifted, and East CG, where initial *p* is shifted to [pf] and further to [f] (isogloss 4a). West CG is also divided into two sections: (1) Central

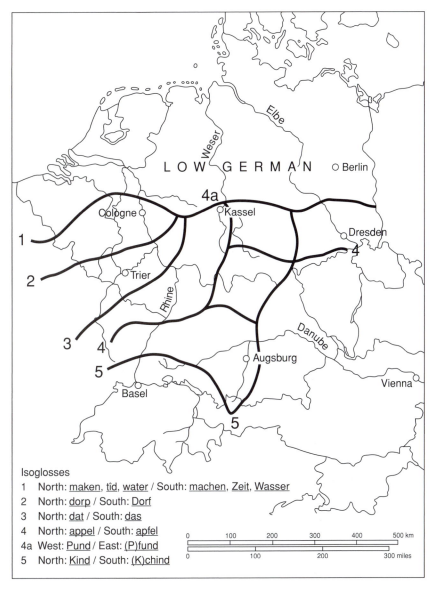

Figure 12.6   Map of German dialects showing the extent of the Second Sound Shift (adapted from Russ 1978)

Franconian, comprising Ripuarian, in which Germanic *p* is unshifted, and Moselle Franconian, and (2) Rhine Franconian, which has shifted the relic words *dat* and *wat* that occur in their unshifted form in Central Franconian (isogloss 3). It is a moot question, however, how far these modern dialect isoglosses reflect the situation in OHG. Figure 12.7 summarizes these changes.

	Labial		Alveolar		Velar	
	Initial	Medial	Initial	Medial	Initial	Medial
CFranc.	**p**	f, ff	[ts]	[s]	**k**	ch [x]
RFranc.	**p** (pf)	f, ff	[ts]	[s]	**k**	ch [x]
East CG	pf/f	f, ff	[ts]	[s]	**k**	ch [x]
UG	pf	f, ff	[ts]	[s]	ch [(k)x]	ch [x]

Figure 12.7   Extent of Sound Shifting (the unshifted sounds are in bold)

Central and Rhine Franconian represent West CG. East CG comprises Thuringian and Upper Saxon. East Franconian, together with Alemannic, Swabian and Bavarian represent Upper German.

12.7.1.2 Theories about the Second Sound Shift

It has traditionally been assumed that the geographical distribution of the sound shift, with more shifted forms in the south than in the north, reflects its actual spread: it started in the south, in the Alemannic dialects, and spread northwards. The first shifted forms of which we have records probably date from the sixth century. However, there have been a number of other theories put forward. One of the main objections to the traditional theory of south-to-north development is that it is counter to the direction of the political and military expansion of the Franks from the north. One explanation, advanced by Schützeichel (1976), suggests that the Sound Shift is older in the north than previously assumed; it perhaps arose independently in the Franconian dialects of CG. Records of very old shifted forms going back to the eighth or ninth century have been discovered, whereas most of the shifted forms in CG were assumed to date from the twelfth century. A more controversial theory, advanced by Theo Vennemann, starts further back with the oldest form of Germanic, a reconstructed paleo-Germanic. The consonant system has three types of consonants: fortis fricatives, fortis plosives and lenis plosives. Of these three the important series are the fortis plosives. These show a twofold development: (1) a series of affricates in High Germanic (*Hochgermanisch*), the CG and UG dialects; (2) a series of aspirated plosives, in Low Germanic (*Niedergermanisch*), the LG dialects and other Germanic languages such as English. This has been labelled the bifurcation theory (*Bifurkationstheorie*). The partial distribution of the Sound Shift in CG is explained by positing a much larger area of the full Sound Shift that is pushed back by the advancing Franks. It is an interesting theory but not generally accepted. A useful summary is Frey (1994: 14–27). Reiffenstein (2004: 82–95) reviews some of the most recent literature. The original bifurcation theory is Vennemann (1984).

12.7.2 Voiced and voiceless plosives and fricatives

The NHG voiced plosives *b*, *d*, *g* probably should be reconstructed as consisting of both plosive and fricative allophones in Germanic. This is mostly based on the fact that they are represented by both plosives and fricatives in German dialects and other Germanic languages.

In OHG the plosive allophones of Germanic *b-v*, *d-ð* and *g-ɣ* were generalized in all positions in the word. The resultant *b*, *g* also became written <p>, <k, c> respectively in some texts in OHG, particularly in Alemannic and Bavarian: *pittan, hapen, këpan, takes, tac* (NHG *bitten, haben, geben, Tages, Tag*). In later OHG the spelling <b> and <g> resumes. The spelling <t> for Germanic *d-dh* is more widespread. <t> occurs initially and medially in Tatian and Notker (*tagun, gotes*). Isidor writes <d> initially (*daghe*), whereas medially <d> and <t> are in free variation. Otfrid has <d> initially (*dâti*), but <t> medially (*guati*). It is not clear whether the spelling of <p> for <b> or <k, c> for <g> represents a sound change. Certainly the spelling of <t> for <d> is a change that is present today. However, in late OHG, there was a regular devoicing of word-final plosives (OHG *wîb, sîd, tag* > MHG *wîp, sît, tac*); even the medial cluster <ng> becomes devoiced to final <nc>: *singen, sanc*.

In many Central and Upper German dialects there is a merger of voiced and voiceless plosives, except *g* and *k*, in all positions. This is known as consonant weakening or lenition (*Konsonantenschwächung*). The standard written language has always maintained the opposition between voiced and voiceless consonants but there has been uncertainty to which phoneme some words have belonged. This has resulted in an interchange between words beginning with *t* and *d*. For example, MHG has *t* in *tam, tihten, tunkel, tump, tiutsch* but they have *d* in NHG: *Damm, dichten, dunkel, dumm, deutsch*. This interchange also occurs medially: MHG *dulten, bortes, kleinôtes*, NHG *dulden, Bordes, Kleinodes*. There is a smaller number of words with *d* in MHG (*dôsen, dôn, under, hinder*), but *t* in NHG (*tosen, Ton, unter, hinter*). An even smaller number of words have *b* in MHG (*bech, bâbest, bredigen*) but *p* in NHG (*Pech, Papst, predigen*). This is not a change in any phonetic features or phonemic pattern but simply in the incidence of some words.

12.7.3 Voiced and voiceless fricatives

Germanic is also assumed to have had the voiceless fricatives *þ, f, s* and *x*. The dental *þ* was probably a voiceless interdental fricative like the [θ] in English *thing*. In the earliest OHG documents it is written <th> and in MHG it is written *d*: OHG *thû*, MHG *du*. It was first written <d> in the eighth century in Bavarian and part of Alemannic but it was not until the eleventh century that it was written <d> in Middle Franconian. The orthographic change from <th> to <d>, reflecting the sound change from fricative to plosive, spread from the south-east to the north-west. In Otfrid the shift of <th> to <d> resulted in a merger with Germanic *d* in initial position: *dohter* < d and *ding* < th. In East Franconian and UG *d* had become *t* and thus there was no merger with the *d* from Germanic *t*, as in NHG *Tochter, Ding*. These two changes are seen as connected. Chronologically the shift of *th* to *d* occurred after the shift of *t* to *d*. This latter change may have come about to fill this 'gap' created by the shift of *d* to *t*. It was part of a 'pull-chain'. In Germanic there were already two dental or alveolar fricatives, *s* and *th*; when Germanic *t* became *z* in medial and final position through the Second Sound Shift, there were three. A contributory factor in the shift of *th* to *d* may also have been the structural pressure to reduce the number of dental or alveolar fricatives. The opposition between /z/ and /s/ continued into MHG: *ëzzen* 'to eat' : *messe* 'mass'; *waz* 'what' : *was* 'was'. These two phonemes merge by the middle of the thirteenth century in a voiceless [s] that is spelt *s, ss* or *ß*.

The other Germanic fricatives were *f, s* and *x*. Germanic *f* becomes voiced in OHG medially between vowels, shown by writing it <u> or <v>: *reue* 'womb', *neue* 'nephew'. Initially and finally it is written <f> (*faran, hof*), which probably shows it was still voiceless in those positions. Medially it is in contrast with the voiceless /f, ff/ from Germanic *p*. Germanic *ff* medially after a short vowel merged with *ff* from Germanic *p*: OHG *heffen* 'to lift', *offan*. In MHG there are not many words that show medial *v*. In NHG medial *v* has merged with medial /f, ff/ in a voiceless labio-dental fricative. The following NHG words were written with medial <v> in MHG but now show a voiceless sound: *Eifer, elf, Geifer* 'spittle', *Höfe* (pl.), *Käfer, Neffe, Ofen, Schaufel, Schiefer* 'slate', *schnaufen, Tafel, Teufel, Ufer, Ungeziefer* 'vermin', *Waffel, Wölfe, Zweifel*. It is not easy to tell when this merger took place, as the phonemes continued to be distinguished in spelling in Early NHG: MHG /v/ is written <f> and MHG /f, ff/ is written *ff*.

It may also be the case that Germanic *s*, which is voiced in NHG, was voiced medially between vowels but since there is no change of spelling we do not know when this came about. Germanic medial *ss*, which only occurred in a few words, merged with MHG /z, zz/ in a voiceless [s]: *missetât : wizzen* becomes *Missetat, wissen*.

Germanic *h*, a voiceless velar fricative, merged with the shifted sound from Germanic *k* medially after a short vowel (OHG *lahhen, brehhan*) and finally (OHG *sah, brah*). In NHG the velar fricative has developed a palatal allophone [ç] after front vowels. Since the spelling has not changed and it is a sub-phonemic change that grammarians did not comment upon, it is difficult to say when it might have started.

12.7.4 The origin of /ʃ/ and merger with /s/

NHG [ʃ] goes back to the OHG cluster *sk* that is sometimes spelt <sc>. In MHG it is spelt <sch> and has become a new phoneme, a voiceless palato-alveolar fricative /ʃ/. The shift of OHG *sk* to [ʃ] is difficult to date. The spelling <sch> is found in a few older sources but it is only in the eleventh century that its frequency increases to any great degree. The phoneme /ʃ/ appears initially (*schaffen, schrîben*), medially (*waschen*) and finally (*visch*). An important pointer to the development of /ʃ/ is its merger with /s/ before initial consonants, which begins from the fourteenth century in UG but does not reach CG before the sixteenth century: NHG *schwer, schlagen, Schmerz, schnell*. Finally after /r/ MHG /s/ (and /z/) have also merged with /ʃ/: MHG *mürsen, bars, hirez* > NHG *morsch, barsch, Hirsch*. There are, however, some exceptions: NHG *Vers, Färse* 'heifer', *Hirse* 'millet'.

12.7.5 Nasals

NHG has three nasal phonemes: /m/ (*schwimmen, schwamm*); /n/ (*sinnen, sann*); and /ŋ/, which only occurs medially and finally (*singen, sang*). MHG had only two nasal phonemes, a bilabial /m/ and an alveolar /n/: *mîn, nein*. The velar nasal occurred, but only as an allophone of /n/ before the palato-velar plosives *k* and *g*: *sinken, singen* [siŋgen]. From being an allophone in MHG, the velar nasal has become a separate phoneme in NHG. This is an example of a phonemic split. This change came about when the MHG medial voiced palato-velar plosive [g] was assimilated to the preceding velar nasal, resulting in a new long nasal /ŋŋ/ that contrasted with MHG /nn/. When long consonants were shortened in NHG, MHG /nn/ and /n/ merged and MHG /ŋŋ/ became /ŋ/.

A similar change affected the MHG cluster *mb*, comprising a bilabial nasal + a voiced bilabial plosive. MHG *kumber* 'care' has become NHG

Kummer. The plosive in the cluster *mb* was assimilated to the nasal – [mm] – and the long nasal subsequently shortened. Phonemically, however, this change was a merger, not a split. The [mm] that resulted from the assimilation of *b* in *mb* merged with an already existing long [mm]: NHG *Kummer, schwimmen.* At first this assimilation and that of *ng* took place in medial position. By analogy the assimilated forms were then levelled out to final position: MHG has *singen, sanc, tumbes, tump* (both with final devoicing); but NHG *singen, sang, dummes, dumm.*

A corresponding merger of MHG *nd, nt* and *nn* does not take place in standard NHG but does occur in Low German and Central German: NHG *Kinder, unter,* LG *kinner, unner.*

QUESTIONS

1   Using the following quotation from Carl Philipp Moritz (1797) discuss how <r> might have been pronounced: 'R wird hervorgebracht, wenn die Zunge mit ihrer Spitze am Zahnfleisch der obern Zähne, fast eben da, wo sie in der Aussprache des *d* und *z* sich andrückt, mit einer zitternden Bewegung anschlägt, daher auch Zitterlaut genannt wird' (Cited in Voge 1978: 121). How reliable are statements of this sort?

2   Using the MHG poem by Walther von der Vogelweide in 12.1.2.1, illustrate the concept of 'series shift' (*Reihenschritt*).

3   Illustrate phonemic merger and phonemic split.

4   Find the English cognates of *Pflicht, Zaun, saufen, gaffen, riechen, Zeichen, Kessel, was,* and then use them to outline the main features of the Second Sound Shift.

5   How far have there been qualitative vowel changes in German? For one example use the rhymes and orthographic conventions of the MHG poem by Walther von der Vogelweide in 12.1.2.1.

6   What effect has umlaut had on the German sound system?

7   Discuss the origin of the NHG velar nasal phoneme /ŋ/ in the light of MHG alternations such as *singen* 'to sing', past tense *sanc*; rhymes in MHG like *lanc – gedanc, kranc – lanc*; and the alternation in English between *strong* and *stronger, long* and *longer.*

8   How did NHG /ŋ/ arise?

9 Using the following OHG version of the Lord's Prayer from Tatian work out what vowels were present in unstressed syllables. What has happened to these in NHG?

Fater unser, thû thâr bist in himile, sî giheilagôt thin namo, queme thin rîhhi, sî thin uuillo, sô her in himile ist, sô her in erdu, unsar tagalîhhaz brôt gib uns hiutu, inti furlâz uns unsara sculdî, sô uuir furlâzamês unsarên sculdîgôn, inti ni gileitêst unsih in costunga (Versuchung), ûzouh arlôsi unsih fon ubile.

10 Using the same OHG Tatian version of the Lord's Prayer, suggest phonetic values for <th> *thû*, <z> *furlâz* and <b> *gib*.

References

Abercrombie, D. 1967. *Elements of General Phonetics*. Edinburgh: Edinburgh University Press.

Ammon, U. 1995. *Die deutsche Sprache in Deutschland, Österreich und der Schweiz. Das Problem der nationalen Varietäten*. Berlin: de Gruyter.

Ammon, U. 1998. 'Die Frage der Teutonismen in der deutschen Gegenwartssprache', in C. V. J. Russ (ed.), *Sprache, Kultur, Nation / Language, Culture, Nation*. (New German Studies Texts and Monographs 12.) Hull: University German Department, 1–14.

Ammon, U. *et al.* 2004. *Variantenwörterbuch des Deutschen*. Berlin: de Gruyter.

Augst, G. 1971. 'Über den Umlaut bei der Steigerung', *Wirkendes Wort* 21: 424–31.

  1975. 'Zum Pluralsystem', in G. Augst, *Untersuchungen zum Morpheminventar der deutschen Gegenwartssprache* (Forschungsberichte des Instituts für deutsche Sprache 25), 5–70.

  1977. 'Wie stark sind die starken Verben?', in G. Augst (ed.), *Sprachnorm und Sprachwandel*. Frankfurt: Athenaion, 125–77.

  1984. 'Der Buchstabe', in G. Drosdowski (ed.), *Die Grammatik: Duden 4*. Mannheim: Dudenverlag, 59–87.

Bach, A. 1965. *Geschichte der deutschen Sprache*. 8th edn. Heidelberg: Quelle and Meyer.

Bach, E. and King, R. D. 1970. 'Umlaut in modern German', *Glossa* 4: 3–21.

Barbour, S. 2001. 'Defending languages and defending nations: Some perspectives on the use of "foreign words" in German', in M. C. Davies, J. L. Flood and D. N. Yeandle (eds.), *'Proper Words in Proper Places': Studies in Lexicology and Lexicography in Honour of William Jervis Jones*. Stuttgarter Arbeiten zur Germanistik 400. Stuttgart: Akademischer Verlag, 361–74.

Barbour, S. and Stevenson, P. 1990. *Variation in German: A Critical Approach to German Sociolinguistics*. Cambridge: Cambridge University Press.

Barker, M. 1925. *A Handbook of German Intonation for University Students*. Cambridge: Heffers.

Becker, T. 1998. *Das Vokalsystem der deutschen Standardsprache*. (Arbeiten zur Sprachanalyse 4.) Frankfurt am Main: Peter Lang.

Benware, W. A. 1986. *Phonetics and Phonology of Modern German*. Washington, D. C.: Georgetown University Press.

Bergmeier, R. and Fries, U. 1979. 'Bemerkungen zum Umlaut im Neuhochdeutschen', *Beiträge zur Geschichte der deutschen Sprache und Literatur* 101: 36–44.

Besch, W. 1988. 'Standardisierungsprozesse im deutschen Sprachraum', *Sociolinguistica* 2: 186–208.

1990. 'Schrifteinheit – Sprechvielfalt. Zur Diskussion um die nationalen Varianten der deutschen Standardsprache', *German Life and Letters* 43: 91–102.

2003. 'Aussprachstandardisierung am grünen Tisch? Der "Siebs" nach 100 Jahren', in J. K. Androutsopoulos and E. Ziegler (eds.), *'Standardfragen': Soziolinguistische Perspektiven auf Sprachgeschichte, Sprachkontakt und Sprachvariation*. Frankfurt am Main: Peter Lang.

Beutler, E. (ed.) 1964. *Johann Wolfgang Goethe: Gedenkausgabe der Werke, Briefe und Gespräche 14*. Zurich: Artemis.

Boase-Beier, J. and Lodge, K. 2003. *The German Language: A Linguistic Introduction*. Oxford: Blackwell.

Boesch, B. (ed.) 1957. *Die Aussprache des Hochdeutschen in der Schweiz: Eine Wegleitung*. Zurich: Schweizer Spiegel.

Boor, H. de and Diels, P. 1955. *Siebs Deutsche Hochsprache: Bühnenaussprache*. 16th edn. Berlin: de Gruyter.

Boor, H. de, Moser, H. and Winkler, C. (eds.) 1969. *Siebs: Deutsche Aussprache. Reine und gemäßigte Hochlautung mit Aussprachewörterbuch*. 19th edn. Berlin: de Gruyter.

Borden, G., Harris, K. S. and Raphael, L. J. 2003. *Speech Science Primer: Physiology, Acoustics and Perception of Speech*. 4th edn. Philadelphia: Lippincott, Williams and Wilkins.

Britain, D. (ed.) 2007. *Language in the British Isles*. Cambridge: Cambridge University Press.

Brockhaus, W. 1995. *Final Devoicing in the Phonology of German*. (Linguistische Arbeiten 336.) Tübingen: Niemeyer.

Brückner, T. and Sauter, C. 1984. *Rückläufige Wortliste zum heutigen Deutsch*. 2 vols. Mannheim: Institut für Deutsche Sprache.

Brundin, G. 2004. *Kleine deutsche Sprachgeschichte*. Munich: Fink.

Brunt, R. J. 1983. *The Influence of the French Language on the German Vocabulary (1649–1735)*. (Studia Linguistica Germanica 18.) Berlin: de Gruyter.

Carr, P. 1993. *Phonology*. London: Macmillan.

Carstensen, B. 1965. *Englische Einflüsse auf die deutsche Sprache nach 1945*. Heidelberg: Winter.

Carstensen, B., Busse, U. and Schmude, R. (eds.) 2001. *Anglizismen Wörterbuch*. 3 vols. Berlin: de Gruyter.

Catford, J. C. 1988. *A Practical Introduction to Phonetics*. Oxford: Clarendon Press.

Chambers, W. W. and Wilkie, J. 1970. *A Short History of the German Language*. London: Methuen.

Chomsky, N. and Halle, M. 1968. *The Sound Pattern of English*. New York: Harper Row.

Clyne, M. 1995. *The German Language in a Changing Europe*. Cambridge: Cambridge University Press.

Cruttenden, A. 1994. *Gimson's Pronunciation of English*. 6th edn. London: Arnold.

Crystal, D. 1987. *The Cambridge Encyclopedia of Language*. Cambridge: Cambridge University Press.

1995. *The Cambridge Encyclopedia of the English Language*. Cambridge: Cambridge University Press.

DAW 2005. = Mangold, M. (ed.) *Duden Aussprachewörterbuch: Duden 6*. Mannheim: Bibliographisches Institut.

DE 2007 = *Herkunftswörterbuch 2007: Etymologie der deutschen Sprache. Duden 7*. Mannheim: Duden.

Delgutte, B. 1997. 'Auditory neural processing of speech', in Hardcastle and Laver (eds.), 507–38.

Dieth, E. 1968. *Vademekum der Phonetik*, 2nd edn. Berne and Munich: Francke Verlag.

DG 1984 = Drosdowski, G. (ed.) *Die Grammatik. Duden 4*. Mannheim: Duden.

Donalies, E. 2002. *Die Wortbildung des Deutschen: Ein Überblick*. Tübingen: Gunter Narr.

DR = *Die deutsche Rechtschreibung. Duden 1*. 2006. 24th edn. Mannheim: Duden.

Drewitz, I. and Reuter, E. (eds.) 1974. *vernünftiger schreiben: reform der rechtschreibung*. Frankfurt: Fischer.

Duden, K. 1880. *Vollständiges Orthographisches Wörterbuch für die Schule: Nach den neuen preußischen, bayerischen und sächsischen Regeln*. Leipzig: Bibliographisches Institut. (Reprinted in facsimile: Mannheim, 1980.)

Duden Grammatik. 1966 = P. Grebe and H. Gipper, *Duden Grammatik*. 2nd edn. Mannheim: Bibliographisches Institut.

Ebner, J. 1998. *Wie sagt man in Österreich? Wörterbuch der österreichischen Besonderheiten*. (Duden Taschenbücher 8.) 3rd revised edn. Mannheim: Bibliographisches Institut.

Egan, A. 1927. *A German Phonetic Reader*. London: University of London Press.

Eichhoff, J. 1977–2000. *Wortatlas der deutschen Umgangssprachen*. 4 vols. Berne and Munich: Francke.

Eichinger, L. M. and Kallmeyer, W. (eds.) 2005. *Standardvariation: Wie viel Variation verträgt die deutsche Sprache?* (Institut für Deutsche Sprache, Jahrbuch 2004.) Berlin: de Gruyter.

Empfehlungen 1959 = *Empfehlungen des Arbeitskreises für Rechtschreibregelung* (1959) *Authentischer Text* (Duden-Beiträge 2). Mannheim: Bibliographisches Institut. Also in Drewitz and Reuter (eds.), 1974: 139–64.

Ernst, P. 2005. *Deutsche Sprachgeschichte*. Vienna: Fakultas.

Essen, O. von. 1964. *Grundzüge der hochdeutschen Satzintonation*. Düsseldorf: Henn.

Fink, H. 1980. 'Zur Aussprache von Angloamerikanischem im Deutschen', in W. Viereck (ed.), *Studien zum Einfluß der englischen Sprache auf das Deutsche / Studies on the influence of the English Language on German*. (Tübinger Beiträge zur Linguistik 132.) Tübingen: Narr, 109–83.

Fleischer, W. and Barz, I. 1992. *Wortbildung der deutschen Gegenwartssprache*. Tübingen: Niemeyer.

Fleischer, W., Helbig, G. and Lerchner, G. (eds.) 2001. *Kleine Enzyklopädie: Deutsche Sprache*. Frankfurt am Main: Peter Lang.

Folz, J. (ed.) 1987. *Wortgeschichte: Herkunft und Entwicklung des deutschen Wortschatzes*. Mannheim: Duden.

Fox, A. C. 1984. *German Intonation: An Outline*. Oxford: Clarendon Press.
    2005. *The Structure of German*. Oxford: Clarendon Press.

Frey, E. 1994. *Einführung in die historische Sprachwissenschaft des Deutschen*. Heidelberg: Groos.

Frings, T. 1957. *Grundlegung einer Geschichte der deutschen Sprache.* Halle: Niemeyer.

Geißler, E. 1933. 'Schriftsprache, Hochsprache, Hochlautung und Gemeinsprache', *Muttersprache* 48: 315–18.

Giegerich, H. J. 1989. *Syllable Structure and Lexical Derivation in German.* Bloomington: Indiana University Linguistics Club.

Göschel, J. 1971. 'Artikulation und Distribution der sogenannten Liquida *r* in den europäischen Sprache', *Indogermanische Forschungen* 76: 84–126.

Griffen, T. D. 1985. *Aspects of Dynamic Phonology.* Amsterdam: John Benjamins.

Grimm, J. 1870. *Deutsche Grammatik I.* 2nd edn, ed. W. Scherer. Berlin: Dümmler. (Reprinted Hildesheim: Olms-Weidmann, 1989.)

Gutachten 1899 = 'Gutachten über die Schrift "Deutsche Bühnenaussprache" (1898)', in *Wissenschaftliche Beihefte zur Zeitschrift des Allgemeinen Deutschen Sprachvereins* 16: 177–212.

GWDA = U. Stötzer and E.-M. Krech (eds.) 1982. *Großes Wörterbuch der deutschen Aussprache.* Leipzig: Bibliographisches Institut.

Haas, W. 1988. 'Schweiz', in U. Ammon, N. Dittmar and K. J. Mattheier (eds.), *Sociolinguistics: An International Handbook.* Berlin: de Gruyter, 2.2: 1365–83.

Hall, C. 2003. *Modern German Pronunciation.* 2nd edn. Manchester: Manchester University Press.

Hall, T. A. 1992. *Syllable Structure and Syllable-Related Processes in German.* (Linguistische Arbeiten 276.) Tübingen: Niemeyer.

Halle, M. 1953. 'The German conjugation', *Word* 9: 45–53.

Hardcastle, W. J. and Laver, J. (eds.) 1997. *The Handbook of Phonetic Sciences.* Oxford: Blackwell.

Hartweg, F. and Wegera, K.-P. 1989. *Frühneuhochdeutsch.* (Germanistische Arbeitshefte 33.) Tübingen: Niemeyer.

Haspelmath. M. 2002. *Understanding Morphology.* London: Arnold.

Haugen, E. 1950. 'The analysis of linguistic borrowing', *Language* 26: 210–31.

   1966. 'Dialect, language, nation', *American Anthropologist* 68: 922–35.

Heller, K. 1996. *Die Rechtschreibreform: Eine Zusammenfassung. Sprachreport Extra-Ausgabe.* Mannheim: Institut für Deutsche Sprache.

Hennig, B. 2001. *Kleines mittelhochdeutsches Wörterbuch.* Tübingen: Niemeyer.

Hoberg, R. 2000. 'Sprechen wir bald alle Denglisch oder Germeng?', in K. Eichhoff-Cyrus and R. Hoberg (eds.), *Die deutsche Sprache um die Jahrtausendwende: Sprachkultur oder Sprachverfall?* Mannheim: Dudenredaktion and Gesellschaft für deutsche Sprache, 303–16.

Hockett, C. F. 1958. *A Course in Modern Linguistics.* New York: Macmillan.

   1960. 'The origin of speech', *Scientific American* 203 (Sept.): 88–109.

Hornung, M. 1988. 'Die richtige Aussprache von Namen in Österreich', in Wiesinger (ed.), 55–70.

Internationaler Arbeitskreis für Orthographie 1992 = *Deutsche Rechtschreibung: Vorschläge zu ihrer Neuregelung.* Tübingen: Narr.

International Phonetic Association 1949. *Principles of the International Phonetic Association.* London: Department of Phonetics, University College.

Jäger, S. 1971. *Der Konjunktiv in der deutschen Sprache der Gegenwart: Untersuchungen an ausgewählten Texten.* (Heutiges Deutsch, Reihe I, 1.) Munich: Hueber.

Jessen, M. 1998. *Phonetic and Phonology of Tense and Lax Obstruents in German.* Amsterdam: Benjamins.

Johnson, S. 2005. *Spelling Trouble? Language, Ideology and the Reform of German Orthography*. Clevedon: Multilingual Matters.

Jones, D. 1967. *The Phoneme*. Cambridge: Heffer.

Josten, D. 1976. *Sprachvorbild und Sprachnorm im Urteil des 16. und 17. Jahrhunderts*. Berne and Frankfurt am Main: Lang.

Keller, R. E. 1978. *The German Language*. London: Faber and Faber.

Kerswill, P. 2007. 'Standard and non-standard English', in Britain (ed.), 34–51.

Kirk, A. 1923. *An Introduction to the Historical Study of New High German*. Manchester: Manchester University Press.

Koekkoek, B. 1965. 'The status of umlaut in standard German morphology', *Journal of English and Germanic Philology* 64: 603–9.

Kohler, K. J. 1995. *Einführung in die Phonetik des Deutschen*. 2nd edn. Berlin: Schmidt.

Kommission für Rechtschreibfragen 1985. *Die Rechtschreibung des Deutschen und ihre Neuregelung*. (Sprache der Gegenwart 66.) Düsseldorf: Schwann.

    1989. *Zur Neuregelung der deutschen Rechtschreibung*. (Sprache der Gegenwart 77.) Düsseldorf: Schwann.

Konferenz 1876. = *Verhandlungen der zur Herstellung größerer Einigung in der deutschen Rechtschreibung berufenen Konferenz*. Berlin.

König, W. 1989. *Atlas zur Aussprache des Schriftdeutschen in der Bundesrepublik*. 2 vols. Ismaning: Hueber.

    1994. *dtv-Atlas Deutsche Sprache*. 10th edn. Munich: dtv.

Korte, B. 1986. 'Die Pluralbildung als Paradigma linguistischer Theorien', *Der Deutschunterricht*: 15–30.

Krech, E.-M. 1961a. 'Zur Entstehung und Kodifizierung der deutschen Hochlautung', *Sprachpflege* 10: 136–41.

    1961b. 'Probleme der deutschen Ausspracheregelung', in H. Krech (ed.), *Beiträge zur deutschen Ausspracheregelung*. Berlin: Henschelverlag, 9–47.

Krech, H. *et al.* 1971. *Wörterbuch der deutschen Aussprache*. 3rd edn. Leipzig: Bibliographisches Institut.

Kühnhold, I. and Wellmann, H. 1973. *Deutsche Wortbildung: Typen und Tendenzen in der Gegenwartssprache*, 1: *Das Verb*. (Sprache der Gegenwart 29.) Düsseldorf: Schwann.

Kühnhold, I., Putzer, O. and Wellmann, H. 1978. *Deutsche Wortbildung: Typen und Tendenzen in der Gegenwartssprache*, 3: *Das Adjektiv*. (Sprache der Gegenwart 43.) Düsseldorf: Schwann.

Kurka, E. 1980. 'Die deutsche Aussprachenorm im 19. Jahrhundert – Entwicklungstendenzen und Probleme ihrer Kodifizierung vor 1898', *Linguististische Studien Reihe A* 66/11: 1–67.

Ladefoged, P. 2005. *Vowels and Consonants*. Oxford: Blackwell.

Lee, D. H. 2005. *Rückläufiges Wörterbuch der deutschen Sprache*. Berlin: de Gruyter.

Leys, O. 1986. 'Zur Geschichte und Formulierung der Pluralregeln der deutschen Substantive', in H. L. Cox, V. F. Vanacker and E. Verhofstadt (eds.), *Wortes anst – verbi gratia. Donum natalicium Gilbert A. R. de Smet*. Leuven, 303–8.

Lipold, G. 1988. 'Die österreichische Variante der deutschen Standardaussprache', in Wiesinger (ed.), 31–54.

MacCarthy, P. 1975. *The Pronunciation of German*. Oxford: Oxford University Press.

Mangold, M. 1984. 'Der Laut', in *Duden Grammatik*. 4th edn. Mannheim: Bibliographisches Institut, 21–58.

Martens, C. and Martens, P. 1961. *Phonetik der deutschen Sprache*. Munich: Hueber.

Martinet, A. 1955. *Économie des changements phonétiques*. Berne: Francke.

Mater, E. 1965. *Rückläufiges Wörterbuch*. Leipzig: Verlag Enzyklopädie.

McQueen, J. and Cutler, A. 1997. 'Cognitive processes in speech perception', in Hardcastle and Laver (eds.), 566–85.

Meier, R. 1984. *Bibliographie zur Intonation*. (Bibliographische Arbeitsmaterialien 5.) Tübingen: Niemeyer.

Meinhold, G. and Stock, E. 1982. *Phonologie der deutschen Gegenwartssprache*. 2nd edn. Leipzig: Bibliographisches Institut.

Meyer, K. 1989. *Wie sagt man in der Schweiz? Wörterbuch der schweizerischen Besonderheiten*. (Duden Taschenbücher 22.) Mannheim: Bibliographisches Institut.

Moore, B. C. J. 1997. 'Aspects of auditory processing related to speech perception', in Hardcastle and Laver (eds.), 539–65.

Moosmüller, S. 1991. *Hochsprache und Dialekt in Österreich: Soziophonologische Untersuchungen zu ihrer Abgrenzung in Wien, Graz, Salzburg und Innsbruck*. (Sprachwissenschaftliche Reihe 1.) Vienna: Böhlau.

Moulton, W. G. 1961. 'Zur Geschichte des deutschen Vokalsystems', *Beiträge zur Geschichte der deutschen Sprache und Literatur* 83: 1–35.

1962. *The Sounds of English and German*. Chicago: University of Chicago Press.

Müller, J. 1882. *Quellenschriften und Geschichte des deutschsprachlichen Unterrichtes bis zur Mitte des 16. Jahrhunderts*. Reprinted with an introduction by M. Rössing-Hager, Darmstadt: Wissenschaftliche Buchgesellschaft, 1969.

Munske, H. H. 1984. 'French transferences with nasal vowels in the graphematics and phonology of the Germanic language', in P. Sture Ureland and I. Clarkson (eds.), *Scandinavian Language Contact*. Cambridge: Cambridge University Press, 231–80.

Muthmann, G. 1988. *Rückläufiges deutsches Wörterbuch: Handbuch der Wortausgänge im Deutschen, mit Beachtung der Wort- und Lautstruktur*. (Reihe Germanistische Linguistik 78.) Tübingen: Niemeyer.

1996. *Phonologisches Wörterbuch der deutschen Sprache*. (Reihe Germanistische Linguistik 163.) Tübingen: Niemeyer.

Nerius, D. 1975. *Untersuchungen zu einer Reform der deutschen Orthographie*. Berlin: Akademie.

2001. 'Graphematik/Orthographie', in Fleischer, Helbig and Lerchner (eds.), 325–50.

Nevalainen, T. and van Ostade, I. T.-B. 2006. 'Standardization', in R. Hogg and D. Denison (eds.), *A History of the English Language*. Cambridge: Cambridge University Press, 271–311.

O'Connor, J. D. 1973. *Phonetics*. London: Penguin.

Paul, H. 1920. *Deutsche Grammatik*. 5 vols. Halle: Niemeyer.

(ed.) 2002. *Deutsches Wörterbuch: Bedeutungsgeschichte und Aufbau unseres Wortschatzes*. 10th edn, revised by H. Henne, H. Kämper and G. Objartel. Tübingen: Niemeyer.

Penzl, H. 1971. *Lautsystem und Lautwandel in den althochdeutschen Dialekten*. Munich: Hueber.

    1975. *Vom Urgermanischen zum Neuhochdeutschen: Eine historische Phonologie*. Berlin: Erich Schmidt.

    1986. *Althochdeutsch*. (Germanistische Lehrbuchsammlung 7.) Berne: Lang.

    1989. *Mittelhochdeutsch*. (Germanistische Lehrbuchsammlung 8.) Berne: Lang.

Pfalzgraf, F. 2003. 'Recent developments concerning language protection organisations and right-wing extremism', *German Life and Letters* 56: 398–409.

    2006. *Neopurismus in Deutschland nach der Wende*. Frankfurt am Main: Peter Lang.

Pfeiffer, W. (ed.) 1993. *Etymologisches Wörterbuch des Deutschen*. Munich: Deutscher Taschenbuch Verlag.

Philipp, M. 1968. *Phonologie des graphies et des rimes: l'alsacien de Thomas Murner*. Paris: Centre National de la Recherche Scientifique.

    1970. *Phonologie de l'allemand*. Paris: Presses Universitaires de France. (German edition, Stuttgart: Kohlhammer, 1974.)

Polenz, P. von. 1994. *Deutsche Sprachgeschichte vom Spätmittelalter*, 2: *17. und 18. Jahrhundert*. Berlin: de Gruyter.

Ramers, K.-H. and Vater, H. 1992. *Einführung in die Phonologie*. Hürtt-Efferen: Gabel Verlag.

Rasch, F. 1998. *The German Language in Switzerland: Mutltilingualism, Diglossia and Variation*. (German Linguistic and Cultural Studies 3.) Berne: Peter Lang.

Rausch, R. and Rausch, I. 1991. *Deutsche Phonetik für Ausländer*. 2nd edn. Leipzig: Verlag Enzyklopädie.

Reiffenstein, I. 2004. *Althochdeutsche Grammatik von Wilhelm Braune*, 1: *Laut- und Formenlehre*. Tübingen: Niemeyer.

Ross, J. R. 1967. 'Der Ablaut bei den deutschen starken Verben', *Studia Grammatica* 6: 47–118.

Russ, C. V. J. 1969. 'Die Ausnahmen zur Dehnung der mhd. Kurzvokale in offener Silbe', *Zeitschrift für Dialektologie und Linguistik* 36: 82–8.

    1977. 'Die Entwicklung des Umlauts im Deutschen im Spiegel verschiedener linguistischer Theorien', *Beiträge zur Geschichte der deutschen Sprache und Literatur* 99: 213–49.

    1978a. *Historical German Phonology and Morphology*. (Oxford History of the German Language 2.) Oxford: Clarendon Press.

    1978b. 'Kausalität und Lautwandel', *Leuvense Bijdragen* 67: 169–82.

    1982. *Studies in Historical German Phonology*. Berne: Peter Lang.

    1986. 'Breaking the spelling barrier: The reconstruction of pronunciation from orthography in historical linguistics', in G. Augst (ed.), *New Trends in Graphemics and Orthography*. Berlin: de Gruyter, 164–78.

    1987. 'Language and Society in German Switzerland. Multilingualism, Diglossia and Variation', in C. V. J. Russ and C. Volkmar (eds.), *Sprache und Gesellschaft in deutschsprachigen Ländern*. Munich: Goethe Institut, 94–121.

    1989. 'Die Pluralbildung im Deutschen', *Zeitschrift für germanistische Linguistik* 17: 58–67.

    (ed.) 1990. *The Dialects of Modern German*. London: Routledge.

Sauer, W. W. 1988. *Der 'Duden': Geschichte und Aktualität eines 'Volkswörterbuchs'*. Stuttgart: Metzler.

Scheuringer, H. 1996. *Geschichte der deutschen Rechtschreibung: Ein Überblick. Mit einer Einführung zur Neuregelung ab 1998.* (Schriften zur diachronen Sprachwissenschaft 4.) Vienna: Praesens.

Schildt, J. 1991. *Kurze Geschichte der deutschen Sprache.* Berlin: Volk und Wissen.

Schindler, F. and Thürmann, E. 1971. *Bibliographie zur Phonetik und Phonologie des Deutschen.* (Bibliographische Arbeitsmaterialien 1.) Tübingen: Niemeyer.

Schirmer, A. and Mitzka, W. 1969. *Deutsche Wortkunde: Kulturgeschichte des deutschen Wortschatzes.* Berlin: de Gruyter.

Schlaefer, M. (ed.) 1984. *Quellen zur Geschichte der deutschen Orthographie im 19. Jahrhundert.* Heidelberg: Winter.

Schmidt, W. (ed.) 1996. *Geschichte der deutschen Sprache.* Stuttgart: Hirzel.

Schmitt, C. 1988. 'Typen der Ausbildung und Durchsetzung von Nationalsprachen in der Romania', *Sociolinguistica* 2: 73–116.

Schützeichel, R. 1976. *Die Grundlagen des westlichen Mitteldeutsch.* Tübingen: Niemeyer.

Schwarz, E. 1967. *Kurze deutsche Wortgeschichte.* Darmstadt: Wissenschaftliche Buchgesellschaft.

Seebold, E. (ed.) 2001. *Chronologisches Wörterbuch des deutschen Wortschatzes: Der Wortschatz des 8. Jahrhunderts.* Berlin: de Gruyter.

Shadle, C. H. 2006. 'Acoustic phonetics', in Brown (ed.), 442–60.

Siebs, T. 1905. *Deutsche Bühnenaussprache: Ergebnisse der Beratungen zur ausgleichenden Regelung der deutschen Bühnenaussprache, die vom 14. bis 16. April 1898 im Apollosaale des Königlichen Schauspielhauses zu Berlin stattgefunden haben.* 3rd edn. Berlin: Albert Ahn.

Siegl, E. 1989. *Duden Ost–Duden West. Zur Sprache in Deutschland seit 1945.* (Sprache der Gegenwart 76). Düsseldorf: Schwann.

Smith, G. 2003. *Phonological Words and Derivation in German.* (Germanistische Linguistik Monographien 13.) Hildesheim: Olms.

Sonderegger, S. 1987. *Althochdeutsche Sprache und Literatur.* 2nd edn. Berlin: de Gruyter.

Stanforth, A. W. 1968. 'Deutsch-englischer Lehnwortaustausch', in W. Mitzka (ed.), *Wortgeographie und Gesellschaft: Festgabe für L. E. Schmitt zum 60. Geburtstag am 10. Februar 1968.* Berlin: de Gruyter, 526–60.

Stevens, K. N. 1997. 'Articulatory-acoustic-auditory relationships', in Hardcastle and Laver (eds.), 462–506.

Stickel, G. 1984. 'Einstellungen zu Anglizismen', in W. Besch *et al.* (eds.), *Festschrift für S. Grosse zum 60. Geburtstag.* (Göppinger Arbeiten zur Germanistik 423.) Göppingen: Kümmerle, 143–73.

Stickel, G. and Volz, N. 1999. *Meinungen und Einstellungen zur deutschen Sprache. Ergebnisse einer bundesweiten Repräsentativenerhebung (amades 2).* Mannheim: Institut für Deutsche Sprache.

Stuttgarter Empfehlungen 1955 = 'Empfehlungen zur Erneuerung der deutschen Rechtschreibung', *Der Deutschunterricht* 3: 125–8. (Reprinted in B. Garbe (ed.), *Die deutsche rechtschreibung und ihre reform 1722–1974.* (Reihe Germanistische Linguistik 10.) Tübingen: Niemeyer, 1978, 137–41.)

Szulc, A. 1987. *Historische Phonologie des Deutschen.* Tübingen: Neimeyer.

Tatzreiter, H. 1988. 'Besonderheiten der Morphologie in der deutschen Sprache in Österreich', in Wiesinger (ed.), 71–98.

Telling, R. 1988. *Französisch im deutschen Wortschatz*. Berlin: Volk und Wissen.

Trautmann, M. 1880. 'Besprechung einiger Schulbücher nebst Bemerkungen über die r-Laute', *Anglia* 3: 204–22 and 376–8.

Trubetzkoy, N. S. 1939. *Grundzüge der Phonologie*. Prague. (Reprinted, Göttingen: Vandenhoeck & Ruprecht, 1967.)

Tschirch, F. 1969. *Geschichte der deutschen Sprache*, 2: *Entwicklung und Wandlungen der deutschen Sprachgestalt vom Hochmittelalter bis zur Gegenwart*. Berlin: Erich Schmidt.

Van der Elst, G. 1987. *Aspekte zur Entstehung der neuhochdeutschen Schriftsprache*. (Erlanger Studien 70.) Erlangen: Palm and Enke.

Vennemann, T. 1982. 'Zur Silbenstruktur der deutschen Standardsprache', in T. Vennemann (ed.), *Silben, Segmente, Akzente*. (Linguistische Arbeiten 126.) Tübingen: Neiemeyer, 261–305.

    1984. 'Hochgermanisch und Niedergermanisch. Die Verzweigungstheorie der germanisch-deutschen Lautverschiebungen', *Beiträge zur Geschichte der deutschen Sprache und Literatur* 106: 1–45.

Viereck, W. 1984. 'Britisches Englisch und Amerikanisches Englisch/Deutsch', in *Sprachgeschichte: Ein Handbuch zur Geschichte der deutschen Sprache und ihrer Erforschung*, vol. 1. Berlin: de Gruyter, 938–48.

    1986. 'The influence of English on German in the past and in the Federal Republic of Germany', in W. Viereck and W.-D. Bald (eds.), *English in Contact with Other Languages*. Budapest: Akademiai Kiado, 107–28.

Viëtor, W. 1885. *Deutsches Aussprachewörterbuch*. Leipzig.

Voge, W. M. 1978. *The Pronunciation of German in the 18th Century*. (Hamburger Phonetische Beiträge 26.) Hamburg: Buske.

Walshe, M. O'C. 1974. *Middle High German Reader*. Oxford: Clarendon Press.

Wängler, H.-H. 1983. *Grundriß einer Phonetik des Deutschen*. 2nd edn. Elwert: Marburg.

Wardale, W. L. 1961. *German Pronunciation*. Edinburgh: Edinburgh University Press.

Wegera, K.-P. (ed.) 1986. *Zur Entstehung der neuhochdeutschen Schriftsprache: Eine Dokumentation von Forschungsthesen*. (Reihe Germanistische Linguistik 64.) Tübingen: Niemeyer.

Weinreich, U. 1953. *Languages in Contact*. The Hague: Mouton.

Wellmann, H. 1975. *Deutsche Wortbildung: Typen und Tendenzen in der deutschen Gegenwartssprache*, 2: *Das Substantiv*. (Sprache der Gegenwart 32.) Düsseldorf: Schwann.

Wells, C. J. 1985. *German: A linguistic history to 1945*. Oxford: Clarendon Press.

Werner, O. 1972. *Phonemik des Deutschen*. Stuttgart: Metzler.

Wiese, R. 1988. *Silbische und lexikalische Phonologie: Studien zum Chinesischen und Deutschen*. (Linguistische Arbeiten 211.) Tübingen: Niemeyer.

    1996. *The Phonology of German*. Oxford: Clarendon Press.

    2003. 'The unity and variation of (German) /r/', *Zeitschrift für Dialektologie und Linguistik* 70: 25–43.

Wiesinger, P. 1970. *Phonetisch-phonologische Untersuchungen zur Vokalentwicklung in den deutschen Dialekten*. 2 vols. Berlin: de Gruyter.

    (ed.) 1988. *Das österreichische Deutsch*. (Schriften zur deutschen Sprache in Österreich 12.) Vienna: Böhlau.

1990. 'The Central and Southern Bavarian dialects in Bavaria and Austria', in C. V. J. Russ (ed.), *The Dialects of Modern German: A Linguistic Survey*. London: Routledge, 438–517.

Wright, J. 1907. *Historical German Grammar*, 1: *Phonology, Word-formation and Accidence*. Oxford: Oxford University Press.

Wurzel, W. U. 1970. *Studien zur deutschen Lautstruktur*. (Studia Grammatica 8.) Berlin: Akademie.

1985. *Konrad Duden*. Leipzig: Bibliographisches Institut.

Index